Date Due

JUL 1 4 '60			
	PRINTED	IN U. S. A.	

AGAINST THE STREAM

AGAINST
THE STREAM

SHORTER POST-WAR WRITINGS
1946-52

KARL BARTH

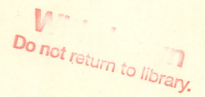
SCM PRESS LTD
56 BLOOMSBURY STREET
LONDON

Acknowledgments are due to *Rencontres Internationales* for the permission to publish VI; to the Author for III, V, VII and IX; to Chr. Kaiser Verlag, München, for VIII; and to Evangelischer Verlag, Zollikon-Zürich, for the remainder.

II 7 (*b*), V, VI, VII and IX were translated by the late Mrs. E. M. Delacour; all the rest by Stanley Godman in consultation with the Editor.

First published 1954

Printed in Great Britain by
The Camelot Press Ltd., London and Southampton

CONTENTS

Editor's Foreword   7

I. THE CHRISTIAN COMMUNITY
   AND THE CIVIL COMMUNITY   13
   (*Christengemeinde und Bürgergemeinde*, 1946)

II. THE CHRISTIAN COMMUNITY IN THE MIDST
    OF POLITICAL CHANGE: DOCUMENTS OF A
    HUNGARIAN JOURNEY   51
    (*Christliche Gemeinde im Wechsel der Staatsord-
    nungen: Dokumente einer Ungarnreise*, 1948)
    1. 'Blessed are the meek, for they shall inherit
       the earth'   53
    2. Modern Youth: its Inheritance and its Re-
       sponsibility   56
    3. The Real Church   62
    4. The Christian Community in the Midst of
       Political Change   77
    5. From the Discussion in Budapest   93
    6. The Reformed Church behind the 'Iron
       Curtain'   101
    7. A Correspondence:
          (A) An Open Letter from Emil Brunner
              to Karl Barth   106
          (B) Karl Barth's Reply   113
    8. To my Friends in the Reformed Church in
       Hungary   118

III. THE CHURCH BETWEEN EAST AND WEST   125
     (*Die Kirche zwischen Ost und West*, 1949)

IV. POLITICAL DECISIONS
    IN THE UNITY OF THE FAITH   147
    (*Politische Entscheidung in der Einheit des Glaubens*,
       1952)

6   *Contents*

V. THE CHRISTIAN MESSAGE IN EUROPE TODAY   165
(*Die christliche Botschaft im heutigen Europa*, 1946)

VI. THE CHRISTIAN MESSAGE
AND THE NEW HUMANISM   181
(*Die christliche Botschaft und der neue Humanismus*,
1949)

VII. THE JEWISH PROBLEM
AND THE CHRISTIAN ANSWER   193
(*Das jüdische Problem und die christliche Antwort*,
1949)

VIII. THE CHRISTIAN UNDERSTANDING
OF REVELATION   203
(*Das christliche Verständnis der Offenbarung*, 1948)

IX. POVERTY   241
(*Armut*, 1949)

A Bibliography of Karl Barth's Writings in English   247

General Index   249

Index of Biblical References   253

EDITOR'S FOREWORD

•

THE reason which led me to compile this volume of shorter post-war writings by Karl Barth is fairly simple. I wanted to make available in English certain writings which would throw light not only on the important themes which engage the author's attention, but also on the author himself. So I have gathered together, with the ready co-operation of Barth himself and of his assistant Charlotte von Kirschbaum, lectures, broadcast talks and even the rapid impromptu replies given to a series of questions put up by a highly intelligent audience in Budapest.

The themes will be unfolded in the assembled material, and I shall not offer my own analysis of them here. It is enough to say that while the preponderance of interest is on political questions—and in particular on the political issue between East and West—the framework of Barth's thought is always unyieldingly Christian, and indeed Christocentric. The lecture on *The Christian Message and the New Humanism*, which he delivered to a gathering of *literati* in Geneva, is in effect an evangelical sermon; but it is composed with such a rare understanding of the situation to which Barth had to address himself that it is at the same time a fruitful exposition for those who will have nothing to do with his theology.

About the light thrown by these writings on the author himself, perhaps a little more may be said here. Ever since I heard Barth giving lectures at Bonn University in the summer of 1947, and got to know him during those months as a private person, working away at the tasks laid upon him by his duties as a Guest Professor at his old University (which he had been forced to leave in 1934), and in particular devoting his time to personal talks with students of every faculty—ever since that time I have felt that fuller justice needed to be done to the personal situation out of which his work has arisen. As he chatted with his friends in his guerilla headquarters in the little basement room in the Geological Institute or developed the theme of 'Revelation' before the crowded audience in the Physics lecture-room of students of all faculties, I was aware of a quality or style about him which is hard to define. It may perhaps best be called *pastoral*, so long as this is not understood as a limitation. Barth's interest has always ranged far and wide over affairs and personalities as well as in the narrower sphere of pastoral care; and in every sphere there is apparent that same urgent yet relaxed concern. A good deal of his more personal and occasional writings has, it is true, been made available in the course of the years in English;[1] and the many volumes of the monumental *Church Dogmatics*, though promised in full by a doughty band of Scots and English translators, have still (with the exception of the first half-volume, published in English in 1936) to appear. But paradoxically, Barth is known to the English-speaking world for his *magnum opus* rather than for those other writings. Yet it would be wrong to separate the two kinds of writing. The quality which is visible in the occasional pieces represented in the present volume is also integral to the *Church Dogmatics*: a quality of personal concern about the pressing actuality and urgency of his theological material which is the basic meaning of *evangelical*.

What I mean is perhaps best illustrated by reflection about the problem of style in translated works, in particular, the problem of translation from German theology. It is unfortunate that the close relationships which formerly existed between English and German literature—and not, of course, merely in the restricted sphere of theological and other learned writing, but also in the great realm of *Dichtung*, of poetry and artistic creation generally —no longer hold today. One reason for this is the comparative neglect of German studies in this country. The universities, under the impact of two wars, have never, I suspect, been wholly liberated from the sense that German literature cannot be expected to compete with the Romance literatures for a major place in the curriculum. And recent developments in German philosophy—indeed since the period of Hegelian domination of all philosophical thought—have not really affected the tradition of academic philosophy in Britain. But there must be other reasons, for the universities are not commonly breeding-grounds of the kind of personal enthusiasm characteristic of Coleridge and Scott and Carlyle in their approach to German literature. I am inclined

[1] See the bibliography on pp. 247–8.

to think that the kind of gibe which associates German thinking and writing with ponderous tomes of recondite speculation under the heavily coloured epithet of 'Teutonic' is really little more than a defence put up against an unknown and therefore presumably alien force. In other words, a great deal of the common suspicion of German scholarship springs from plain ignorance. One does not need to have read widely among the *Novellen* of modern German literature or among the great novels of the nineteenth century in order to find displayed a subtle and profound sensibility and a fine instrument of style, simple or complex, in the German language itself.

Barth's style is massive and complex; yet I hope that the present volume indicates, even in translation, something of the wit as well as the sobriety, the humour and cheerfulness as well as the serious purpose, the robust and merry character of Barth's faith as well as its unyielding strength. Even if no translation can properly capture these qualities, yet I think it worth saying explicitly that characteristic of Barth's style (and reminiscent of Luther's) is an earthy tang, an athletic sinewy idiom of common speech, which gives pith and vigour to his thinking. His style is not up in the clouds, but down to earth; his manner as a dogmatist is not dogmatic; and his significance as a theologian is not separable from his personal style both in his writing and in his work as a pastor.

The relation of the man himself to his theology might still seem irrelevant to those who know only of his theological significance. For the impact of his theology, in this country at least, seems to be of a kind which is relatively independent of personality or of the passing topics of the day. It seems to many that Barth's theology is a prime example of what Paul Tillich calls 'heteronomous' thinking. That is, it elaborates an intricate and massive system of dogmatic propositions which hang together in an orderly and therefore beautiful fashion. But if, it is supposed, you were to try to apply or interpret these propositions in the light of the needs of an actual situation which really matters for an individual or a society (for a student, say, whose faith has been devoured by nihilism, or for a political or cultural group which wants to know the Church's prescription for peace, or antidote for political bigotry, or the like) then, the suspicion runs,

Barth's theological structure remains alien and remote, like his own Swiss Alps, grand, impressive, full of splendid light and shade, but cold and—in their highest reaches, at least— uninhabitable.

I should like to persuade readers of this volume that Barth's theology is, so to speak, more like the towns and villages of Switzerland than its mountains: as life flows into them from the mountains, but they themselves are most efficient and up-to-date, so this theology flows across Europe, and beyond, meeting need at many points, even where the theology as a system is not recognised, or not accepted. If I understand the essence of that theology aright, then Barth himself would not ask for anything better. I mean that his alleged heteronomous thinking is capable, in application, of being transformed into the most apt power, whether that power is expressed in prophetic or pastoral or political form. For in fact Barth does not provide a *system* of theology at all, which might claim a general efficacy for the various sores of men; he is too good a student of Kierkegaard ever to fall back into the idealist camp; but his theological writing is, if I may put it inelegantly, a kind of clearing of the throat before the real telling speech breaks forth. Perhaps the metaphor, beside being inelegant, is a little askew; for the theology is not, taken by itself, a merely meaningless rumble. Nevertheless, its amplitude as a Christocentric and Trinitarian exposition is most alive when it flows into the heart of Christian life, which is to be found on the one hand in the society of Christian people, the Church, and on the other hand in the world of today, in which the faithful Christian is rightly involved.

I do not mean by this that Barth adapts his Christian message, chameleon-like, to the demands of passing or alien fashions of thought. But in the proper sense he is all things to all men; his theology is existentially involved in the tragedies and the aspirations of our time. This is not the result of a deliberate effort on Barth's part to disguise himself, as it were, to hide the black gown until people grow accustomed to his presence. Rather, it is of the marrow of his theology that it should discern no *a priori* superiority in the merits or claims of one group as against another (whether the group be ecclesiastical, or political, or cultural). The author himself suggested the title for this English collection—not, I suspect, because he imagines himself *contra mundum* in his whole concern; but rather because his concern keeps so closely to the inner stream of the Christian message that it is bound to appear (as in the controversy about the proper attitude of the Church in the West to the Church in Communist-controlled lands) to move against the stream of political thought in the West.

I hope that the present collection of writings, addressed to widely different occasions, nevertheless will reflect a theology which is truly human, and filled with compassion, because it flows from a coherent faith in the One Triune Lord.

RONALD GREGOR SMITH.

Whitsun, 1953.

I

THE CHRISTIAN COMMUNITY
AND THE
CIVIL COMMUNITY

A revision and enlargement of
a talk given by Barth in Berlin,
Göttingen, Papenburg and Stuttgart, in the summer of 1946.

THE CHRISTIAN COMMUNITY
AND THE
CIVIL COMMUNITY

B Y the 'Christian community' we mean what is usually called 'the Church' and by the 'civil community' what is usually called 'the State'.

The use of the concept of the 'community' to describe both entities may serve at the very outset to underline the positive relationship and connexion between them. It was probably with some such intention in mind that Augustine spoke of the *civitas coelestis* and *terrena* and Zwingli of divine and human justice. In addition, however, the twofold use of the concept 'community' is intended to draw attention to the fact that we are concerned in the 'Church' and the 'State' not merely and not primarily with institutions and offices but with human beings gathered together in corporate bodies in the service of common tasks. To interpret the 'Church' as meaning above all a 'community' has rightly become more recognised and normal again in recent years. The Swiss term 'civil community'—in Swiss villages the residential, civil and ecclesiastical communities often confer one after the other in the same inn, and most of the people involved belong to all three groups—the 'civil community' as opposed to the 'Christian community' may also remind Christians that there are and always have been communities outside their own circle in the form of States, i.e. political communities.

The 'Christian community' (the Church) is the commonalty of the people in one place, region or country who are called apart and gathered together as 'Christians' by reason of their knowledge of and belief in Jesus Christ. The meaning and purpose of this 'assembly' (*ekklesia*) is the common life of these people in one Spirit, the Holy Spirit, that is, in obedience to the Word of God in Jesus Christ, which they have all heard and are all needing and eager to hear again. They have also come together in order to pass on the Word to others. The inward expression of their life as a Christian community is the one faith, love and hope by which they are all moved and sustained; its outward expression is the Confession by which they all stand, their jointly acknowledged and exercised responsibility for the preaching of the Name of Jesus Christ to all men and the worship and thanksgiving which they offer together. Since this is its concern, every single Christian community is as such an ecumenical (catholic) fellowship, that is, at one with the Christian communities in all other places, regions and lands.

The 'civil community' (the State) is the commonalty of all the people in one place, region or country in so far as they belong together under a constitutional system of government that is equally valid for and binding on them all, and which is defended and maintained by force. The meaning and purpose of this mutual association (that is, of the *polis*) is the safeguarding of both the external, relative and provisional freedom of the individuals and the external and relative peace of their community and to that extent the safeguarding of the external, relative and provisional humanity of their life both as individuals and as a community. The three essential forms in which this safeguarding takes place are (*a*) legislation, which has to settle the legal system which is to be binding on all; (*b*) the government and administration which has to apply the legislation; (*c*) the administration of justice which has to deal with cases of doubtful or conflicting law and decide on its applicability.

2

When we compare the Christian community with the civil community the first difference that strikes us is that in the civil community Christians are no longer gathered together as such but are associated with non-Christians (or doubtful Christians). The civil community embraces everyone living within its area. Its members share no common awareness of their relationship to God, and such an awareness cannot be an element in the legal system established by the civil community. No appeal can be made to the Word or Spirit of God in the running of its affairs. The civil community as such is spiritually blind and ignorant. It has neither faith nor love nor hope. It has no creed and no gospel. Prayer is not part of its life, and its members are not brothers and sisters. As members of the civil community they can only ask, as Pilate asked: What is truth? since every answer to the question abolishes the presuppositions of the very existence of the civil community. 'Tolerance' is its ultimate wisdom in the 'religious' sphere—'religion' being used in this context to describe the purpose of the Christian community. For this reason the civil community can only have external, relative and provisional tasks and aims, and that is why it is burdened and defaced by something which the Christian community can, characteristically, do without: physical force, the 'secular arm' which it can use to enforce its authority. That is why it lacks the ecumenical breadth and freedom that are so essential to Christianity. The *polis* has walls. Up till now, at least, civil communities have always been more or less clearly marked off from one another as local, regional, national and therefore competing and colliding units of government. And that is why the State has no safeguard or corrective against the danger of either neglecting or absolutising itself and its particular system and thus in one way or the other destroying and annulling itself. One cannot in fact compare the Church with the State without realising how much weaker, poorer and more exposed to danger the human community is in the State than in the Church.

3

It would be inadvisable, however, to make too much of the comparison. According to the fifth thesis of the *Theological Declaration* of Barmen (1934), the Christian community also exists in 'the still unredeemed world', and there is not a single problem harassing the State by which the Church is not also affected in some way or other. From a distance it is impossible clearly to distinguish the Christian from the non-Christian, the real Christian from the doubtful Christian even in the Church

B

itself. Did not Judas the traitor participate in the Last Supper? Awareness of God is one thing, Being in God quite another. The Word and Spirit of God are no more automatically available in the Church than they are in the State. The faith of the Church can become frigid and empty; its love can grow cold; its hope can fall to the ground; its message become timid and even silent; its worship and thanksgiving mere formalities; its fellowship may droop and decay.

Even the Church does not simply 'have' faith or love or hope. There are dead churches, and unfortunately one does not have to look far to find them anywhere. And if, normally, the Church renounces the use of physical force and has not shed blood, sometimes the only reason has been lack of opportunity; struggles for power have never been entirely absent in the life of the Church. Again, side by side with other and more far-reaching centrifugal factors, local, regional and national differences in the Church's way of life have been and still are strong. The centripetal forces which it needs are still weak enough to make even the unity of Christian communities among themselves extremely doubtful in many places and a special 'ecumenical' movement both desirable and urgently necessary. There is then no cause for the Church to regard the civil community too superciliously.

4

More important still, however, is the positive relationship between the two communities which results from the fact that the constitutive elements of the civil community are also proper and indispensable to the Christian community. The very term *ekklesia* is borrowed from the political sphere. The Christian community also lives and acts within the framework of an order of law which is binding on all its members, of a 'canon law' which it cannot regard as an end in itself but which it cannot neglect to institute as a 'token of the Lordship of Christ' (A. de Quervain, *Kirche, Volk und Staat*, 1945, p. 158). The Christian community exists at all times and places as a *politeia* with definite authorities and offices, with patterns of community life and divisions of labour. What the legislature, the executive and the administration of the law are in the life of the State has its clear parallels in the life of the Church, however freely and flexibly it may be shaped and however 'spiritually' it may be established and intended. And though the Christian community does not embrace all men, but only those who profess themselves Christians and would like, more or less seriously, to be Christians—it reaches out, instituted as it is to be the 'light of the world', from these few or many, to all men. The gospel, with which it is commissioned, is preached to all, applies to all. To serve all the people within range of the place, region or country where it is established, is the purpose of its existence no less than it is that of the civil community. In I Tim. 2.1-7 we read that the God in whose sight it is good and acceptable that Christians as such may lead a quiet and peaceable life in all godliness and honesty, will have all men to be saved and to come to the knowledge of the truth, and that Christians are therefore to pray for all men and especially for 'kings', that is, for those who bear special responsibility in the political sphere (which embraces all men).

In this sense, therefore, the existence of the Christian community is political. Furthermore, the object of the promise and the hope in which the Christian community has its eternal goal, consists, according to the unmistakable assertion of the New Testament, not in an eternal Church but in the *polis* built by God and coming down from heaven to earth, and the nations shall walk in the light of it and the kings of the earth will bring their glory and honour into it (Rev. 21.2, 24)—it consists in a heavenly *politeuma* (Phil. 3.20)—in the *basileia* of God—in the judgment of the King on the throne of His glory (Matt. 25.31f.). Bearing all this in mind, we are entitled and compelled to regard the existence of the Christian community as of ultimate and supremely political significance.

5

The Christian community is particularly conscious of the need for the existence of the civil community. For it knows that all men (non-Christians as well as Christians) need to have 'kings', that is, need to be subject to an external, relative and provisional order of law, defended by superior authority and force. It knows that the original and final pattern of this order is the eternal Kingdom of God and the eternal righteousness of His grace. It preaches the Kingdom of God in this eternal form. But it also thanks God that His Kingdom has an external, relative and provisional embodiment 'in the world that is not yet redeemed', in which it is valid and effective even when the temporal order is based on the most imperfect and clouded knowledge of Jesus Christ or on no such knowledge at all. This external, relative and provisional, but not on that account invalid or ineffective, form of legal order is the civil community. The Christian community is aware of the need for the civil community, and it alone takes the need absolutely seriously. For—because it knows of the Kingdom and grace of God—it knows of man's presumption and the plainly destructive consequences of man's presumption. It knows how dangerous man is and how endangered by himself. It knows him as a sinner, that is as a being who is always on the point of opening the sluices through which, if he were not checked in time, chaos and nothingness would break in and bring human time to an end. It can only conceive the time that is still left to it as a 'time of grace' in the twofold sense of being the time which it is given in order to know and lay hold of God's grace—and as the time which it is given for this very purpose by the grace of God. The Christian community itself exists in this time which is given to man, that is, in the space where man's temporal life is still protected from chaos— and on the face of it chaos should have broken in long ago. It sees as the visible means of this protection of human life from chaos the existence of the civil community, the State's effort to achieve an external, relative and provisional humanising of man's life and the political order instituted for all (for non-Christians as well as Christians—they both need it, for human arrogance is alive in both), under which the evil are punished and the good rewarded (Rom. 13.3; I Pet. 2.14) and which guarantees that the worst is prevented from happening. It knows that without this political order there would be no Christian order. It knows and it thanks God that—as the inner circle within the wider circle (cf. O. Cullmann, *Königsherrschaft Christi und Kirche im Neuen Testament*, 1941)—it is allowed to share the protection which the civil community affords.

6

Knowing that, it recognises in the existence of the civil community—disregarding the Christianity or lack of Christianity of its members and officials and also disregarding the particular forms which it assumes—no less than in its own existence the operation of a divine ordinance (*ordinatio*, i.e. institution or foundation), an *exousia* which is and acts in accordance with the will of God (Rom. 13.1*b*). However much human error and human tyranny may be involved in it, the State is not a product of sin but one of the constants of the divine Providence and government of the world in its action against human sin: it is therefore an instrument of divine grace. The civil community shares both a common origin and a common centre with the Christian community. It is an order of divine grace inasmuch as in relation to sinful man as such, in relation to the world that still needs redeeming, the grace of God is always the patience of God. It is the sign that mankind, in its total ignorance and darkness, which is still, or has again become, a prey to sin and therefore subject to the wrath of God, is yet not forsaken but preserved and sustained by God. It serves to protect man from the invasion of chaos and therefore to give him time: time for the preaching of the gospel; time for repentance; time for faith. Since 'according to the measure of human insight and human capacity' and 'under the threat and exercise of force' (Barmen Thesis No. 5), provision is made in the State for the establishment of human law and (in the inevitably external, relative and provisional sense) for freedom, peace and humanity, it renders a definite service to the divine Providence and plan of salvation, quite apart from the judgment and individual desires of its members. Its existence is not separate from the Kingdom of Jesus Christ; its foundations and its influence are not autonomous. It is outside the Church but not outside the range of Christ's dominion—it is an exponent of His Kingdom. It is, according to the New Testament, one of the 'powers' created through Him and in Him and which subsist in Him (Col. 1.16f.), which cannot separate us from the love of God (Rom. 8.37f.) because they are all given to Him and are at His disposal (Matt. 28.18). The activity of the State is, as the Apostle explicitly stated (Rom.

13.4, 6), a form of divine service. As such it can be perverted
just as the divine service of the Church itself is not exempt from
the possibility of perversion. The State can assume the face and
character of Pilate. Even then, however, it still acts in the power
which God has given it ('Thou couldest have no power at all
against me, except it were given thee from above': John 19.11).
Even in its perversion it cannot escape from God; and His law
is the standard by which it is judged. The Christian community
therefore acknowledges 'the benefaction of this ordinance of His
with thankful, reverent hearts' (Barmen Thesis No. 5). The benefaction which it acknowledges consists in the external, relative
and provisional sanctification of the unhallowed world which is
brought about by the existence of political power and order.
In what concrete attitudes to particular political patterns and
realities this Christian acknowledgment will be expressed can
remain a completely open question. It makes one thing quite
impossible, however: a Christian decision to be indifferent; a
non-political Christianity. The Church can in no case be indifferent or neutral towards this manifestation of an order so clearly
related to its own mission. Such indifference would be equivalent
to the opposition of which it is said in Rom. 13.2 that it is a
rebellion against the ordinance of God—and rebels secure their
own condemnation.

7

The Church must remain the Church. It must remain the
inner circle of the Kingdom of Christ. The Christian community
has a task of which the civil community can never relieve it and
which it can never pursue in the forms peculiar to the civil co-
munity. It would not redound to the welfare of the civil
community if the Christian community were to be absorbed by
it (as Rothe has suggested that it should) and were therefore
to neglect the special task which it has received a categorical
order to undertake. It proclaims the rule of Jesus Christ and the
hope of the Kingdom of God. This is not the task of the civil
community: it has no message to deliver; it is dependent on a
message being delivered to it. It is not in a position to appeal to

the authority and grace of God; it is dependent on this happening elsewhere. It does not pray; it depends on others praying for it. It is blind to the Whence? and Whither? of human existence; its task is rather to provide for the external and provisional delimitation and protection of human life; it depends on the existence of seeing eyes elsewhere. It cannot call the human *hybris* into question fundamentally, and it knows of no final defence against the chaos which threatens it from that quarter; in this respect too it depends on ultimate words and insights existing elsewhere. The thought and speech of the civil community wavers necessarily between a much too childlike optimism and a much too peevish pessimism in regard to man—as a matter of course it expects the best of everybody and suspects the worst! It obviously relies on its own view of man being fundamentally superseded elsewhere. Only an act of supreme disobedience on the part of Christians could bring the special existence of the Christian community to an end. Such a cessation is also impossible because then the voice of what is ultimately the only hope and help which all men need to hear would be silent.

8

The Christian community shares in the task of the civil community precisely to the extent that it fulfils its own task. By believing in Jesus Christ and preaching Jesus Christ it believes in and preaches Him who is Lord of the world as He is Lord of the Church. And since they belong to the inner circle the members of the Church are also automatically members of the wider circle. They cannot halt at the boundary where the inner and outer circles meet, though the work of faith, love and hope which they are under orders to perform will assume different forms on either side of the boundary. In the sphere of the civil community the Christian community shares common interests with the world and its task is to give resolute practical expression to this community of interest. The Christian community prays for the civil community. It does so all the more since the civil community as such is not in the habit of praying. But by praying for it, it also makes itself responsible for it before God, and it would not be taking this responsibility seriously if it did no more than pray, if it did not also work actively on behalf of the civil community. It also expresses its active support of the civil community by acknowledging that, as an operation of a divine ordinance, the civil power is also binding on Christians and significant and just from the Christian point of view. It expresses its active support of the civil community by 'subordinating' itself, in the words of the Apostle (Rom. 13.1) to the cause of the civil community under all circumstances (and therefore whatever the political form and reality it has to deal with *in concreto*). Luther's translation speaks of 'being *subject*' (cf. English A.V.: 'Let every soul be *subject* to the higher powers'—Trans.), which is something dangerously different from what is meant here. The last thing this instruction implies is that the Christian community and the Christian should offer the blindest possible obedience to the civil community and its officials. What is meant is (Rom. 13.6f.) that Christians should carry out what is required of them for the establishment, preservation and maintenance of the civil community and for the execution of its task, because, although they are Christians and, as such, have their home elsewhere, they also live in this outer circle. Jesus Christ is still its centre: they too are therefore responsible for its stability. 'Subordination' means the carrying out of this joint responsibility in which Christians apply themselves to the same task with non-Christians and submit themselves to the same rule. The subordination accrues to the good of the civil community however well or however badly that community is defended, because the civil cause (and not merely the Christian cause) is also the cause of the one God. In Rom. 13.5 Paul has expressly added that this 'subordination' is not optional but necessary, and necessary not merely 'for fear of punishment', for fear of the otherwise inevitable conflict with an obscure commandment of God, but 'for conscience sake': in the clear evangelical knowledge of the divine grace and patience, which is also manifested in the existence of the State and, therefore, in full responsibility towards the will of God which the Christian sees revealed in the civil community. The 'subordination' will be an expression of the obedience of a free heart which the Christian offers to God in the civil sphere as in the sphere of the Church—although with a different purpose (he

renders to Caesar what is Caesar's and to God what is God's—
Matt. 22.21).

9

In making itself jointly responsible for the civil community,
the Christian community has no exclusive theory of its own to
advocate in face of the various forms and realities of political
life. It is not in a position to establish one particular doctrine as
the Christian doctrine of the just State. It is also not in a position
to refer to any past realisation of the perfect State or to hold out
any prospect of one in the future. There is but one Body of
Christ, born of the Word of God, which is heard in faith. There
is therefore no such thing as a Christian State corresponding to
the Christian Church; there is no duplicate of the Church in the
political sphere. For if, as the effect of a divine ordinance, as the
manifestation of one of the constants of divine Providence and
of the historical process which it governs, the State is in the
Kingdom of Christ, this does not mean that God is revealed,
believed and perceived in any political community as such. The
effect of the divine ordinance is that men are entrusted (whether
or not they believe it to be a divine revelation) to provide 'according to the measure of human insight and human capacity' for
temporal law and temporal peace, for an external, relative and
provisional humanisation of man's existence. Accordingly, the
various political forms and systems are human inventions which
as such do not bear the distinctive mark of revelation and are
not witnessed to as such—and can therefore not lay any claim to
belief. By making itself jointly responsible for the civil community, the Christian community participates—on the basis of
and by belief in the divine revelation—in the human search for
the best form, for the most fitting system of political organisation; but it is also aware of the limits of all the political forms
and systems which man can discover (even with the co-operation
of the Church), and it will beware of playing off one political
concept—even the 'democratic' concept—as *the* Christian concept,
against all others. Since it proclaims the Kingdom of God it has
to maintain its own hopes and questions in the face of all purely
political concepts. And this applies even more to all political

achievements. Though the Christian will be both more lenient and more stern, more patient and more impatient towards them than the non-Christian, he will not regard any such achievement as perfect or mistake it for the Kingdom of God—for it can only have been brought about by human insight and human ability. In the face of all political achievements, past, present and future, the Church waits for 'the city which hath foundations, whose builder and maker is God' (Heb. 11.10). It trusts and obeys no political system or reality but the power of the Word, by which God upholds all things (Heb. 1.3; Barmen Thesis No. 5), including all political things.

10

In this freedom, however, the Church makes itself responsible for the shape and reality of the civil community in a quite definite sense. We have already said that it is quite impossible for the Christian to adopt an attitude of complete indifference to politics. But neither can the Church be indifferent to particular political patterns and realities. The Church 'reminds the world of God's Kingdom, God's commandment and righteousness and thereby of the responsibility of governments and governed' (Barmen Thesis No. 5). This means that the Christian community and the individual Christian can understand and accept many things in the political sphere—and if necessary suffer and endure everything. But the fact that it can understand much and endure everything has nothing to do with the 'subordination' which is required of it, that is, with the share of responsibility which it is enjoined to take in the political sphere. That responsibility refers rather to the decisions which it must make before God: 'must' make, because, unlike Christian understanding and suffering, Christian intentions and decisions are bound to run in a quite definite direction of their own. There will always be room and need for discussion on the details of Christian intentions and decisions, but the general line on which they are based can never be the subject of accommodation and compromise in the Church's relations with the world. The Christian community 'subordinates' itself to the civil community by making its knowledge of the

Lord who is Lord of all its criterion, and distinguishing between the just and the unjust State, that is, between the better and the worse political form and reality; between order and caprice; between government and tyranny; between freedom and anarchy; between community and collectivism; between personal rights and individualism; between the State as described in Rom. 13 and the State as described in Rev. 13. And it will judge all matters concerned with the establishment, preservation and enforcement of political order in accordance with these necessary distinctions and according to the merits of the particular case and situation to which they refer. On the basis of the judgment which it has formed it will choose and desire whichever seems to be the better political system in any particular situation, and in accordance with this choice and desire it will offer its support here and its resistance there. It is in the making of such distinctions, judgments and choices from its own centre, and in the practical decisions which necessarily flow from that centre, that the Christian community expresses its 'subordination' to the civil community and fulfils its share of political responsibility.

II

The Christian decisions which have to be made in the political sphere have no idea, system or programme to refer to but a direction and a line that must be recognised and adhered to in all circumstances. This line cannot be defined by appealing to the so-called 'natural law'. To base its policy on 'natural law' would mean that the Christian community was adopting the ways of the civil community, which does not take its bearings from the Christian centre and is still living or again living in a state of ignorance. The Christian community would be adopting the methods, in other words, of the pagan State. It would not be acting as a Christian community in the State at all; it would no longer be the salt and the light of the wider circle of which Christ is the centre. It would not only be declaring its solidarity with the civil community: it would be putting itself on a par with it and withholding from it the very things it lacks most. It would certainly not be doing it any service in that way. For the thing the civil community lacks (in its neutrality towards the Word and Spirit of God) is a firmer and clearer motivation for political decisions than the so-called natural law can provide. By 'natural law' we mean the embodiment of what man is alleged to regard as universally right and wrong, as necessary, permissible and forbidden 'by nature', that is, on any conceivable premise. It has been connected with a natural revelation of God, that is, with a revelation known to man by natural means. And the civil community as such—the civil community which is not yet or is no longer illuminated from its centre—undoubtedly has no other choice but to think, speak and act on the basis of this allegedly natural law, or rather of a particular conception of the court of appeal which is passed off as *the* natural law. The civil community is reduced to guessing or to accepting some powerful assertion of this or that interpretation of natural law. All it can do is to grope around and experiment with the convictions which it derives from 'natural law', never certain whether it may not in the end be an illusion to rely on it as the final authority and therefore always making vigorous use, openly or secretly, of a more or less refined positivism. The results of the politics based on such considerations were and are just what might be expected. And if they were and are not clearly and generally negative, if in the political sphere the better stands alongside the worse, if there were and still are good as well as bad States—no doubt the reality is always a curious mixture of the two!—then the reason is not that the true 'natural law' has been discovered, but simply the fact that even the ignorant, neutral, pagan civil community is still in the Kingdom of Christ, and that all political questions and all political efforts as such are founded on the gracious ordinance of God by which man is preserved and his sin and crime confined.

What we glimpse in the better kind of State is the purpose, meaning and goal of this divine ordinance. It is operative in any case, even though the citizens of the particular State may lack any certain knowledge of the trustworthy standards of political decision, and the overwhelming threat of mistaking an error for the truth may be close at hand. The divine ordinance may operate with the co-operation of the men and women involved, but certainly without their having deserved it: *Dei providentia hominum confusione*. If the Christian community were to base its political responsibility on the assumption that it was also interested in the problem of natural law and that it was attempting to base its decisions on so-called natural law, this would not alter the power which God has to make good come of evil, as He is in fact always doing in the political order. But it would mean that the Christian community was sharing human illusions and confusions. It is bad enough that, when it does not risk going its own way, the Christian community is widely involved in these illusions and confusions. It should not wantonly attempt to deepen such involvement. And it would be doing no less if it were to seek the criterion of its political decisions in some form of the so-called natural law. The tasks and problems which the Christian community is called to share, in fulfilment of its political responsibility, are 'natural', secular, profane tasks and problems. But the norm by which it should be guided is anything but natural: it is the only norm which it can believe in and accept as a spiritual norm, and is derived from the clear law of its own faith, not from the obscure workings of a system outside itself; it is from knowledge of this norm that it will make its decisions in the political sphere.

12

It is this reliance on a spiritual norm that makes the Christian community free to support the cause of the civil community honestly and calmly. In the political sphere the Church will not be fighting for itself and its own concerns. Its own position, influence and power in the State are not the goal which will determine the trend of its political decisions. 'My Kingdom is not of this world. If my Kingdom were of this world, then would my servants fight that I should not be delivered to the Jews, but now is my Kingdom not from hence' (John 18.36). The secret contempt which a Church fighting for its own interests with political weapons usually incurs even when it achieves a certain amount of success, is well deserved. And sooner or later the struggle generally ends in mortifying defeats of one sort or another. The Christian community is not an end in itself. It serves

God and it thereby serves man. It is true that the deepest, ultimate, divine purpose of the civil community consists in creating opportunities for the preaching and hearing of the Word and, to that extent, for the existence of the Church. But the only way the State can create such opportunities, according to the providence and ordinance of God, is the natural, secular and profane way of the establishment of law, the safeguarding of freedom and peace, 'according to the measure of human insight and capacity'. The divine purpose is therefore not at all that the State should itself gradually develop more or less into a Church. And the Church's political aim cannot be to turn the State into a Church, that is, make it as far as possible subservient to the tasks of the Church. If the State grants the Church freedom, respect and special privileges in any of the ways which are open to it (guarantees of one kind or another, a share in education and broadcasting, the defence of the Sabbath, financial reliefs or subsidies and the like), the Church will not immediately start dreaming of a Church-State. It will be thankful for the State's help, seeing in such help a result of the divine providence and ordinance: and it will show its gratitude by being a Church all the more faithfully and zealously within the broader frontiers that the State's gifts make possible, thereby justifying the expectation which the State evidently reposes in it. But it will not claim such gifts as a right. If they are refused, it will look in itself for the reason, not in the State. 'Resist not evil!' is an injunction that applies here. The Church will ask itself whether it has already given proof to the State of the Spirit and the power of God, whether it has already defended and proclaimed Jesus Christ to the world to the extent that it can expect to be considered an important, significant and salutary factor in public life. It will ask, for example, whether it is in a position to say the tremendous things that are certainly entitled to be heard in schools. It will first and foremost do penance—when and where would it not have cause for so doing?—and it will do that best by concentrating on its own special work in the, possibly, extremely small space left to it in public life, with all the more confidence and intensity and with redoubled zeal, 'with the greatest force applied at the narrowest point'. Where it has first to advertise its desire to play a part in public life, where it must first establish its claim to be considered a factor of public importance, it only proves that its claim to be heard is irrelevant and it thoroughly deserves not to be heard at all, or to be heard in a way that will sooner or later afford it no pleasure. Whenever the Church has entered the political arena to fight for its claim to be given public recognition, it has always been a Church which has failed to understand the special purpose of the State, an impenitent, spiritually unfree Church.

13

The Church cannot, however, simply take the Kingdom of God itself into the political arena. The Church reminds men of God's Kingdom. This does not mean that it expects the State gradually to become the Kingdom of God. The Kingdom of God is the Kingdom where God is without shadow, without problems and contradictions, where He is All in All: it is the rule of God in the redeemed world. In the Kingdom of God the outward is annulled by the inward, the relative by the absolute, the provisional by the final. In the Kingdom of God there is no legislature, no executive, no legal administration. For in the Kingdom of God there is no sin to be reproved, no chaos to be feared and checked. The Kingdom of God is the world dominion of Jesus Christ in honour of the Father, revealed in the clear light of day. The State as such, the neutral, pagan, ignorant State knows nothing of the Kingdom of God. It knows at best of the various ideals based on natural law. The Christian community within the State does know about the Kingdom of God, however, and it brings it to man's attention. It reminds men of the Jesus Christ who came and is to come again. But it cannot do this by projecting, proposing and attempting to enforce a State in the likeness of the Kingdom of God. The State is quite justified if it refuses to countenance all such Christian demands. It belongs to the very nature of the State that it is not and cannot become the Kingdom of God. It is based on an ordinance of God which is intended for the 'world not yet redeemed' in which sin and the danger of chaos have to be taken into account with the utmost seriousness and in which the rule of Jesus Christ, though in fact already established, is still hidden. The State would be disavowing its own purpose if it were to act as though its task was to become the Kingdom of God. And the Church that tried to induce it to develop into the Kingdom of God could be rightly reproached for being much too rashly presumptuous. If its demand were to have any meaning at all, it would have to believe that its own duty was also to develop into the Kingdom of God. But, like the State, the Church also stands 'in the world not yet redeemed'. And even at its best the Church is not an image of the Kingdom of God. It would appear that when it makes this demand on the State, the Church has also confused the Kingdom of God with a mere ideal of the natural law. Such a Church needs to be reminded again of the real Kingdom of God, which will follow both State and Church in time. A free Church will not allow itself to be caught on this path.

14

The direction of Christian judgments, purposes and ideals in political affairs is based on the analogical capacities and needs of political organisation. Political organisation can be neither a repetition of the Church nor an anticipation of the Kingdom of God. In relation to the Church it is an independent reality; in relation to the Kingdom of God it is (like the Church itself) a human reality bearing the stamp of this fleeting world. An equating of State and Church on the one hand and State and Kingdom of God on the other, is therefore out of the question. On the other hand, however, since the State is based on a particular divine ordinance, since it belongs to the Kingdom of God, it has no autonomy, no independence over against the Church and the Kingdom of God. A simple and absolute heterogeneity between State and Church on the one hand and State and Kingdom of God on the other is therefore just as much out of the question as a simple and absolute equating. The only possibility that remains—and it suggests itself compellingly—is to regard the existence of the State as an allegory, as a correspondence and an analogue to the Kingdom of God which the Church preaches and believes in. Since the State forms the outer circle, within which the Church, with the mystery of its faith and gospel, is the inner circle, since it shares a common centre with the Church, it is inevitable that, although its presuppositions and its tasks are its own and different, it is nevertheless capable of reflecting indirectly the truth and reality which constitute the Christian community. Since, however, the peculiarity and difference of its presuppositions and tasks and its existence as an outer circle must remain as they are, its justice and even its very existence as a reflected image of the Christian truth and reality cannot be given once and for all and as a matter of course but are, on the contrary, exposed to the utmost danger; it will always be questionable whether and how far it will fulfil its just purposes. To be saved from degeneration and decay it needs to be reminded of the righteousness which is a reflection of Christian truth. Again and again it needs a historical setting whose goal and content is the moulding of the State into an allegory of the Kingdom of God and the fulfilment of its righteousness. Human initiative in such situations cannot proceed from the State itself. As a purely civil community the State is ignorant of the mystery of the Kingdom of God, the mystery of its own centre, and it is indifferent to the faith and gospel of the Christian community. As a civil community it can only draw from the porous wells of the so-called natural law. It cannot remind itself of the true criterion of its own righteousness, it cannot move towards the fulfilment of that righteousness in its own strength. It needs the wholesomely disturbing presence, the activity that revolves directly around the common centre, the participation of the Christian community in the execution of political responsibility. The Church is not the Kingdom of God, but it has knowledge of it; it hopes for it; it believes in it; it prays in the name of Jesus Christ, and it preaches His Name as the Name above all others. The Church is not neutral on this ground, and it is therefore not powerless. If it only achieves the great and necessary *metabasis eis allo genos* which is the share of political responsibility which it is enjoined to assume, then it will not be able to be neutral and powerless and deny its Lord in the other *genos*. If the Church takes up its share of political responsibility, it must mean that it is taking that human initiative which the State cannot take: it is giving the State the impulse which it cannot give itself; it is

c

reminding the State of those things of which it is unable to remind itself. The distinctions, judgments and choices which it makes in the political sphere are always intended to foster the illumination of the State's connexion with the order of divine salvation and grace and to discourage all the attempts to hide this connexion. Among the political possibilities open at any particular moment it will choose those which most suggest a correspondence to, an analogy and a reflection of, the content of its own faith and gospel.

In the decisions of the State the Church will always support the side which clarifies rather than obscures the Lordship of Jesus Christ over the whole, which includes this political sphere outside the Church. The Church desires that the shape and reality of the State in this fleeting world should point towards the Kingdom of God, not away from it. Its desire is not that human politics should cross the politics of God, but that they should proceed, however distantly, on parallel lines.

It desires that the active grace of God, as revealed from heaven, should be reflected in the earthly material of the external, relative and provisional actions and modes of action of the political community. It therefore makes itself responsible in the first and last place to God—the one God whose grace is revealed in Jesus Christ—by making itself responsible for the cause of the State. And so, with its political judgments and choices, it bears an implicit, indirect but none the less real witness to the gospel.

Even its political activity is therefore a profession of its Christian faith. By its political activity it calls the State from neutrality, ignorance and paganism into co-responsibility before God, thereby remaining faithful to its own particular mission. It sets in motion the historical process whose aim and content is the moulding of the State into the likeness of the Kingdom of God and hence the fulfilment of the State's own righteous purposes.

15

The Church is based on the knowledge of the one eternal God, who as such became man and thereby proved Himself a neighbour to man, by treating him with compassion (Luke 10.36f.). The inevitable consequence is that in the political sphere the Church will always and in all circumstances be interested primarily in human beings and not in some abstract cause or other, whether it be anonymous capital or the State as such (the functioning of its departments!) or the honour of the nation or the progress of civilisation or culture or the idea, however conceived, of the historical development of the human race. It will not be interested in this last idea even if 'progress' is interpreted as meaning the welfare of future generations, for the attainment of which man, human dignity, human life in the present age are to be trampled underfoot. Right itself becomes wrong (*summum ius summa iniuria*) when it is allowed to rule as an abstract form, instead of serving the limitation and hence the preservation of man. The Church is at all times and in all circumstances the enemy of the idol Juggernaut. Since God Himself became man, man is the measure of all things, and man can and must only be used and, in certain circumstances, sacrificed, for man. Even the most wretched man—not man's egoism, but man's humanity—must be resolutely defended against the autocracy of every mere 'cause'. Man has not to serve causes; causes have to serve man.

16

The Church is witness of the divine justification, that is, of the act in which God in Jesus Christ established and confirmed His original claim to man and hence man's claim against sin and death. The future for which the Church waits is the definitive revelation of this divine justification. This means that the Church will always be found where the order of the State is based on a commonly acknowledged law, from submission to which no one is exempt, and which also provides equal protection for all. The Church will be found where all political activity is in all circumstances regulated by this law. The Church always stands for the constitutional State, for the maximum validity and application of that twofold rule (no exemption from and full protection by the law), and therefore it will always be against any degeneration of the constitutional State into tyranny or anarchy. The Church will never be found on the side of anarchy or tyranny. In its politics it will always be urging the civil community to treat this fundamental purpose of its existence with the utmost seriousness: the limiting and the preserving of man by the quest for and the establishment of law.

17

The Church is witness of the fact that the Son of man came to seek and to save the lost. And this implies that—casting all false impartiality aside—the Church must concentrate first on the lower and lowest levels of human society. The poor, the socially and economically weak and threatened, will always be the object of its primary and particular concern, and it will always insist on the State's special responsibility for these weaker members of society. That it will bestow its love on them—within the framework of its own task (as part of its service), is one thing and the most important thing; but it must not concentrate on this and neglect the other thing to which it is committed by its political responsibility: the effort to achieve such a fashioning of the law as will make it impossible for 'equality before the law' to become a cloak under which strong and weak, independent and dependent, rich and poor, employers and employees, in fact receive different treatment at its hands: the weak being unduly restricted, the strong unduly protected. The Church must stand for social justice in the political sphere. And in choosing between the various socialistic possibilities (social-liberalism? co-operativism? syndicalism? free trade? moderate or radical Marxism?) it will always choose the movement from which it can expect the greatest measure of social justice (leaving all other considerations on one side).

18

The Church is the fellowship of those who are freely called by the Word of grace and the Spirit and love of God to be the children of God. Translated into political terms, this means that the Church affirms, as the basic right which every citizen must be guaranteed by the State, the freedom to carry out his decisions in the politically lawful sphere, according to his own insight and choice, and therefore independently, and the freedom to live in certain spheres (the family, education, art, science, religion, culture), safeguarded but not regulated by law. The Church will not in all circumstances withdraw from and oppose what may be practically a dictatorship, that is, a partial and temporary limitation of these freedoms, but it will certainly withdraw from and oppose any out-and-out dictatorship such as the totalitarian State. The adult Christian can only wish to be an adult citizen, and he can only want his fellow citizens to live as adult human beings.

19

The Church is the fellowship of those who, as members of the one Body of the one Head, are bound and committed to this Lord of theirs and therefore to no other. It follows that the Church will never understand and interpret political freedom and the basic law which the State must guarantee to the individual citizen other than in the sense of the basic duty of responsibility which is required of him. (This was never made particularly clear in the classic proclamations of so-called 'human rights' in America and France.) The citizen is responsible in the whole sphere of his freedom, political and non-political alike. And the civil community is naturally responsible in the maintenance of its freedom as a whole. Thus the Christian approach surpasses both individualism and collectivism. The Church knows and recognises the 'interest' of the individual and of the 'whole', but it resists them both when they want to have the last word. It subordinates them to the being of the citizen, the being of the civil community before the law, over which neither the individuals nor the 'whole' are to hold sway, but which they are to seek after, to find and to serve—always with a view to limiting and preserving the life of man.

20

As the fellowship of those who live in one faith under one Lord on the basis of a Baptism in one Spirit, the Church must and will stand for the equality of the freedom and responsibility of all adult citizens, in spite of its sober insight into the variety of human needs, abilities and tasks. It will stand for their equality before the law that unites and binds them all, for their equality in working together to establish and carry out the law, and for their equality in the limitation and preservation of human life that it secures. If, in accordance with a specifically Christian insight, it lies in the very nature of the State that this equality must not be restricted by any differences of religious belief or unbelief, it is all the more important for the Church to urge that the restriction of the political freedom and responsibility not only of certain classes and races but, supremely, of that of women, is an arbitrary convention which does not deserve to be preserved any longer. If Christians are to be consistent there can only be one possible decision in this matter.

21

Since the Church is aware of the variety of the gifts and tasks of the one Holy Spirit in its own sphere, it will be alert and open in the political sphere to the need to separate the different junctions and 'powers'—the legislative, executive and the judicial—inasmuch as those who carry out any one of these functions should not carry out the others simultaneously. No human being is a god able to unite in his own person the functions of the legislator and the ruler, the ruler and the judge, without endangering the sovereignty of the law. The 'people' is no more such a god than the Church is its own master and in sole possession of its powers. The fact is that within the community of the one people (by the people and for the people) definite and different services are to be performed by different persons, which, if they were united in one human hand, would disrupt rather than promote the unity of the common enterprise. With its awareness of the necessity that must be observed in this matter, the Church will give a lead to the State.

22

The Church lives from the disclosure of the true God and His revelation, from Him as the Light that has been lit in Jesus Christ to destroy the works of darkness. It lives in the dawning of the day of the Lord and its task in relation to the world is to rouse it and tell it that this day has dawned. The inevitable political corollary of this is that the Church is the sworn enemy of all secret policies and secret diplomacy. It is just as true of the political sphere as of any other that only evil can want to be kept secret. The distinguishing mark of the good is that it presses forward to the light of day. Where freedom and responsibility in the service of the State are one, whatever is said and done must be said and done before the ears and eyes of all, and the legislator, the ruler and the judge can and must be ready to answer openly for all their actions—without thereby being necessarily dependent on the public or allowing themselves to be flurried. The statecraft that wraps itself up in darkness is the craft of a State which, because it is anarchic or tyrannical, is forced to hide the bad conscience of its citizens or officials. The Church will not on any account lend its support to that kind of State.

23

The Church sees itself established and nourished by the free Word of God—the Word which proves its freedom in the Holy Scriptures at all times. And in its own sphere the Church believes that the human word is capable of being the free vehicle and mouthpiece of this free Word of God. By a process of analogy, it has to risk attributing a positive and constructive meaning to the free human word in the political sphere. If it trusts the word of man in one sphere it cannot mistrust it on principle in the other. It will believe that human words are not bound to be

empty or useless or even dangerous, but that the right words
can clarify and control great decisions. At the risk of providing
opportunities for empty, useless and dangerous words to be
heard, it will therefore do all it can to see that there is at any
rate no lack of opportunity for the *right* word to be heard. It
will do all it can to see that there are opportunities for mutual
discussion in the civil community as the basis of common
endeavours. And it will try to see that such discussion takes
place openly. With all its strength it will be on the side of those
who refuse to have anything to do with the regimentation, con-
trolling and censoring of public opinion. It knows of no pretext
which would make that a good thing and no situation in which
it could be necessary.

24

As disciples of Christ, the members of His Church do not
rule: they serve. In the political community, therefore, the
Church can only regard all ruling that is not primarily a form of
service, as a diseased and never as a normal condition. No State
can exist without the sanction of power. But the power of the
good State differs from that of the bad State as *potestas* differs
from *potentia*. *Potestas* is the power that follows and serves the
law; *potentia* is the power that precedes the law, that masters
and bends and breaks the law—it is the naked power which is
directly evil. Bismarck—not to mention Hitler—was (in spite of
the *Daily Bible Readings* on his bedside table) no model states-
man because he wanted to establish and develop his work on
naked power. The ultimate result of this all-too-consistently pursued aim was inevitable: 'all that draw the sword shall perish
by the sword'. Christian political theory leads us in the very
opposite direction.

25

Since the Church is ecumenical (catholic) by virtue of its very
origin, it resists all abstract local, regional and national interests

in the political sphere. It will always seek to serve the best interests of the particular city or place where it is stationed. But it will never do this without at the same time looking out beyond the city walls. It will be conscious of the superficiality, relativity and temporariness of the immediate city boundaries, and on principle it will always stand for understanding and co-operation within the wider circle. The Church will be the last to lend its support to mere parochial politics. *Pacta sunt servanda? Pacta sunt concludenda!* All cities of the realm must agree if their common cause is to enjoy stability and not fall to pieces. In the Church we have tasted the air of freedom and must bring others to taste it too.

26

The Church knows God's anger and judgment, but it also knows that His anger lasts but for a moment, whereas His mercy is for eternity. The political analogy of this truth is that violent solutions of conflicts in the political community—from police measures to law court decisions, from the armed rising against a régime that is no longer worthy of or equal to its task (in the sense of a revolt undertaken not to undermine but to restore the lawful authority of the State) to the defensive war against an external threat to the lawful State—must be approved, supported and if necessary even suggested by the Christian community—for how could it possibly contract out in such situations? On the other hand, it can only regard violent solutions of any con-flict as an *ultima ratio regis*. It will approve and support them only when they are for the moment the ultimate and only possi-bility available. It will always do its utmost to postpone such moments as far as possible. It can never stand for absolute peace, for peace at any price. But it must and will do all it can to see that no price is considered too high for the preservation or restoration of peace at home and abroad except the ultimate price which would mean the abolition of the lawful State and the practical denial of the divine ordinance. May the Church show her inventiveness in the search for other solutions before she joins in the call for violence! The perfection of the Father in heaven, who does not cease to be the heavenly Judge, demands the earthly perfection of a peace policy which really does extend to the limits of the humanly possible.

27

These are a few examples of Christian choices, decisions and activities in the political sphere: examples of analogies and corollaries of that Kingdom of God in which the Church believes and which it preaches, in the sphere of the external, relative and provisional problems of the civil community. The translation of the Kingdom of God into political terms demands Christian, spiritual and prophetic knowledge on every side. The points of comparison and the decisions we have quoted are in no sense equivalent to the paragraphs of a political constitution. They are merely intended to illustrate how the Church can make decisions on a Christian basis in the political sphere. We might have taken twice or three times as many or only half as many examples or just one example to make the vital point clear. We used examples because we were concerned to illuminate the analogical but extremely concrete relationship between the Christian gospel and certain political decisions and modes of behaviour. The only more concrete way of discussing the relationship would be to refer to individual historical decisions. The reason why we mentioned many examples was that we wanted to demonstrate that the essence of Christian politics is not a system or a succession of momentary brainwaves but a constant direction, a continuous line of discoveries on both sides of the boundary which separates the political from the spiritual spheres, a correlation between explication and application. The list of such explications and applications that we have offered here is naturally incomplete. And it is of the very nature of all such points of contact and decision as have been or could have been mentioned that the translations and transitions from the one sphere to the other will always be open to discussion as far as the details are concerned, will only be more or less obvious and never subject to absolute proof. What we have said here needs to be extended, deepened and particularised. The more one studies the problems of translation from one sphere to the other, the more one will realise that it is not possible to deal with every problem in this way. But the clarity of the message of the Bible will guarantee that all the explications and applications of the Christian approach will move in one unswerving direction and one continuous line. What we were concerned to show was the possibility and the necessity of comparisons and analogies between the two spheres and of the decisions which have to be made in the transition from one to the other.

28

Let me add a comment on the constancy and continuousness of the line of Christian political thought and action that we have indicated. We have argued not from any conception of 'natural law' but from the gospel. It cannot be denied, however, that in the list of examples quoted we have more than once made assertions which have been justified elsewhere on the basis of natural law. We bear no grudge against anyone who may have been reminded of Rousseau—and who may have been pleased or angry on that account. We need not be ashamed of the affinity. We have seen that the divine ordinance of the State makes it perfectly possible for theoretical and practical insights and decisions to be reached, which are objectively right, where one would inevitably expect only errors and false steps, in view of the turbid source from which they derive. If our results really did coincide with theses based on natural law, it would merely confirm that the *polis* is in the Kingdom of Jesus Christ even when its office holders are not aware of the fact or refuse to admit it, and therefore are unable to use the insight into the nature of the *polis* which this fact suggests. Why should it be impossible that, in spite of the State's blindness, objectively correct insights have been and are being reached again and again? The pagan State lives because such leadership of the blind has repeatedly made its stability and its functions possible. All the more reason, surely, why the Church cannot and must not withhold its witness to an insight based on clearly defined and consistently applicable facts.

29

A further comment on the constancy and continuity of the Christian approach in politics: it may be remarked (again, with pleasure or annoyance) that the Christian line that follows from the gospel betrays a striking tendency to the side of what is generally called the 'democratic' State. Here again, we shall be careful not to deny an obvious fact, though 'democracy' in any technical meaning of the word (Swiss, American, French, etc.), is certainly not necessarily the form of State closest to the Christian view. Such a State may equally well assume the form of a monarchy or an aristocracy, and occasionally even that of a dictatorship. Conversely, no democracy as such is protected from failing in many or all of the points we have enumerated and degenerating not only into anarchy but also into tyranny and thereby becoming a bad State. It must be admitted that the word and the concept 'democracy' ('the rule of the people') is powerless to describe even approximately the kind of State which, in the Christian view, most nearly corresponds to the divine ordinance. This is no reason, however, why it should be overlooked or denied that Christian choices and purposes in politics tend on the whole towards the form of State, which, if it is not actually realised in the so-called 'democracies', is at any rate more or less honestly clearly intended and desired. Taking everything into account, it must be said that the Christian view shows a stronger trend in this direction than in any other. There certainly is an affinity between the Christian community and the civil communities of the free peoples.

30

In conclusion, we propose to discuss the problem of how Christian decisions in the political sphere may be put into action.

The first method that suggests itself is the formation and activity of a special Christian party. This has long been adopted in Holland and later in Switzerland (Evangelical People's Party), and in recent times especially in France (Mouvement Républicain Populaire) and Germany (Christian Democratic Union). On the Protestant side it has been deemed possible and necessary to join forces with Roman Catholic fellow-citizens with the same political views. But parties are one of the most questionable phenomena in political life: they are in no sense its constitutive elements, and it is possible that from the very outset they have been pathological or at least no more than secondary phenomena. I wonder if the Christian community is well advised to add one more to the number of these organisations in order to fulfil its own share of political responsibility? Can there be any other 'Christian' party in the State but the Christian fellowship itself, with its special mission and purpose? And if what we want is a political corollary of the Church in political life, can anything else be permissible and possible but—please do not be scared!—a single State party excluding all others, whose programme would necessarily coincide with the tasks of the State itself, understood in the widest sense (but excluding all particularist ideas and interests)? How can there be a special Christian party alongside other political parties?—a party to which some Christians belong, whilst others do not—a party opposed by other non-Christian parties (which it must nevertheless recognise as legitimately non-Christian). To institute special Christian parties implies that the Christian community as such has no claim on the support of all its members for its own political line. It implies that it cannot help but allow the non-Christians in the State to consolidate themselves in a non-Christian bloc in order to enforce their own anti-Christian line. The Church's supreme interest must be rather that Christians shall not mass together in a special party, since their task is to defend and proclaim, in decisions based on it, the Christian gospel that concerns all men. They must show that although they go their own special way, they are not in fact against anybody but unconditionally for all men, for the common cause of the whole State.

In the political sphere the Christian community can draw attention to its gospel only indirectly, as reflected in its political decisions, and these decisions can be made intelligible and brought to victory not because they are based on Christian premises but only because they are politically better and more calculated to preserve and develop the common life. They can only witness to Christian truths. The claim to be witnesses to Christian truths does not necessarily make them such, however! Surely it will be inevitable that the Christian qualities for which it can have no use in the political sphere will become an embarrassment to a Christian party? And will not the aims and methods which it needs if it is to be effective as a political party (the winning of majorities and political strongholds, propaganda and the benevolent toleration and even encouragement of non-Christian or problematically Christian sympathisers and even leaders; compromises and coalitions with 'non-Christian' parties and so on) compel it to deny the specifically Christian content of its policy or at any rate obscure rather than illuminate it? Will such a party not inevitably be compromising the Christian Church and its message all the time? In the political sphere Christians can only bring in their Christianity anonymously. They can break through this anonymity only by waging a political battle for the Church and by so doing they will inevitably bring discredit and disgrace on the Christian name. In the authentically political questions which affect the development of the civil community Christians can only reply in the form of decisions which could be the decisions of any other citizens, and they must frankly hope that they may become the decisions of all other citizens regardless of their religious profession. How can Christians mass together in a political party at all in these circumstances? The thing is only possible—and the suspicious alliance of the Protestants with the Romans in the French M.R.P. and the German C.D.U. shows that it only becomes successful, where the Kingdom of God is interpreted as a human goal founded on natural law, where an allegedly Christian law, which is in fact a mere amalgam of humanitarian philosophy and morality, is set alongside the gospel in the political sphere. When it is represented by a Christian party the Christian community cannot be the political salt which it is its duty to be in the civil community.

31

The opportunity that it is offered to fulfil this duty is simply the one that lies nearest to hand: the preaching of the whole gospel of God's grace, which as such is the whole justification of the whole man—including political man. This gospel which proclaims the King and the Kingdom that is now hidden but

will one day be revealed, is political from the very outset, and
if it is preached to real (Christian and non-Christian) men on
the basis of a right interpretation of the Scriptures it will necessarily be prophetically political. Explications and applications of
its political content in an unmistakable direction will inevitably
take place (whether in direct or indirect illumination of the political problems of the day) where the Christian community is
gathered together in the service of this gospel. Whether this
happens or not will depend on the preachers, but not only on
them. It is a bad sign when Christians are frightened by 'political'
sermons—as if Christian preaching could be anything but political. And if it were not political, how would it show that it is
the salt and the light of the world? The Christian Church that
is aware of its political responsibility will demand political preaching; and it will interpret it politically even if it contains no direct
reference to politics. Let the Church concentrate first, however,
on seeing that the whole gospel really is preached within its own
area. Then there will be no danger of the wider sphere beyond
the Church not being wholesomely disturbed by it.

32

The Christian community acts within the meaning and limits
of its own mission and competence when it speaks, through the
mouth of its presbyterial and synodal organs, in important situations in political life, by making representations to the authorities
or by public proclamations. It will be careful to select, as wisely
as possible, the particular situations in which it deems it right to
speak, and it will have to choose its words very prudently and
very definitely if it is to be heard. It must not give the impression
that it never wakes from the sleep of an otherwise non-political
existence until such matters as gambling or the abuse of alcohol
or the desecration of the Sabbath or similar questions of a religious and ethical nature in the narrower sense are under discussion,
as if such problems were not in fact only on the verge of real
political life. The Church must see that it does not make a habit
of coming on the scene too late, of entering the fray only when
its opinions no longer involve any particular risk and can no
longer exert any particular influence. It must see above all that

the idea of the Church as the representative of a definitive class-conditioned outlook and morality is not allowed to gain ground, thereby confirming those who already loyally believe in this 'law' and arousing the disapproval of those who are, on the contrary, unable to regard such a 'law' as in any sense eternal. All this applies just as much to the Christian journalism and writing that is carried on with or even without the authority of the Church. Christian publicists and writers must place themselves honestly in the service of the gospel which is intended for all men and not devote their gifts to some Christian fad or another.

33

Perhaps the most important contribution the Church can make is to bear in mind in the shaping of its own life that, gathered as it is directly and consciously around the common centre, it has to represent the inner within the outer circle. The real Church must be the model and prototype of the real State. The Church must set an example so that by its very existence it may be a source of renewal for the State and the power by which the State is preserved. The Church's preaching of the gospel would be in vain if its own existence, constitution, order, government and administration were not a practical demonstration of the thinking and acting from the gospel which takes place in this inner circle. How can the world believe the gospel of the King and His Kingdom if by its own actions and attitudes the Church shows that it has no intention of basing its own internal policy on the gospel? How can a reformation of the whole people be brought about if it is common knowledge that the Church itself is bent only on self-preservation and restoration—or not even that? Of the political implications of theology which we have enumerated there are few which do not merit attention first of all in the life and development of the Church itself. So far they have not received anything like enough attention within the Church's own borders.

What nonsense it is, for example, that in a country like Germany which has diligently to learn the rudiments of law, freedom, responsibility, equality and so on, that is, the elements of the democratic way of life, the Church considers it necessary to act more and more hieratically and bureaucratically and becomes a refuge for nationalism in a situation in which it ought supremely to appear as the holy catholic Church, and thereby help to lead German politics out of an old defile. The Church must not forget that what it is rather than what it says will be best understood, not least in the State.

34

If the Church is a Christian community it will not need a Christian party. If it is a true fellowship it will perform with its words and its whole existence all the functions which the disastrous enterprise of 'Christian' parties is evidently intended to fulfil. There will be no lack of individual Christians who will enter the political arena anonymously, that is, in the only way they can appear on the political scene, and who will act in accordance with the Christian approach and will thereby prove themselves unassuming witnesses of the Gospel of Christ, which can alone bring salvation in the political sphere no less than elsewhere. Any fame that they acquire will not be founded on the fact that they are 'nice, pious people' but simply that from their own distinctive point of view they will know better than others what is best for the civil community. It is not the presence and co-operation of 'Christian personalities' that helps the State. One thinks of Bismarck again: assuming for the moment that he was something like the 'Christian personality' that legend describes him to have been, what difference did it make to the unfortunate tendency of his politics? What help was it to poor Germany? The way Christians can help in the political sphere is by constantly giving the State an impulse in the Christian direction and freedom to develop on the Christian line. Let it not be said that there are too few of such Christians and that these few in their isolation are helpless. How much one individual can do whose heart and soul is really wrapped up in the cause! And in any case Christians are not asked to do something in their own strength, but only what they are required to do by the grace of God.

What does it matter if they are isolated and if—since there are such things as parties—they are members of different parties, that is, of one of the various 'non-Christian' parties? They will take the party programme, party discipline, party victories and party defeats in which they are involved, as seriously and humorously as the cause deserves. In every party they will be against narrow party policies and stand up for the interests of the whole community. By that token they will be political men and women in the primary meaning of the word. Scattered in different places, and known or unknown to one another, in touch with one another or out of touch, they will all be together—as citizens, and will make the same distinctions and judgments, choose and desire one cause, work for one cause. Let us pray that the Church may supply the State with such Christians, such citizens, such political men and women in the primary meaning of the word! For in their existence the Church will be fulfilling its share of political responsibility in the most direct form.

35

Let me remind you once again of the fifth thesis of the *Theological Declaration* of Barmen, which I have quoted from several times already:

> The Bible tells us that, in accordance with a divine ordinance, the State has the task of providing for law and peace in the world that still awaits redemption, in which the Church stands, according to the measure of human insight and human capacity, and upheld by the threat and use of force. The Church acknowledges the benefaction of this divine ordinance with a thankful, reverent heart. It reminds men of God's Kingdom, God's Commandment and justice, and thereby of the responsibility of governors and governed alike. It trusts and obeys the power of the Word by which God sustains all things.

I think that I have dealt with 'The Christian Community and the Civil Community' within the terms of this thesis, and therefore in accordance with the mind of the Confessional Church in Germany. Some things would be different now if that Church had itself given more attention to this section of the Declaration in good time. But it cannot be too late to return to it now with a new seriousness, deepened and strengthened by experience.

II

THE CHRISTIAN COMMUNITY IN THE MIDST OF POLITICAL CHANGE

Documents of various kinds, lectures, *ex tempore* discussion, letters, etc., from a journey to Hungary in the spring and summer of 1948.

THE CHRISTIAN COMMUNITY
IN THE MIDST OF
POLITICAL CHANGE

1. 'BLESSED ARE THE MEEK
FOR THEY SHALL INHERIT THE EARTH' (Matt. 5.5)

*A Sermon preached in the Great Church in Debrecen
on Good Friday 1948.*

WE are gathered here today to hear the message of Good
Friday, the tidings of the suffering and death of our Lord Jesus
Christ. Let me say straight away that these tidings are not tidings
of disaster or tidings of mourning. We do not stand beneath the
Cross of Christ as did His disciples and the women that stood by
the Cross. For He who was crucified at that time and in that
place rose again on the third day. His suffering and death were
thus revealed to be our life and salvation. Properly understood,
there is no difference between the message of Good Friday and
the message of Christmas: 'Behold I bring you good tidings of
great joy, which shall be to all people.' Blessed are those who
are called to hear and accept this message.

For those who do hear and accept it the message of Good
Friday means the promise: 'they shall inherit the earth'. They
are already appointed heirs and will one day be able to enter
into possession. This inheritance is the land, the earth, the dwelling
place created by God beneath His heaven. Here they are to be
allowed to live as God determined and intended that man
should live.

They will not be strangers and fugitives in the world created
by God: they will be at home, they will be in their native land.
This world with its heights and depths, with its growth and decay,
its miracles and mysteries, will belong to them and they will no
longer be servants but masters therein. No troubles will torment
them any more, for the land will feed and water them. No fear

will trouble them, for there will be no enemies to harm them.
They will not be prisoners but free men and women. They will
no longer know the evil longing and desire to do wrong to
secure right for themselves, for they will all come into their
rightful inheritance. They will no longer need to resist one
another, to vie and quarrel, for they will have a common cause
to be thankful and rejoice. God will wipe away all tears from
their eyes and death will be no more, nor sorrow, nor crying,
nor pain, for the first things are passed away.

This is the promise of Good Friday for those for whom it is
intended and who can hear and accept it.

But who are those for whom the message of Good Friday is
intended to be a good and a joyful message? 'Blessed are the
meek, for they shall inherit the earth.' Note that it was Jesus
who said this. To understand who the meek are we shall have
to hold fast to Him. In the language of the Bible the meek are
those who have truly humbled themselves, those who have been
truly humiliated, those who have truly fallen from the height
to the depths.

In the real and precise meaning of the word, however, Jesus
Christ alone was ever meek. And so the promise which is given
to the meek is wholly contained in Him and its fulfilment is to
be found in Him alone. We men and women can be humbled
and humiliated too. Perhaps we have once been rich and become
poor. Perhaps we have fallen from honour to disgrace, perhaps
we once lived securely and must now live in great insecurity.
But none of us has come down from the height and majesty
of God. We may know something of what it means to live in
the depths and in loneliness: but none of us has ever been in
the depths of hell and rejected by God. And when we are humbled
and humiliated it is against our will. None of us wants to be
humiliated, none of us wants to accept humiliation freely and
willingly. Even when we are humbled and humiliated we are
still proud in the bottom of our hearts, because we have not
humbled and humiliated ourselves before God. The truly humbled
and humiliated and therefore the meek are those who are humbled
before God. But Jesus Christ alone was truly meek. 'I am meek
and lowly in heart.' Only He was able to say that. And in this
very meekness, this true submission and humiliation before God

Jesus Christ, rejected by the Jews and condemned by the Gentiles, was a free man, a lord, a prince, a sovereign, the King of all kings, the liberator of His people Israel, the Saviour of the nations.

For in this His meekness which we remember today, He achieved the mightiest of all deeds ever fulfilled on earth: in His own person He restored and re-established the violated law of God and the shattered law of man. In this meekness the grace of God appeared in His person, and the obedient man, at peace with God and in whom God has pleasure, was revealed. In this meekness of His, Jesus Christ, nailed to the Cross as a criminal, created order in the realm of creation, the order in which man can live eternally, as the redeemed, converted child of God.

The whole fullness of the promise is contained in this one person: the possession of the land, freedom and life and our appointment as heirs. In Him who was betrayed by Judas and forsaken by all His disciples, who was condemned by the High Priest and sentenced by Pilate, who was mocked by the mercenaries and died on the gallows, in Him all this is contained.

In Him the clear promise to all holds good: 'I know what thoughts I cherish about you, thoughts of peace and not of sorrow.' In Him, the truly meek! This was revealed in His resurrection.

And now He comes into our midst wherever His Word is preached and His Holy Meal celebrated. He comes, the Holy One, to us, to His people, who still understand Him so badly and bear witness to Him so imperfectly and whom He has yet loved and still loves and will love to eternity. He passes through our modern world with all its anxiety, dissension and misery. He is passing through this congregation now. And He cries: 'Blessed are the meek!' What else can that mean except that He is calling us to Himself?

My friends, we shall never be able to compare ourselves with Him. We shall never rival Him; we shall never be meek as He was meek. But we shall be allowed to be numbered among those who bend their knees in His name. And this bending of the knees is the meekness to which He invites us, who are wholly unlike Him. He invites us to remember that He was meek for us, that He became a servant for us and was obedient even unto death on the Cross; that He who was rich became poor that we, through His poverty, might become rich.

He invites us to believe in Him. He calls us: 'Come unto me all ye that labour and are heavy laden and I will give you rest.' The meek who inherit the earth are those who hear the voice of the eternal God in the bitter suffering and shameful death of Jesus: 'I have loved thee with an everlasting love: therefore with loving kindness have I drawn thee.'

Amen.

2. MODERN YOUTH:
ITS INHERITANCE AND ITS RESPONSIBILITY

A talk given in Sarospatak and Budapest in March and April 1948.

My friends! When a representative of the older generation spoke to young people forty years ago, when I was a student myself, he was able to do so with the self-assurance of a father with a fine and precious inheritance to show and later to pass on to his son. He had a strong background: centuries of the richest imaginable achievement, of almost uninterrupted progress in all fields, the whole structure of a venerable civilisation. He had a solid platform to stand on. He had the right to demand a respectful hearing, and the young people would have been wrong to deny it to him.

Perhaps even forty years ago the inheritance was not quite so marvellous and the platform not quite so high as it seemed. Even at that time there were more problems and anxieties in the air, more cracks in the timbers than the older generation were willing to admit, and we younger people able to perceive. But the walls of old Europe were still standing; its light, though already somewhat clouded over, was still shining. Today it shines no more. Western civilisation is out of joint. Instead of leading us to still further heights, the progress of the centuries has suddenly brought us to the depths of two world wars which have left a sea of ruin behind them and destroyed millions upon millions of lives, though no one can say what they all really died for. And now the wars are over humanity is divided into more mutually hostile camps than ever before. Science and technics have been concentrated on forging more and more terrible weapons of death and destruction. And if it has not actually taught crime and corruption, Western philosophy has at any rate, in defiance of its great history, not proved a restraining and conserving force.

We have seen how the morality of modern civilised man has turned out to be a terribly thin covering of ice over a sea of primitive barbarity. We have an art that can apparently offer us nothing better than a confirmation of our own disintegration. And we have Christian churches which have only occasionally borne a clear witness in the midst of disaster; and there is no doubt but that in recent years the whole conception of a Christian civilisation in the West has been pitilessly exposed as an illusion—not least in the eyes of the heathen and Mohammedan world.

This then is the world we older people have to show and pass on to you younger folk. This is what it was developing into in the years of our prime, when we were in positions of leadership or responsibility. How can we claim a respectful hearing from you? The usual complaint of the old about the young might well be reversed today, and you might ask us what we really feel about not being able to bequeath you anything better; how we feel about having to send you on your journey from such unworthy beginnings. But I shall probably not be wrong if I assume that you are far too preoccupied with yourselves to worry us with such questions—too preoccupied with your own question: where do we go from here? It will indeed be far more your own question since you will have to rely on yourselves for the answer to a much greater degree than we did forty years ago and than did very many generations before us. In many matters it will be almost impossible for you to establish any link with the past. I wonder if you realise what a privilege that is, however? We have no right at all to prevent you examining very freely and very strictly everything that has been transmitted to you and forming your own opinions. Your poverty implies a splendid freedom from preconceived ideas and judgments which we of the older generation used secretly to yearn for, but which could not be our lot at that time. I know and you know even better how much is denied to you. But do let me tell you that it is a mark of distinction for a younger generation to be forced

to accept the freedom of individual responsibility as you are
today—perhaps for the first time for a very long age in the
history of the relationship between young and old.

Let me say a few more words to you as you set out on your
way; they come from one who lived through the end of the
age that has now gone, but who still knew its fragile, though
far from empty, glory, and who may for that very reason be
able to give you some advice. Your freedom will really have to
be the freedom to accept responsibility. It will therefore be no
cheap or easy freedom. The fact that we have so clearly made
a mess of our affairs does not absolve you from the task of
making the very best of yours. We cannot discharge you from
that responsibility. The conditions under which you are forced
to take up your task today are not favourable. You may be forgiven by later generations if your success is only partial. But you
must not expect to be forgiven if you do not take your life in
hand, just as it is, with the utmost seriousness. It is the only life
you have. And your turn has come.

A younger generation confronted by so much emptiness will
inevitably be tempted to yield to certain fears remote from freedom and responsibility. I should not be advising you well if I
did not implore you to resist them. One of them might consist
in trying to drown the miseries of the time with as much technics,
sport and aesthetic amusement as possible, with all the worldly
pleasures that are still available. No one will begrudge you for
wanting to make up for long years of darkness by indulging in
one or two pastimes of that kind. But see that you do not repeat
the error which the younger generation before you certainly
made. By over-indulging itself in technics, sport and aesthetic
amusements it developed a state of mind or rather mindlessness
in which, through neglecting its responsibilities, it also lost its
freedom and fell an easy prey to the slogans and catchwords of
the charlatans and dictators.

Another temptation to which the younger generation may
succumb is once again to look around for leadership and authority, for some binding prescription or other. There is no lack
of pigeon-holes, old and new, where such recipes, or rather,
marching orders, are all prepared for those who know not the
value of freedom. The Roman Church promises the security of

a firm authority throughout the world; and one has only to submit to some of the political systems already in existence to be rid very quickly of personal responsibility and to learn discipline in plenty. I wonder if you are aware that all propaganda is an invention of the devil, and whether you are determined to deal with it accordingly even though it may be easier, and less troublesome, to allow it to ensnare you?

You may also be tempted to find refuge in the scepticism and intellectual nihilism which considers neither freedom nor discipline, good nor evil worthy of more than a weary smile. In Western Europe we have a philosophy the most advanced champions of which have just reached the point of informing us that the true humanist, the one whose life is most fulfilled, is the person who is capable of the greatest boredom; and—according to Sartre—even hell itself has no fire and torment, but is merely a place without windows and exits, a place filled with the boredom which three men, distributed among three sofas, are bound to feel for one another for ever more. 'Continuons!' is the last word of this remarkable drama (its name is *Huit clos*) before the curtain falls. My advice is this: Let us not even begin like this, let alone 'continue', or if we have already made a start in this direction, let us turn back again as quickly as possible! Perhaps this was the worm that was only too much at home in the timbers of the old house. It is not worth feeding the animal. Take it from me that the tiniest spark of simple faith in life and readiness to accept responsibility is better than a whole load of this wisdom of the worms.

In this sense then let us cry: *Vivat libertas!* If the youth of today is going to be free, then it must use its freedom to test its inheritance and to confer new honour on what is worthy of honour. Much, though not everything, had to be consumed by the fire and cannot and must not return. But some of the inheritance is waiting for the understanding ears and eyes and faithful hands of this very generation, that it may come into its own.

That twice two are four and not five was and is a precious truth which must still remain in force in the coming age for which you will bear responsibility. The Ten Commandments will also remain in force or rather return to force after having been transgressed so violently. The serpent's counsel, Let us do

evil that good may come out of it! should continue to be banned
in the future. A lie must still be called a lie and injustice injustice.
For there is no doubt that God will remain God and will know
how to find and to judge all who would have it otherwise, as
He has done from the beginning.

Again and again in time past there have been men both able
and determined to think for themselves. It would not be a good
thing if there were to be no such men in your generation. Listen
to a few sentences from old Immanuel Kant's treatise, *What is
Enlightenment?*:

> Enlightenment is man's departure from the mental infancy
> for which he has only himself to blame. Mental infancy is the
> inability to use one's intelligence without the guidance of
> someone else. It is one's own fault if the cause lies not in the
> lack of intelligence but in lack of decision and the courage to
> use it without someone else's guidance. *Sapere aude!* Have the
> courage to use your own intelligence! is therefore the motto
> of the Enlightenment.

It would be a bad thing if the youth of today was no longer
receptive to the spirit which inspired these sentences. On the contrary, it would be a good thing if the second half of the twentieth
century were to become an age of 'Enlightenment' in the best
sense of the word, after the first half has unexpectedly brought
us so much dark insanity. It will be up to you to do all you can
to bring this about.

We hope that the coming age—your age—will be an age in
which the music of Mozart and the poetry of Goethe will be
received with ever more sensitive ears and open hearts. And I
do not think that an age which had no room for a federated
State like the Swiss Confederation, founded on the freely con-
stituted and freely expressed will of the people, could be called
a good age. It certainly could not develop into a good age, however, if the gospel of Jesus Christ, the message of free grace, the
word of the Christian who is in faith lord of all things and in
love the servant of all things, were to become silent or no longer
heard.

My friends, I cannot have given you the impression that I

speak to you as a *laudator temporis acti*. It is my earnest belief that everything we see before us today is more or less polluted, diluted and devalued. But the freedom of youth will be tested by its daring to rediscover, recognise and acknowledge (better than we did) the things that were and will therefore remain true and right, and good and beautiful even in the shadows which cloud them in the present. Do not waste your inheritance on any account, mean though it may seem to you today. One day you too will have to pass it on to those who come after you. Perhaps you will think of me when those as yet unborn stand before you and ask what you have done, not to diminish but to increase, the inheritance that was entrusted to you in this time of great affliction which is, for all that, a time of great opportunity for the exercise of freely accepted responsibility.

I have almost finished. If your freedom is to be strong and genuine it will have to have a foundation. What was called freedom in the European age now passed collapsed, and was bound to collapse, because for a long time and at an amazingly deep level it had degenerated into a freedom for godlessness and inhumanity—not merely in its secular and evil form but in its religious and moral form too. Do not hesitate to describe and treat anyone as a 'reactionary' who attempts to commend this kind of freedom to you under whatever name. Freedom means freedom for God and one's neighbour. Wherever it is something different from that it is not freedom for responsibility. In the freedom for God and one's neighbour you will find the right words and instinctively take the right steps and grow into defiance against the idols of yesterday and those of today. You will not become doctrinaires: not conservative nor revolutionary nor even democratic doctrinaires! The New Testament calls this freedom the freedom of the children of God, our freedom in Jesus Christ. Why? Because as true God and true man Jesus Christ has brought God and man together. 'If the Son shall make you free ye shall be free indeed.' This Word was also spoken to our generation. We did not understand it very well. Will it be granted to your generation to understand it a little better? May it be granted to you! What is certain is that we the old and you the youth of today, are members one of another as we listen to this Word.

3. THE REAL CHURCH

A lecture delivered in Miskolc, Debrecen, Budapest, Papa and Sopron in March and April, and to the Bernese Pastors' Association, Burgdorf, in June, 1948.

The word 'Church' has again acquired a stronger and more significant sound in our time. In 1926 the then General Superintendent and present Bishop of Berlin, Otto Dibelius, published a book entitled *The Century of the Church*, meaning this twentieth century of ours. The author has certainly been proved correct in that there has been more discussion about the Church in the three decades since the end of the first world war than in the whole of the eighteenth and nineteenth centuries put together. Who would have dreamed that this could have happened, even around 1910, when the writing of Hermann Kutter, for example, was at the height of its influence? Perhaps the almost complete breakdown of the political, economic and cultural pattern of Europe which began with the first world war may have suggested the question whether it might not fall to the lot of the Church to save this old Europe once again and perhaps revive it in a new form, just as it once helped to found it. The Roman Catholic Church seems to be particularly full of hope in this respect and to awaken much public and private expectation. The fact that its outward life has become much more imposing again, and the very vigorous advances it is making in some directions, are certainly among the reasons why the word 'Church' has come so much more into the foreground of Christian awareness and theological 'conversations' even outside its own ground. The Roman Church certainly owes something of its strength to its outstanding ability to put across the idea that it is the 'real Church'. It must not be forgotten, however, that during the great crisis which lasted from 1933 to 1945 certain 'proofs of the Spirit and the power' were manifested in the Protestant Church, first of all in Germany, then especially in Holland and Norway and elsewhere too, which should neither be overestimated nor underestimated, and which were in fact more or less unexpected wherever they were found. These manifestations of the power of the Spirit made a good many people inside and outside these churches aware that the inner disintegration of the Protestant Church was not so far advanced as had sometimes been supposed.

The concept of the Church has been impressed on us from a quite different angle through the ecumenical movement which has been with us for nearly a quarter of a century now. This movement, by bringing the weaker churches in touch with the other actually or allegedly stronger and at any rate more self-confident churches, has suggested to them that they might put more trust in their own cause. And finally, the abandonment by evangelical theology at least in some fields of the traditional liberalism and individualism of the fathers of the eighteenth and nineteenth centuries, and a fresh appreciation of the belief in the communion of saints, may well have helped to move the thoughts of many in this direction, in spite of the many other ways in which the change has taken place.

Now, the more urgently the 'Church' is discussed today, the more reason there obviously is to be clear about what is really meant by this word and concept—in so far of course as it is not being used without any meaning at all. What is the Church really? What is the 'real Church'? That is the question to which we want to attempt to give as simple and central an answer as possible.

I

The real Church becomes visible in so far as it emerges and shines forth from its seclusion in ecclesiastical organisation, tradition and custom, in the power of the Holy Spirit.

We shall begin by asking where and how is the real Church to be seen? According to the third article of the old Creed it is one of the realities in which as Christians we must believe. This means, however, that even Christians can see the real Church only through faith. The real Church is not visible in the way the State is directly visible in its citizens and officials, laws and institutions. What is seen in faith is seen in the radiant emergence of the content of faith, over which the believer has no power, in which he can share only by grace. The real Church is truly not invisible but visible. But it is visible only where it is rendered visible by the action of God, by the witness of the Holy Spirit. This is the visibility in which the Church is seen by faith.

What is seen in the same place without faith and without this revelation and witness is not the real Church at all. Obviously, as a religious society the Church can be seen just as a State can be seen. What is seen are simply the church members and officials, church ordinances and constitutions, church buildings and church history, the Bible, dogma and ritual, churchgoers and parsons in all their divers activities, and the like. But all this is merely the outward image and semblance of the Church. What is visible is the 'something' that claims, in all places and under many different names, to be the 'Church'. Clearly, this 'something' can be seen without any faith at all. But the real Church is seen only when it comes forth as the original behind the image, as the truth behind the semblance. And when it comes forth it comes forth unmistakably. It really can be seen. In the very place where before only the image and the semblance were seen, the real Church is seen. Just as the dark letters of an illuminated advertisement become visible, legible, speaking when the current is switched on. And as we gaze at this real Church which is visible only to the eye of faith, we believe in the holy catholic Church, as we believe in the Holy Spirit and therefore in God. It is in fact not the Church itself which makes its reality visible, but the Holy Spirit, and therefore God, whose pleasure it is to confer this visibility on the Church. Yet whenever the Church is mentioned we all tend to think first of the image and semblance. We so rarely believe what we say when we use the word. It is well to realise then that what the word brings to mind is not the real Church at all. The opportunity to think of the real Church is given to us only through the mercy of God. He acknowledges the image and the semblance and therefore ourselves, and He makes us, by believing in Him, believe in the real Church and see the real Church.

2

*The real Church will therefore always and everywhere be
visible only to a very few, very frightened and very joyful
'Christians' and to these only by the free grace of God.*

What has been said so far should be a warning. We talk about the Church nowadays too easily, too glibly, too positively and too directly, as if (because we have again realised, perhaps owing to better exegesis and dogmatics, that such a thing exists at all) it simply 'existed' and were visible and available to us as Christians along with its authority and all its spiritual treasures. I am thinking of many of our younger theologians, who have not themselves taken part in the Exodus from Egypt and the crossing of the Jordan, and who now find it difficult to realise that the way from seeing to believing and from believing to a new kind of seeing is a way which it is no foregone conclusion that one will go or rather be led. The image of the Church is after all merely an image and its semblance merely a semblance, if the mercy of God does not intervene and cause us to see the real Church. It is possible to talk very importantly, very solemnly, very ecclesiastically and no doubt very impressively and movingly and yet all the time quite emptily about the Church, if all one really sees is the image and semblance, if faith with its insight has not intervened, if the Church, which is worthy of the highest praise, has not yet come into sight at all, if all the praise of the Church in fact refers merely to the 'something' that all the world can see, if it does not stem from faith. The Church seen without faith cannot be a credible Church: it can rouse no faith. We need to be warned against the dangerous successes that are won too easily to last.

The belief in and therefore the seeing of the real Church is not everyone's affair, for this believing and seeing are inevitably dependent on the revelation of God and the witness of the Holy Spirit. Here, too, many are called, but few are chosen. The matter can be put to the test. The real Church is the lowliest, the poorest, meanest, weakest thing that can possibly exist under God's heaven, gathered as it is around a manger and a Cross. But who is frightened by this stark fact when he says the word 'Church'? Who really considers what a deep disgrace he takes upon himself when he acknowledges the Church? If we saw the real Church how frightened we should be! And the real Church is also the highest, richest, most radiant and mighty thing under God's heaven, just as surely as the one born in a manger and crucified on Golgotha rose from the dead and reigns at God's right hand. But who really rejoices in this fact when he utters the word 'Church'? Who really thinks of the incomparable

E

honour that is conferred on him by being allowed to acknowledge the Church? If we were to see the real Church, with what joy we should rejoice! There is certainly no lack of timid believers, and plenty of only too confident believers too. But where are those who are both frightened and joyful; where are those who have knowledge of the real Church? 'When the Son of man cometh, shall he find faith on the earth?' (Luke 18.8). Is it not true that those who know the real Church will never be the many but only the few? Do not misunderstand me: the offer and the challenge are issued to all. Who could not, who would dare not to see the real Church? But the mystery of free grace and the mystery of free faith stand winnowing in the midst even of those who seriously desire to be Christians. When one realises that, one will be careful not to be too glib and dogmatic in this matter, since we can speak of the real Church only with fear and trembling—only with very great fear and very great joy.

3

The real Church lives as the congregation of its Lord, i.e. as the assembly of lost sinners called by Him, and living by the consolation and admonition of the biblical witness to the reconciliation of the world with God, which has taken place in Him.

We shall now attempt to give an initial answer to the all-important question: how and from what and for what does the real Church live? With our eyes fixed simply on its establishment by Jesus Christ, we answer:

A. It lives as His congregation, bound to and inseparable from Him. It lives with Him and from Him but He always leads the way and His Church follows—He always stands above: the Church always stands below; He always speaks: the Church always merely answers. It belongs not to itself but to Him. It does not live from and for itself, but because and in that He lives, He, the Head, and the Church the body in its members. It sits at His feet. It serves Him. All it can do is to try to please Him. It knows no wisdom, no holiness and no law that is not His. It knows of no power and glory apart from that which is in Him. It has no desire to exist at all except in Him, and if it did so desire it could not. The real Church is so lowly that it has all things in Him alone and it is so majestic because it has all things in Him.

B. The real Church lives as the gathering called together by Him. No one belongs to it by birth and descent; no one belongs to it because he belongs to a Christian family or a Christian nation; no one belongs to it because of some provision that others have made for him; neither does anyone belong to it by virtue of his own decision and enrolment, nor by virtue of his religious experience or some other sort of spiritual conversion. The Church is the assembly called together, united, held together and governed by the Word of its Master—or it is no real Church at all. A commander calls his officers and N.C.Os. to the front, to make certain communications to them and give them their orders. It is in this act of calling, this reception of communication and command that the real Church exists. Thus and in no other way!

C. The members of the real Church are, however, in no sense 'dignitaries'. Those who are gathered together in the real Church are lost sinners, and hence neither religious virtuosi nor a moral élite. Where the Church represents 'the best circles' it is certainly no real Church. The only thing that can distinguish its members from other men is the fact that they know, admit and acknowledge that we men are, taken as a whole, not by nature good members of society but rather 'tend to hate God and our neighbour'. The members of the Church are 'better' than others only in so far as they are more aware of the extent of human guilt before God, are more aware than others of the indissoluble solidarity of all men as sinners.

D. The real Church therefore lives as if constantly held and sustained over an abyss. When it imagines it can find comfort and encouragement in itself it is certainly not the real Church. The real Church lives on the comfort and exhortation which it is allowed to receive despite the folly and perversity of man. It lives in the power of the life of its Lord, which is superior to and other than its own life. It lives by allowing itself to be shamed by His goodness. It lives only in so far as its own religiosity and pious habits, its whole ritual, ordinary as well as extraordinary, are constantly being reduced to dust and ashes in the fire of His

Word and Spirit. It lives in His mercy. Only His mercy keeps it from tiring. The unreal church is always weary because it refuses to be ashamed, refuses to be burnt to dust and ashes, rejects His mercy. It would get on much better if it was a real Church!

E. The new comfort from outside itself and the exhortation from above which the real Church is allowed to receive and to live by are entirely and exclusively the comfort and exhortation of the biblical testimony. The real Church lives not from two or three or even from many sources, but from this one source alone. Why only from this one source? Because it is only here that an answer can be found to the question which alone can move the real Church. That question is: What is to become of such offenders against God and our neighbour as we human beings all are? Moses and the Prophets, John the Baptist and the evangelists and apostles all take their origin from the answer to this question. There are many answers to other questions. But this is the question of the real Church. It is not wilfulness or narrow-mindedness but simple realism if the real Church holds fast to the Scriptures that are holy because they were written for the unholy: they testify to the life that has appeared and is promised to all the unholy.

F. This is the life, however, on which the real Church is permitted to live without ceasing: the reconciliation of the world with God, which has taken place in Jesus Christ, the covenant of grace established in Him between God and lost sinners. This is the law of the gospel, to which the real Church is subject, from which it cannot withdraw, which it cannot praise enough: it must believe, it is bound to believe that God in spite of His great anger towards our human unbelief, was, is and remains faithful and has given Himself in His Son and has thereby restored the divine law which man had infringed and the human law which man had forfeited; and has thus established an eternal peace. There is no human being in any human time and situation for whom that has not happened and to whom it does not apply. What is the solidarity of human guilt beside the solidarity in which all are set by the grace of God? In order to be able readily to admit the first—the solidarity of human guilt—one must know the second—the solidarity in which all are set by the grace of God. The real Church is the assembly of those who are allowed by God's grace to know of His grace for all men, who, as the first-born of the whole creation, are allowed to know the Lord of the world, who is the Lord of that covenant, as their own Lord. The real Church lives in this knowledge.

4

The real Church lives in the intimate association of those who are comforted and exhorted in this way, on the basis of their common relationship to the Son of God who was born, crucified and rose again as man for all men.

In attempting a second answer, we shall take a more horizontal view of the Church, and say that the real Church lives in the absolute solidarity of its members one with another. There are other human solidarities. It is true, right and necessary that there are families, nations and classes, associations of every kind representing common interests, aims and convictions. But none of these other human associations even approaches the unity of those who are members of the real Church. They are all limited associations, they lay hold of man only partially, only in certain components of his existence, not in his existence as such. Hence they also overlap. Family can stand against family, nation against nation, class against class, interests, aims and convictions against other interests, aims and convictions. In so far as they are gathered into the real Church men are called out of, taken out of these limited associations—and out of the family before all else, as we all know. It is not that the real Church is necessarily opposed to these other associations. But it does not coincide with any of them. It stands above them all. It has no part in their overlappings and altercations. It signifies the unconditional solidarity of man. It is the solidarity of human life before God and before our neighbour. The fact that its members are called and taken out of all their other human associations means that they are called and taken into the real and true human solidarity.

In the real Church we know one another: everyone knows the other for what he really is: a lost sinner in whom there is no help, a sinner comforted and exhorted by Jesus Christ, in whom is his only help. According to the Gospel this is the life in which, in spite of all their other differences, all men are relations, brothers and sisters. In the real Church all are known to one another as brothers and sisters. In the real Church men can and must have an ultimate, natural and basic trust in one another—otherwise they would not be in the real Church. One immediately recognises one's own character in the characters of the others and the others' character in one's own, and this inevitably makes a final alienation and an ultimate fear of one another impossible.

The members of the real Church love one another. In the real Church loving means neither esteeming, nor admiring nor revering. Loving means simply accepting the other in his place and in his way of life exactly as he is. One would not want to exist oneself unless the other existed in his place and way of life. It is impossible to see how men could really love one another if they knew nothing of the judgment and grace of God and of the consequent solidarity of all human kind. But it is also impossible to see how, if this foundation of human existence is kept in sight, as it is in the real Church, man can avoid loving his fellowmen. As this is the very root of Christian love, there is no need to worry about the necessary reservations which we owe to truth, to our neighbour and to ourselves. As this is the root of Christian love, it is impossible to face one another in the real Church with any ultimate reservations.

In the real Church people help one another. Not in the way that God helps His creatures, but in the way human beings can help each other. In the real Church people help one another not with any intention of doing good, of showing how selfless they are (which no one is), nor to give God pleasure and make an impression on the public by their sacrifices (a superfluous undertaking anyway, since the one sacrifice that counts has long since been made for us), but because they have in the real Church a common cause which makes its claim on all its members. Look how woodmen lend each other a hand when a tree is being felled. Look and listen—a really edifying spectacle that I cannot admire enough here in Hungary—how in a gipsy band every individual player has his ears and eyes glued on the leading fiddler, concentrating absolutely on the leader's improvisations, and hence playing inevitably and happily with all the others. This is the way we help one another in the purely practical sphere. And so it is in the real Church where we are confronted by a common task and dedicated to a common mission and are invited, without any moralising on the subject, to be mutually responsible for one another, to bear one another's burdens.

We are not speaking of the striving after an ideal of some kind, we are speaking of the fulfilment of no other law but the law of Christ. This knowing, loving and helping one another in the real Church is life lived from the gospel, life lived in a common and universally acknowledged relationship to the Word of God that became flesh for us. Christians are not doing anything outstanding, they are under no monastic rule when they treat one another a little differently from what is normal in human behaviour. But they must 'let their moderation be known unto all men' (Phil. 4.5). In this they are merely provisional representatives and heralds for all who do not yet know, have not yet heard, cannot yet grasp that the reconciliation of the world with God has also been effected for them, that the order rooted in this event has also come into force for them. They cannot yet live in the light of this knowledge. Or are they perhaps already doing so, to the shame of Christians themselves? Many hard things can be said against certain children of this world, but it cannot be denied that they are at any rate amongst themselves better friends than most members of ministers' fraternal societies throughout the world. Perhaps this happens to prove that that order operates for all whether they are aware of it or not, since the reconciliation of the world with God took place for all. Perhaps it is also intended to show that it is quite common for Christians to lose the real Church.

5

*The real Church lives in the fellowship of the Holy Spirit,
i.e. from the knowledge that the Kingdom of God has come,
in prayer for the revelation of His Glory and therefore for
the commission to tell all men that God was, is and will be
for them all.*

We shall attempt a third answer to the question what is the life of the real Church, by looking at the event, the action and the story that takes place in what the New Testament calls the 'fellowship of the Holy Spirit'. As the vertical is related to the horizontal, so the fellowship of the Holy Spirit is related to the fellowship of Christians among themselves. The real Church lives because God who was in Christ, because Christ who is at the right hand of God, does not cease to live for us. It lives because the fact that He is in heaven and man on earth and that He has done on earth once for all that which was needed for man's salvation, is not the end of the matter. The Church lives because day by day new life comes from God's eternal throne. It lives because it is allowed to see, hear and receive this new life from day to day. It lives in ever renewed knowledge of what God has done for man in Jesus Christ for love of us men. How could it ever come to an end of its vision and understanding of the depth, the height and the breadth of this work achieved by God? What generation can ever do anything but begin at the beginning again in its own way? Emmanuel: 'God with us': even the small child can grasp it, yet the old man may safely admit that he is still very far from understanding it, since ever new dimensions and aspects of God's presence with us are revealed on every side; ever new light is shining; ever new growth in knowledge is possible and necessary. The real Church lives in this growing knowledge. And it lives in ever renewed prayer for the revealing of Jesus Christ as the Lord, which shall surpass all knowledge and all Christian knowledge, and for the final vision of His glory. The real Church still stands with the whole world in the midst of so much temptation and weakness, so much care and tribulation, so much limitation and error. The people that sees the great light is still a people walking in darkness. Therefore our prayer can still only be that what has been achieved by God in man and the whole creation, and in the real Church as well, may acquire a definite form. But the real Church differs from the mere image and semblance of the Church in that it penetrates to this sphere again and again and in that it can leave behind all self-sufficiency and self-satisfaction, but also all brooding and despair over the particular enigmas of the present, and can sigh as it prays: 'Hallowed be Thy name, Thy Kingdom come, Thy will be done'; or, summing up all things: 'Amen, yea, come, Lord Jesus, come!' And this sighing, as Luther once described it, because it is the sighing of the Holy Spirit, itself becomes a cry that resounds through all heaven, so loudly that all the angels listen: they never remember hearing a louder sound than this.

It is in such constantly renewed knowledge and prayer that the real Church lives in every new movement of its life. The real Church is by nature not an end in itself, but serves God by serving all men. Even when it withdraws to its interior lines, retreat can and will be merely the preparation for an all the more powerful appeal to the outside world. When officers and N.C.Os. have received their instructions, they go—that is the only reason why they have been called—back to the troops, in order to pass on the orders. 'God so loved'—not the Christian, but—'the world'. 'I am the light of the world', says the Lord, and by His own self-giving He passes the light on to His disciples: 'Ye are the light of the world!' It is the duty of the real Church to tell and show the world what it does not yet know. This does not mean that the real Church's mission is to take the whole or even half the world to task. It would be the servant of quite a different Master if it were to set itself up as the accuser of its brethren. Its mission is not to say 'No', but to say 'Yes'; a strong 'Yes' to the God who, because there are 'godless' men, has not thought and does not think of becoming a 'manless' God—and a strong 'Yes' to man, for whom, with no exception, Jesus Christ died and rose again. How extraordinary the Church's preaching, teaching, ministry, theology, political guardianship and missions would be, how it would convict itself of unbelief in what it says, if it did not proclaim to all men that God is not against man but for man. It need not concern itself with the 'No' that must be said to human presumption and human sloth. This 'No' will be quite audible enough when as the real Church it concerns itself with the washing of feet and nothing else. This is the obedience which it owes to its Lord in this world. This is the cause which is worthy of its burning zeal, this is the exercise it will carry out again and again. As long as this exercise is being carried out, together with the exercise of knowledge and prayer, the real Church will live: from above, from heaven to earth, in the fellowship of the Holy Spirit. If it did not live thus constantly renewed, how could it be more than a mere image and semblance of the Church, how could it be a real Church?

6

*The real Church lives under the order and government which
its Lord Himself exercises by endowing the congregation
gathered in His name with the gifts it needs for the fulfilling
of its service.*

We shall now attempt a fourth and final answer to our question and say: the real Church lives by being ruled by its Lord
and by Him alone. It does not live according to its own dis-
cretion: neither does it live on its own responsibility and at its
own risk. If it has ever tried to speak and act in obedience, it will
not regard itself as eternally, infallibly and unshakably bound
by any of its actions and decisions, by any of its own traditions
and customs, nor by any of its newly made decisions; it will
rather always hold itself ready to receive new orders. This applies
to its preaching and worship, to its theology and its theoretical
and practical laws. What we men understand and conceive as
right and true in the life of the Church, what we have agreed
on after the most conscientious enquiry, it may be for many
centuries, can be really significant as a guide for future reference, but it must never be the power by which the Church
is ruled. That would mean that we had made ourselves
or our forefathers the masters of the Church, and it would also
mean that we had become the slaves of an ecclesiastical demonism, which has not a jot more claim to our souls simply because
it is ecclesiastical than has any other form of demonism. This is
a parting of the ways where the mere image and semblance of
the Church on the one hand, and the real Church on the other
hand, divide particularly clearly.

The Lord of the Church must be allowed to rule it by Himself and on His own. The fact that He has declared Himself to
the prophets and apostles, and that the real Church hears His holy
word and witness, means that He speaks to it again and again,
and that it can always distinguish His voice from the voice of
other masters. All that is needed that He may really exercise His
government is that His people should really be, and remain, the
Church which proclaims and hears Him in its preaching, Baptism
and Holy Communion. Then He will be in the midst of His
Church—'with us on the battlefield with His spirit and His gifts'.

And it is in fact through the gifts of His spirit that He governs the real Church, makes it capable, willing and ready to perform its duties properly, the many duties which fall to it as part of its one, all-embracing service because the men, conditions and times it is called to serve are themselves so varied. In Rom. 12 and I Cor. 12 we read of the multiplicity of these gifts, and we surmise that this multiplicity may be infinite. The real Church has no fear of this wealth. It may well be asked whether it is not because we all want to build the Church too much according to our own wisdom and are for ever deadening the Spirit, and are to that extent not yet the real Church at all, that the gifts of the Spirit are so few amongst us and there is so much mutual suspicion amongst the bearers of such gifts as we may have— between the teachers and ministers, the prophets and the exhorters, and between all these and those who are called to lead. What is derived from ourselves will always be incomplete, insufficient and therefore exclusive, i.e. separating and disintegrating, in the Church as much as anywhere else.

The gifts of the Spirit will not disintegrate the Church, but will rule and regulate it, inasmuch as they come from the One Lord. But we must not be afraid of them or try to barricade ourselves off against them with the works of man. We must not say 'gift' and mean our own ability; we must not say 'service' and mean office; we must not say 'confession' and mean denomination; we must not say 'prayer' and mean rite; we must not say 'order' and mean regimentation; we must not say 'Christ' and mean the Fathers—or simply ourselves, and so on.

The doors must remain open for the Lord to come in at all times and in all places. The real Church is free in that it trusts the spirit—the spirit of the Word of its Master, to guide it certainly into all truth. This means that it is tied to the extent that it can rely on no other guidance but this, not on its tradition, or on any kind of inspiration, on no hierarchy and on none of the more or less powerful experiences of which its members may boast. The best that can be said in this respect, however, is probably that it has pleased the Lord again and again and that it has been possible for Him to come to His own even through closed doors and to create a real Church from a mere image and

semblance of a Church, in other words, to create a Church
governed by Him and by the gifts of His Spirit.

7

*The real Church is the one, holy, universal, apostolic
Church, which we are invited to follow and be living
members of, in that Jesus Christ calls us to be His followers.*

We shall close by asking: How does one come to the real
Church, how does one participate in its life? One comes to it by
not shutting one's eyes and ears, not making a fuss, not saying
'Yes—but!' whenever one sees or hears about it from one point
of view or another. Few see the real Church. Many could and
should see it. Why do so few see it? Because a whole wall of
pious and impious human wilfulness, of ancient and modern
cleverness and clumsiness stands between us and the real Church.
Why do we not break through this wall? Why do we not leap
over it with God? And why do we ask how the real Church
could become a reality for us when we know somewhere in the
depths of our being that we would refuse to break through or
leap over the wall even if an angel from heaven itself were to
invite us?

But let us not close with an accusation. All are doubtless called
to the real Church, for it lives from Jesus Christ and from Him
the call goes forth again and again to the pseudo-Church, the
call that is in fact powerful enough to create the real Church.
His call is very friendly and very stern. He calls the sleepers and
the overburdened, the weary and the sad, he calls the hypocrite
in the Church, open and unconfessed alike. He calls them all to
repentance, to conversion and to belief. He calls for the humble
and the courageous.

It will appear later whether too much or too little has been
attempted in the great forthcoming enterprise in Amsterdam.
Its success or failure will depend on whether it will please God
to make His call heard there. Where its members turn to and
profess their faith in the real Church with heart and mind and
voice, the smallest village church can be more important than
the whole great Amsterdam Conference, if such profession is
made in accordance with the 54th Question of the *Heidelberg*

Catechism, where, in answer to the question what we believe of the Church, it is stated that the real Church can be touched and felt:

That the Son of God may gather, defend and preserve from the whole human race a chosen congregation for eternal life through His Spirit and Word in the unity of the true faith from the beginning of the world even to the end, and that I may be and remain a living member of the same to eternity.

4. THE CHRISTIAN COMMUNITY IN THE MIDST OF POLITICAL CHANGE

A lecture delivered in Sarospatak and Budapest in March 1948.

I

The Christian Church commemorates the great change in earthly and heavenly history, which has already taken place in the death of Jesus Christ in judgment on human sin and for the justification of sinful man, which has already been proclaimed in His resurrection from the dead and will be revealed in His second coming, as the goal of all the temporal ways of God.

Our title refers to 'changing political order'. That makes it topical. Our generation has had much, only too much, experience of this matter. We know what political changes mean in the way of excitement, tension and brutality, humiliation and insults, human fates, deserved and undeserved, the revelation of human character, good and bad, practical and spiritual problems, the disruption of all standards and perspectives. Is it possible to discuss this matter—particularly whilst it is still in progress—without taking sides and therefore becoming excited, nervous, passionate and indignant, without using the demonised language of propaganda with all its foreshortenings and exaggerations, with its slogans that kill all thought in speaker and listener alike, which reduce discussion to the dealing and receiving of blows? Is there any other way of discussing the matter?

At any rate that is precisely what we propose to attempt in

this talk. Our subject is 'The Christian Church in the midst of political change.' The Christian Church lives not in heaven but on earth. We are assuming therefore at the very outset that the Church is not uninterested but on the contrary supremely interested, both as a fellowship and individually, in 'the changing political order' and in everything involved in such changes. The other assumption, however, is even more important: that the Church must be and must remain a Christian fellowship and live for its own concerns even in the midst of political changes. The point that interests us here is the nature of these Christian concerns. To discuss this question we shall first of all have to try and detach ourselves a little from the immediately topical aspect of the subject, not in order to lose sight of it but rather to acquire a calmer, clearer and better sight of it.

There is—and this must be said before all else—a change which is infinitely more incisive and important than all the changes in the political realm. We may call this great change quite simply Jesus Christ in the twofold aspect of His death on the Cross and His second coming in glory, as made known in His resurrection. The Christian Church knows that not only itself but the whole world exists in the time between these two events; between the action God has already taken and the action He has still to take for man through His only Son. Political changes, along with all other changes, take part within this intermediary time. And they are significant for the Christian Church because they take place within this framework. Their beginning and their goal—the beginning and the goal of what we call world history—is at all events the history of God's salvation of man.

The beginning from which we come is the death of Jesus Christ with the intimation of its significance in His resurrection. What happened in the death of Jesus Christ was that God passed sentence on human sin by taking it upon Himself in the person of His own Son, by suffering its bitter consequence and punishment Himself and thereby making human sin forgiven, settled and done with once for all. And in the death of Jesus Christ God justified sinful man by restoring human dignity in the Person of His Son and by restoring law between man and man, by accepting man as His child. This is the great change from which the world of today derives. The old things are passed away.

Satan has fallen from heaven like a flash of lightning. The Kingdom of God has come nigh. What had to happen for the reconciliation, for the redemption and the peace of man, has happened really, fundamentally, completely. 'Thanks be to God, which giveth us the victory through our Lord Jesus Christ.' That is the message the Christian Church has had in its ears since the first Easter Day, and which it cannot help but proclaim with its lips. This is its real concern: the unequivocal news that the world, whether it knows it or not—it must be brought to hear it— derives from this beginning, from the great change already brought about by the death of Jesus Christ.

The goal to which we are moving is the second coming of Jesus Christ which has already been announced in His resurrection and is already under way: the general and final revelation of what took place in His death and hence the revelation of the Kingdom, of the Judgment and the righteousness, of the consummated reconciliation, of the divine deliverance. The covering which lies over all things and over all eyes will then be removed. We shall see directly what we can now see only distorted in a mirror. We shall then know God even as we are known by Him now. That is the message of the Christian Church, the message of hope which it has for itself but also for the whole world, for everything and everyone. This is its real concern: to call men to watch and pray, to serve and to endure. Everything is moving towards this goal, this great change that is still to come as the end of time in the revelation of Jesus Christ.

The alternation and the changes of political systems stand in the light of this great change which is called Jesus Christ. This is the standpoint from which we must view political change to see it clearly. It would be curious if it were not possible and permissible to speak of these smaller changes with a certain calm and clarity in the Church which believes in and acknowledges this one great change.

2

*The Christian fellowship lives in the sphere of the political
systems in whose existence it will see in all circumstances an
ordinance of divine wisdom and patience, for which it will
therefore be grateful and for which it will know itself responsible in the freedom of its mission, in memory of that change
and in the expectation of His revelation.*

The history of the world is involved in and belongs to the
history of salvation. But the time in which it takes place—and
hence our time—is the time of faith and not yet the time of
seeing. Not a time of blindness but a time of seeing in a mirror.
Not a time of darkness or lack of knowledge but a time of veil-
ing. Not a lost time, but a time of testing. It is in a particular
sense the time of the Christian community, in which it remembers and waits, in which it gathers and prepares, the time of its
mission and consolation, of its trust and struggle, of its sifting
and temptation.

It is, however, not only the time of the Christian community:
it is also the time of political systems. Political systems are the
attempts undertaken and carried out by men in order to secure
the common political life of man by certain co-ordinations of
individual freedom and the claims of the community, by the
establishing of laws with power to apply and preserve them.
Political organisation means a system of law based on power,
a system of power in honour of law.

The Christian Church knows only one Lord, His system, His
law, His power. But it knows this Lord as the Lord of all lords.
It therefore sees His order, His will, His institution and His hand
in political systems, with all their provisional and limited aims.
It realises that political systems are run by men. But it sees a divine
commission above and behind this provisional and limited work
of man. It sees a necessary and wholesome gift of God in this
work of man. What is at issue is the preservation of the common
life from chaos. Political systems create and preserve a space for
that which must happen in the time between the beginning and
the end of which we have spoken: a space for the fulfilment of
the purpose of world history, a space for faith, repentance and
knowledge. They create a space for the life and mission of the

Christian Church and therefore a space for something the whole world needs. Those who bear the burden of political systems, the peoples and their governments, may seldom know or even have any idea what the Church is for. The Church knows all the more what political systems are for. Political systems may be as unecclesiastical as they like, but the Church cannot on any account be unpolitical, and that applies to all its members too.

On principle they will always be grateful for the existence of political systems as such. In any case they will understand them as a divine precaution, as an ordinance of divine wisdom and patience—even when the imperfections and errors caused by the men who run them and their follies, trivial as well as grave and tragic, are all too obvious. Such imperfections are to some extent inevitable. There is no such thing as a perfect political system. There are only better and worse systems. None of them can do more than refract the gift of God. But something of God's wisdom and patience (though it may be only a reasonable traffic regulation!) will be revealed by even the worst political system. It has often been observed, and rightly, that the 'government' of whose divine institution the Apostle Paul spoke, was the 'State' of the Emperor Nero. It may well be that even in the best State Christians will never be able to express their gratitude for God's gift and ordinance except in the form of serious opposition. But this implies that they will never be able to regard and treat even the worst State as wholly diabolical. If they have to remember on the one hand that it would be pure foolishness to expect any political system to be the Kingdom of God, they must not forget that 'the devil has already lost his ancient right to the whole human race', so that, much as he would like to, he does not in fact stand a chance of incarnating himself in any political system. If it may be their duty to raise an undeniably necessary protest, they will have no right whatsoever to consider themselves exempt from the duty to take their share in the life of the State. The concrete form in which the Christian gratitude for God's gift and ordinance is expressed is its sharing of political responsibility. The Church cannot simply leave this work to others. The apostles could not have emphasised this Christian co-responsibility more forcibly than by their call to the Church to pray for the holders of political office. How can one pray seriously about a matter

F

in which one has no share? It was Paul again who said conscience
makes the Christian participation in the political order necessary
and imperative. The more serious such participation is, the more
critical it will be: Christians will never be the easiest citizens for
any government, ruling majority or minority, clique or individual. But they will never be able to take the line of sterile
negation. For who knows better than the Christian the purpose
of and need for political systems as such? Who ought to be more
qualified for genuine political action than the Christian? The fact
that Christians do prove themselves to have a special vocation
in this direction ought not to be something to be ashamed of.

3

*In political changes the Christian Church perceives signs
of the judgment that has already been accomplished and
omens of its future revelation, but it also sees them as offers
of a new divine provision for all men and, for itself, new
opportunities for repentance, meditation and witness.*

Political systems change. How could it be otherwise? The
elements that make up every State—freedom, community, law,
power—can be conceived and realised in very different ways
both separately and in their interrelationships. Political history
may be said to consist in a constant variation of these different
elements. I come from a country where there has been no change
of political system for a hundred years. But what are a mere
hundred years? When I was in Hungary twelve years ago I heard
a lot about the thousand-years-old Crown of St. Stephen. No one
mentions it today: I gather it is supposed to be in the Vatican
now. Political systems come and go, even though they often last
for a long time. What was called political freedom four hundred
years ago was something very different from what goes by that
name today, and even today there does not seem to be any
general agreement about it. Yesterday's right can become today's
wrong; what is right in one country may be wrong in another.
And what one generation thought was a real community may
be spurned as 'social dissolution' at another time and place.
Unfortunately, the only constant factor appears to be the element
of force. In every other respect the search for new political forms

and patterns seems to be never-ending. Even in an age of political
stability the process usually continues underground. When it
enters an acute stage we talk about 'political change'. All or
almost all the old coins are then sent to the melting-pot to be
melted down and recast. Does the process, seen as a whole,
develop progressively? Even forty years ago most historians
boldly assumed and asserted that it does. Meanwhile, however,
we have seen the emergence of political systems which discourage
this belief. Is that any reason, however, for assuming that the
decline is universal or that the cycle of political change moves
inevitably from bad to better and then back again? Perhaps the
least pretentious and most accurate metaphor might be that of
a great undulation. There is no need to decide on this one way
or the other, however. One thing is certain: the alternation of
political systems is the only completely certain continuity in
this field.

If we ask ourselves what the Christian Church should think
and say about political change in general, one thing must be
absolutely certain: every such change takes place between the
death and the second coming of Jesus Christ and under His
dominion. This means that whenever such changes occur the
Christian reaction cannot be one of extreme joy or extreme
horror, not because the Christian is indifferent to or contemp-
tuous of political matters but simply because the Christian already
has something which calls for extreme joy and extreme horror.
A 'small' change like this cannot in any sense compete with the
great change from which the Christian takes his bearings. If
that is agreed, then it must be added that the 'small' changes,
precisely because they occur in the era and under the Lordship of Jesus Christ, are entitled to our serious interest and
attention.

They are in the nature of signs and omens of the great change
which lies behind and before us—thus they are interpreted in
particular in the Old Testament. Men were never good, however, are not good, and never will be good. They live on God's
forgiveness, not from their own righteousness. Manifestations of
perfect righteousness are therefore not to be expected in this
sphere: in no political formula or system of any kind, and certainly not in any political achievement or personality. When the

limitations, the fragility and frailty, the injustice of this work of man are shown by the fall of one system and its replacement by another, it should serve to remind us that our whole existence is not based on itself, that we live rather in a world and can only build a world which stands in need of redemption from evil and must wait for the revelation of this redemption. The very instability of political history should serve to confirm the Christian assurance that only the love of God is eternal. Changing political systems will be indirect evidence of the Kingdom that has no end—the Kingdom from which the world derives and towards which it moves. 'When these things begin to come to pass, then look up, and lift up your heads; for your redemption draweth nigh.'

The Christian Church will certainly not omit to see in such changes a new offer of the divine provision for all men. When one political system, the work of men's hands, collapses to make way for another, it means at least that the work of divine patience and wisdom is not yet completed. Once again, a limit has been set to some abuse of law and freedom, of community and power. A new political system means that men have been allowed a new chance to order their common life differently, and, possibly, better. The providence of God has enabled them to make a fresh start. It is impossible to see how the Christian Church could refuse to be prepared to take a hopeful interest in such an event, at any rate as a matter of principle.

The most important thing to be said in this matter in general terms is that the Christian Church will see in such changes above all an opportunity to do penance itself. Can an old political system collapse without the Christian Church having failed in some way or other to fulfil its responsibilities towards people and government? And can a new political system arise without the Christian Church asking itself how, with what fresh insight and strength, it can make a new and better appeal to men in the new situation? For the Christian Church a new political system necessarily means an occasion to revise the foundations of its own activities, a challenge to renewed concentration, a summons to fresh witness, all of which is appropriate since a time of political upheaval provides the incentive to seek a better knowledge of the Word of God.

4

The Christian Church is independent in relation to political
change inasmuch as, grounded in the Word of God and
committed solely to His Word, it can see in no ancient or
modern political system more than an imperfect, threatened
and restricted human effort, the furthering or opposing of
which should never be confused with its own proper mission.

New political systems will always be a temptation to the
Christian Church to surrender its own freedom and to lose confidence in its own mission. This may happen because it imagines
it must remain loyal to God's gift and institution by thought-
lessly holding on to the old régime and therefore identifying
itself with the conservative forces, the men of yesterday. No
doubt the old régime that is falling or has already fallen had its
good points, and the old men may have had their merits. Possibly the old régime offered the Church opportunities which it
cannot expect from the new or at any rate not directly. And it
is true that a political revolution rarely occurs without creating
some fresh injustice: injustice that may easily seem more terrible
at the moment because it strikes quite different groups and individuals. If the Christian Church is badly advised it will be a
party to the ideological glorification and support of yesterday's
régime and ideological discrimination against the new system.
It will make the cause of political reaction the Church's cause
and God's cause. But in so doing it will surrender its freedom—
or rather, by this attitude it will show that it had already lost
its freedom under the old system, that it had already been guilty
of identifying its own mission with the dominant ideals of the
old system, that it had already lost confidence in its own mission
—and now refuses to see that the moment has come to recollect
its freedom and rejoice in its own mission.

Fundamentally, the same thing can also happen the other way
round: in this case the Church will side with the new régime.
The spirit of a new period of history can be mistaken for the
Holy Spirit; the proclamations and actions of the 'progressives',
the radical, revolutionary forces and the waves of the flood to
which they give rise, may be mistaken for a revelation of God.
There may be some reason for this too. The change may in fact

be directed towards a better State. Much old falsehood and injustice may be brought to well-merited judgment. Many people may really be helped by the change. Serious Christians may have been working for the change for a long time. On the other hand, it may well be no more than a simple instinct of self-preservation which urges the Christian Church not to 'miss the bus'. Or, on a higher and better plane: it may be allured by the possibility of reaching entirely new circles with its message: the liberators and the liberated. Great circumspection is required lest the price be too high. The price might consist in the Christian Church allowing itself to be persuaded in its enthusiasm to make the new cause its own cause and the cause of God. Ideological glorifications and discriminations—in the reverse direction now —might be indulged in which have nothing at all to do with a Christian view of the situation. The Church would surrender its freedom on this path too. And it would probably happen simply because for a long time past it had not known how to use its freedom, had long since lost all confidence in its mission, and because this confidence had been replaced by a vacuum which can now be filled with a quite un-Christian enthusiasm for the new régime.

In both cases the Christian Church would be serving strange gods, forgetting that the Kingdom of Him who is its Lord 'is not of this world' but has come into the world as the light of God. In both cases it would be allowing the Word of God to be taken captive, and would be making itself a prisoner of the new régime. It must remember the clear and decisive reason why it should resist this temptation in both the forms in which it may appear, and why it must remain free at any cost in the midst of political change. It is grounded in the Word of God and committed to Him alone. It can accompany every political system. But it cannot serve strange gods. It cannot therefore ally itself with any political system, old or new, for better or for worse, just as it cannot oppose any system unconditionally. It can offer absolute and abstract obedience or resistance to none but to each only the relative concrete obedience or resistance which it is commanded to offer by the Word of God. The Word of God is not tied to any political system, old or new. It justifies and judges all of them. It passes through, because it is superior to, all political change. It is neither old nor new, but eternal. The Christian Church must be guided by the Word of God and by it alone. It must follow the logic and ethics of the Word of God and no other. It must hearken to its instructions and to no other. It must not forget for an instant that all political systems, right and left alike, are the work of men. If it is forced by the Word of God to say Yes here and No there and No here and Yes there, it must not be a Yes and No by which it is compromised and disturbed in its own mission. It must hold itself free to carry out its own mission and to work out a possibly quite new form of obedience or resistance. It must not sell this birthright for any conservative or revolutionary mess of pottage.

5

The independence of the Christian Church vis-à-vis political change is restricted by its participation in the rights and wrongs, in the weal and woe of all men and above all by the freedom of the Word of God, which may call the Church to take particular decisions and attitudes in relation to particular events.

The Church cannot make an absolute principle of its freedom. Its primary and fundamental concern is the freedom of the Word of God and only secondarily its own freedom, which is in any case bound up with the first. Its freedom is based on but also restricted by its mission, which is to preach the Word of God to man. It must proclaim the Word of God to man. It can therefore not fail to take an interest in the rights and wrongs of man, in his weal and woe. The world cannot be a matter of indifference to the Church, for it is the world which God loved and reconciled to Himself in Jesus Christ. It cannot escape its share in the world's suffering, its guilt and responsibility for the world's ways. No guarantee of its own freedom would justify it leaving the world in the lurch in the critical situation caused by political changes. It would then be passing by on the other side with the Pharisee and the Levite. If it thinks that its duty is to keep out in certain circumstances, the reason must not on any account be a fear of soiling its hands. Even a decision to keep out must spring from a positive attitude. It must not be an escape

into neutrality. It must be one expression of its utmost interest
and sympathy.

It has to proclaim the Word of God to man. No consideration
for its own freedom must allow the Church to impose a silence on
the Word of God. It may be that the Word of God calls the
Church apart into the stillness of retreat. But it may also be that
it calls it to decision, to battle, and summons it to take sides.
Relative, concrete obedience in relation to the old or the new
system may become a necessity. The Church must then have
no fear of unexpected enemies or unexpected friends. The fact
that both sides are the work of man must not prevent it from
saying Yes to one side as definitely as it says No to the other.
If the Word of God requires it to enter the fray and soil its
hands, then it must enter it in the name of God and soil its hands.
It is His honour, not the Church's, that is at stake. And if it
does not enter the fray and soil its hands, that too may be not
an escape into neutrality but an act of utter obedience.

These are the two ways in which its freedom is limited. But
it may not be a twofold frontier at all. If the Church is truly
human, it will be open to the Word of God which may call it to
decision or restraint. And if it is open to the Word of God, it
will inevitably have to profess its belief in man—whether by
decision or restraint.

6

*The Christian Church participates in political changes
inasmuch as every such event must give it cause to allow
itself to be renewed by the Word of God, in order to achieve
a prophetic appreciation of the background and consequences
of the change.*

Let us try to think over what we have said in the two preceding
theses, but in the reverse direction.

Political changes will always tempt the Church to surrender
its life and fail to carry out its mission. In such times it can refer
to its sacred neutrality, its position above the parties. What lies
behind this reference, however, is not freedom but weakness:
the Church's inability to see, to understand and illuminate the
political situation—its failure in the prophetic role for which it

should be prepared and equipped. Or the Church may be careful and restrained for very worldly diplomatic reasons, although this is the very moment when it ought to say and do something brave for the sake of God and man. Or, in view of the problems all around it, it may be accidentally engaged in a self-sufficient withdrawal into the interior where, unaffected by political changes, it imagines it is well occupied with its private affairs: this may take the form of a withdrawal into an other-worldly Christianity or the cultivation of 'inwardness', or well-meaning efforts at individual moral rearmament; or it may take the form of a withdrawal into theology or into some 'liturgical' movement, or preoccupation with other Christian accessories. It will then construct a wonderfully restored ecclesiastical heaven with creeds and dogmas, prayers and hymns, devotions and offerings, and perhaps a bustling round of good works (inspired by the Epistle of James no doubt), or a triumphal hierarchy after the old pattern or of new invention, high above the wicked earth with its changing political systems. But all this will be far, far away from the humanity it has left completely in the lurch.

This is just what must not be allowed to happen. The Church cannot live in permanent retreat, however pleasant its dreams as it sleeps away its mission to mankind. If the Church must remain free, above the changing political systems, this very freedom necessarily implies that the Church should participate in these events.

No doubt such events must give the Church cause to allow itself to be renewed by the Word of God—renewal by the Word of God is what it must seek, not renewal by bringing itself into line with the new régime or by taking up some religious hobby or other that may have entered somebody's head. When political conditions change, Christians will simply take it as an occasion to read the Scriptures anew and to rediscover how dangerously and how beneficially, how consistently and how gently, how profoundly and how practically the Word of God speaks to those who know it is their only refuge. The Church that does that will then learn an entirely new kind of praying, based on the assurance of being heard. The result will inevitably be that its witness, its interpretation of the Bible and the Catechism will acquire new strength and a fundamental relationship to the present. And this new appreciation of the Bible, this new belief in prayer and this new witness are the way the Church can participate in political change. All the other things can only follow from this foundation. All other things would be in vain, a mere snatching at the wind, if the Church were to neglect this one all-important contribution.

Thus renewed by the Word of God, however, it will be able to make to some extent a direct contribution to political events in a revolutionary age. If it lives in the Bible, in prayer and for its witness, then it need have no fear of the complexities of the political problem or of its own loneliness, which will be noticed quickly enough on both sides. For it will have a fixed point from which it can see and understand the events of the days and the years calmly, penetratingly and impartially. It will know to what extent the past gives it cause for turning back and turning round, and it will be able to say with some precision in what this turning back and turning round must consist. It will be able to see the possibilities of the immediate future which give cause for encouragement, hope and concrete decision. Though it will studiously refrain from all programme-making, it will certainly be in a position to give advice and instructions for a few immediate, it may be minute, but anyway, forward-leading steps. In doing that it will be exercising the prophetic guardianship which it behoves it to fulfil. It must not neglect it. It must have no fear. And it will exercise this office all the more confidently, the more unassumingly it behaves, and the less it omits to return to the source again and again, and the clearer it is and remains that it, the guardian, must be the first to submit to the prophetic Word. It is and will remain safe by venturing out into freedom.

7

The participation of the Christian Church in political changes is limited by its mission to proclaim under all circumstances and therefore with its prophetic word nothing but the joyful message of Jesus Christ, its promise and its admonition.

The duty of the Church to participate in political changes cannot become a principle with rigidly predictable consequences.

It is not bound to participate at any price and under any circumstances. Its participation cannot and must not become an end in itself; it has its limits and they must be carefully observed. In all cases and under all circumstances its participation must bear the stamp of its own mission. The Church cannot act ecclesiastically and then indulge in political action as an unrelated sideline. Its politics must be merely one expression of its own unique life. This means that, even in the exercise of its prophetic office of guardian, its business must not be the proclaiming and advocacy of some mixture of religion and politics, but solely the preaching of the one gospel, the joyful message of God's free grace in Jesus Christ. It can and must bear witness to this Lord alone, to His comfort and admonition, and thus to the one hope for the whole creation. The important issue is the political implications of this preaching of the gospel. The Church's business is to proclaim that God is on man's side and therefore opposed to man's destruction; to defend the cause of man in whom God Himself has taken such a personal interest and to defend it under all circumstances whatsoever. In this way and only in this way will the Church's preaching be genuinely prophetic. If its preaching was bereft of this purpose, it would be mere fanatical raving, however imposing it might sound. And that is what it must never be allowed to become.

The Church can never defend and proclaim—or even attack—abstract norms, ideals, historical laws and socio-political ideologies as such. Its concern must never be with political principles, creeds and catechisms but only with definite and concrete political constellations. It cannot make itself responsible either for any -ism or for rejecting it.

Whenever it is pressed to do so, it must say No! however wonderful or terrible the particular -ism may be. It has no system of its own and is not interested in systems. It can therefore on no account become a political party. It recognises no political supporters and no political enemies—it only recognises human beings. On this point our Protestant view must differ from the Roman Catholic with the utmost rigour. Our Church can only comment on political changes according to the particular circumstances. It must refuse absolutely to be tied down to a political line. Only in the rarest cases will its position be the same today as it was fifty or even ten years ago. It remains free simply because it has no other law to proclaim but the law of Christ which is the gospel. It may have to speak very conservatively today and very progressively or even revolutionarily tomorrow—or vice versa. It cannot have a 'programme' because it has a living Master whom it has to serve in the most varied circumstances and situations. The ground from which it lives and the loyalty it obeys are different from the ground and loyalty of all the political parties—Left and Right alike—with which it may work today only to have to work against them tomorrow. Christian politics are always bound to seem strange, incalculable and surprising in the eyes of the world—otherwise they would not be Christian.

Just because it has to speak so independently, the Church must also be allowed to be silent when necessary, in order thereby to speak the more clearly. It cannot and must not be a harum-scarum, demanding to be heard on every occasion and in every situation. It can and must speak only when an inner compulsion of its own impels it to speak. It must not allow itself to be forced by violent threats to give an answer to every allegedly 'burning' question. It must be allowed to find the way to freedom—if it should ever be obstructed—possibly through its own fault—by making itself invisible for long stretches of the road.

8

The Church best performs its service in the midst of political change when its attitude is so independent and at the same time so sympathetic that it is able to summon the representatives of the old and new order alike, winners and losers alike, to humility, to the praise of God and to humanity, and can invite them all to confide in the great change and to hope in His revelation in glory.

Finally, the criterion of the proper service which the Christian community can render in the midst of political change may be expressed as follows:

Its first and final concern is with God and man, with its witness to the relationship of God and man in Jesus Christ. It is concerned with political systems, and their changes, with political parties, with their points of views, ideas and power only inasmuch as all these things belong to man. The question the Church asks is what difference will these things make to the men on whom God has bestowed His grace in Jesus Christ, for whom Christ died and rose again? All those involved in political upheavals, those in the right and those in the wrong, the victors and the defeated, the advocates and the opponents of the old and the new order—all these are men for whom Jesus Christ died and rose again. The Church must bear them all in mind under all circumstances. It will not be indifferent to the distinctions in their position and rank and above all, in their responsibilities. But it will see them all as human beings, each in his own place, and not just as badge-wearers, as mere exponents of a 'cause'. It will speak with them and pray for them just as they are. Though very much involved in all the conflicts and arguments it will also be very free: 'I am here not to hate with you but to love with you.'

The criterion of the Church's real service will therefore be whether it is in a position to summon all involved in political changes to humility and modesty one with another—and to the praise of God, by raising their heads together and rejoicing—and to call them to humanity, that is to a situation in which they not only dispute but are tolerant one with another.

Faith in the great change that occurred in Jesus Christ, towards the revelation of which the Church moves forward with the whole world, will give it the strength it needs for this proper service. He is the Alpha and Omega, the beginning and the end, the standpoint from which it must always be judged whether or not the Church is on the right road. He is the 'whole', within which the change of political systems takes place, within which the Church has its mission and commission. It must therefore pray that it may always be ready and willing to serve its Lord with an integrity in accordance with His wholeness.

5. From the Discussion in Budapest on the Morning of April 1st 1948[1]

When I left Hungary ten years ago after a fortnight's stay only one word of the difficult Hungarian language had made

[1] The questions were submitted to me in writing.

an indelible impression on me. The word—if I can pronounce it correctly—is *Felelete*! (the answering of questions). It may be no mere chance that I have remembered this one word, since even at that time answering questions was the most difficult part of my task. It is easier to deliver lectures than to answer questions, especially when one does not know the questioners personally and only knows the situation as far as a foreign observer can know it. I must therefore ask you to bear with me if I do not fulfil all your expectations. I will do my best, but I must admit that I approach the task with some hesitation, since I am afraid I don't quite understand some of the questions or, alternatively, understand some of them only too well and am afraid I may say something that might lead to new questions. I shall need a special measure of wisdom and confidence this morning, and I must also ask you to make a wise and sensible use of what I have to say.

First of all, I shall try to deal with a group of questions concerned with the State.

Question: According to the Christian interpretation, does the State belong to the sphere of creation or the sphere of redemption? *Answer:* The State belongs to the order of redemption. It is no accident that the place where the State appears in the Creed is in the second article ('suffered under Pontius Pilate') and not in the first article. It is pertinent to add that if we understand the State as an institution of the wisdom and patience of God and do not split up the work of God into various departments but see it as an undivided whole, we shall see the State strictly related to the mercy of God. It is God's intention to see that His mercy may have scope to unfold on earth. This is in fact the purpose of creation in general, to provide a *theatrum gloriae suae* (Calvin). In the sphere of nature there is intended to be an order of the grace of God, and this space is guaranteed by the State. If our interpretation of the relationship between the State and the heavenly powers and forces, as expounded in the New Testament, is correct, we shall know that these powers are not almighty but subject to Christ, so that even in the State we are fundamentally in the *regnum Christi*, which has its centre, however, in the Church. It is also no accident that there is a linguistic affinity between the inner and the outer circle. Christ is called

the Messiah, the King of Israel, who has brought in the Kingdom, the basileia. And the *polis* is the expectation of Christians;
they themselves are called citizens and dwellers in the same house
together—all these are primarily political concepts which are
naturally used metaphorically in the Church, but they do show
that the political sphere is related to the ecclesiastical. We have
to interpret creation from the standpoint of redemption and not
the other way round.

Question: Is it in accordance with the Christian mind to assume
that there will ever be a stateless society?
Answer: In accordance with the Christian mind, the answer is
definitely No. One's view of man would have to be quite gro-
tesquely optimistic to believe in a possibility which can occur
only to dreamers and visionaries. Those who no longer need
the State are in the Kingdom of the God who will one day be
all in all. But so long as our life is lived in faith and not in the
direct vision of God we shall need the State as much as we need
the Church (in the New Jerusalem the Church will also come
to an end). Whoever disputes that cannot know what he is saying.

Question: What is to be understood by the concept of the constitutional State?
Answer: That is a large question. I will try to answer it as briefly
and clearly as possible. Let us recall what we mean by a State
in general. A State is an attempt undertaken by men to organise
the outward life of man, with the intention of preventing individual encroachments on the rights of the whole community and
at the same time encroachments of the community on the rights
of individuals. The order set up is guaranteed by force—it is part
of the nature of the State, that it depends in the final resort on
the availability of force. But this must not be isolated from the
other point, that the State must be supported by the free responsibility of its members. The State cannot be drawn down over
men's heads like a hood. Rightly understood, there is such a
thing as '*l'Etat c'est moi*'. A proper State will be one in which
the concepts of order, freedom, community, power and responsibility are balanced in equal proportions, where none of these
elements is made an absolute dominating all the others. A State

in which only individual freedom was valid would not be a constitutional State, but one about to slide into anarchy. And if mere power predominates in a State it is not a constitutional State but a mere tyranny. And if the principle of community were to enforce itself to the exclusion of all the other elements we should have an ant-State. The proper State is the one in which no such excesses occur, in which there is a certain balance between the various constituent elements. Actually, one can do no more than merely indicate the direction in which the proper State can be found. It goes without saying that there has never been a perfect constitutional State, and that there never will be this side of Judgment Day. The sense and the non-sense of world history is that the elements which make up the State are involved in a constant movement which makes it possible to speak of a better or a worse State but never of an absolutely good State— nor, thank God!—ever of an absolutely bad State.

Question: What is the relationship between Rom. 13 and Rev. 13? *Answer:* It is curious that both these strange passages in the New Testament occur in a chapter 13! The early Christians evidently saw no contradiction here or any necessity to cancel one of the passages. On the contrary, they read in Paul's Epistle that there is no *exousia* that is not from God, and in Rev. 13 that the same political system can take on the form of the beast from the abyss. One and the same State, Nero's Roman State, is described in the New Testament as a divine institution and as a beast from the abyss. These are the two poles, between which we have to see the State in the context of time. We have to reckon with both, but obviously first with Rom. 13, and then with Rev. 13 as the great question mark. The fact that these two aspects exist: the good *ordinatio Dei* on the one hand and the *corruptio hominum* on the other, is not a hopeless, but it certainly is a very serious problem. What we call political responsibility has to find expression between these two poles. Rom. 13 must be the starting point. On the basis of this command ('Every soul must be submissive to its lawful superiors') the Christian sees reality as it is, and may feel some cause for fear when he remembers that the beast from the abyss is waiting at the end of the inclined plane on which the State may find itself. But in fact we shall never

see the State either in its pure form as the ordinance of God or
in its entirely diabolical perversion. These two poles are the
frontiers between which reality moves. Only the dreamers and
fanatics can imagine they are in a *civitas Dei*, possibly a *civitas*
in the old style with God-sent kings and kingdoms which last
a thousand years, where the kings sit on thrones and priests pay
homage to them; or they may imagine themselves in a *civitas*
in the modern style: the coming society in which all men will
enter into their rights, in which freedom will rule and all problems will be solved and the evil one be vanquished. All such
fancies are mere day-dreaming. But, you know, it is no less a
day-dream to imagine you can see the beast from the abyss
walking about alive in the streets! Fortunately we are spared
that sight. There is a hell, but it is a frontier; there is no hell
that we can actually see. Jesus Christ has gone down into hell
and locked it up for us, and sealed it off. We no longer have to
reckon with the possibility of hell becoming a reality. It is the
sign of the *regnum Christi* that in this era everything has its limits,
in good and in evil. I would recommend you to read both these
chapters very carefully and very seriously. You will come to
see that we live between them. When you have grasped that,
you will not dramatise our situation, but you will judge it soberly.
(There is a proverb: 'When the donkey's feeling too well, he
goes dancing on the ice.' I can't say that I feel too well at the
moment; I don't want to dance, and I hope I'm not merely a
donkey—but all the same I must now move on to some slippery
ice!! The questions you have put to me are becoming more and
more burning and more and more dangerous. Up till now they
have moved in the theological, the dogmatic and the exegetical
sphere: that will now no longer be the case.)

Question: What should the Christian attitude be to a State that
pays no attention to justice, which may be a godless State,
nevertheless pretends to be a friend of the Church, but which
must turn out sooner or later to be an enemy of the Church,
for inescapable ideological reasons? What should the Church's
attitude be to a State which allows the Church to carry on independently for the time being for purely tactical reasons, but also
intimates that it will fight the Church in the future?

G

Answer: 'Nightingale, I hear thy warbling!' I would first like to give you a serious and weighty answer to these questions—a whole series on similar lines has been submitted—in general terms. To the extent that 'somewhere or other' the State does appear in the way described in the questions, the only possibility open to the Christian will be to hold fast to the word: 'We ought to obey God rather than men.' Let that be the strong foundation supporting all that follows.

When that word has been said and heard, I should like to add a second and somewhat less formidable answer: in such a situation the main thing for us Christians is not to lose our calm and our sense of humour. For—let me remind you of what I said a short while ago—we shall not meet a perfect Christian State until the Day of Judgment—nor the devil's State either. We shall always be moving between the two. And so, even if the State begins to show signs of the beast from the abyss, as Christians we shall not immediately clutch at the *ultimo ratio*: Yes or No? Consent or martyrdom? Just because we are Christians we shall be free to wait a little and give ourselves time to examine the whole situation in detail. No State can exist that is able to escape from the ordinance of God. One must begin with Rom. 13 and not with Rev. 13. Why not hold fast to the order that still exists or again exists even in a menacing and dangerous State? The Christian life is based primarily on affirmation of the good and only secondarily on condemnation of the evil. I am no loyalist and am perfectly prepared to slam the table. But the occasion must be quite clear. And I am afraid that these questions betray the uneasiness of a mistrust that is not Christian. What I should like to do, therefore, would be to put my hand on the shoulders of those who have sent in these questions and ask: 'Ferryman, tell me honestly: is the situation really as dangerous as all that?'[1] Already so dangerous today? It might become more dangerous—I know the way these things work out. But does it not still hold good that we should not fret over tomorrow, even though there may be good cause to ask anxiously: What will they do tomorrow? If we face them openly and calmly today then we may pray: 'Give us our bread today for tomorrow' (which is the exact translation). Then we shall not need to let

---

[1] From the song, *Als wir jüngst in Regensburg waren.*

tomorrow cast a gloom over today. 'Cast all your cares on Him.' What has the Christian Church to fear if it has faith? What can the kind of State adumbrated in these questions do to it? There is not a trace in the New Testament of the Church being afraid of the State. Therefore I should like to say to all the friends who have put these questions: Let us not be afraid. It is easy to be afraid anywhere in the world today. The whole of the Western world, the whole of Europe is afraid, afraid of the East. But we must not be afraid. We shall then be able to enter the morrow with a quiet conscience. The morrow may be quite different from what we think. Great dangers in the life of individuals and nations have often only appeared on the horizon. Everything is in the hands of God. We must certainly offer resistance if necessary, but why be nervous and despondent? We shall never act aright in this State if we indulge in that mood.

Question: Is it possible to carry out one's duties as a citizen without belonging to a party?
Answer: Certainly, it is possible in all circumstances. The fact that there are parties in political life is really only a secondary phenomenon in the life of the State. Parties are a necessary evil, and can easily become a very great evil. In such cases one's duty as a citizen is best fulfilled by keeping away from them. Indeed, in certain circumstances it may well be one's duty as a citizen to protest against all political partisanship.

Question: Can a Christian join any party, even a non-Christian party?
Answer: I don't think we have any right to talk about 'Christian parties'. Christian parties are just as non-existent as Christian States. States and parties are organs in which all can participate without being asked about their faith. That is the difference between States and parties on the one hand and the Church on the other. Even if a party consisted entirely of Christians, it could not practise its Christianity as such in the political sphere. That would be an illusion. The question here, however, is, Can a Christian join any party?—to which I would say that a Christian will join the party in which he sees the greatest approximation to what we described as a striving after the proper State. Such

a party will not be absolutely in the right, but it may be a bit
more so than the others. The Christian will join this party without fanaticism but with clear-sighted conviction that it is the
best party for him to be associated with. I can only imagine one
case of a party which a Christian should not join under any circumstances: this would be a party which was not only a party
but clandestinely also a Church, demanding that its members
should subordinate their relationship to God and their neighbour
to the ideals of the party. Such parties existed in ancient times
and exist today. The Christian cannot enter such a party since
he already belongs to a real Church. He might possibly associate
himself with the practical aims of such a party, but he could not
share its creed. He would refuse the invitation to join it, with
a friendly smile.

Question: Has the State the right to force its citizens to join a
definite party?
Answer: Here I can only answer with a frank 'No!' In making
this demand the State would not be a proper State at all. One
can join a party only if one is convinced that it stands for the
right. If the State were to force its citizens into a particular party
it would be attacking its own foundations. It would be forcing
its citizens to lie. How could the State expect to be really sustained by such a society? Here then I must reply with a frank
No! And—*Honi soit qui mal y pense*!

Question: Is it permissible to join a party in order to keep one's
job?
Answer: I have recently learnt two words in Hungary: *Igen* (Yes)
and *Nem* (No). In this case too I can only say *Nem*. It is not permissible. For it is not good and advisable to do anything against
one's conscience. I am of the opinion that the Christian answer
to this must be perfectly clear and plain. There may be many
reasons for evading this answer. And I have every sympathy for
anyone who does evade it under overwhelming pressure. We
human beings are constantly doing many things which we know
to be wrong. But I think it would be cruel if I were to reply to
this question: perhaps one may, perhaps one may not. There is
no Yes and No about it, only No. And that No must be the

basis of anything one says afterwards. Anyone who does join
a party to keep his job must infringe his conscience somewhere.
And it is not good to have to walk around with a broken conscience. I saw it happening in Germany fifteen years ago, and
I know what I'm talking about. I know how many thousands
upon thousands of broken men were walking about. And what
help is it to the party if these men are deceiving it? The party
is not doing itself any good: it ought not to allow such people
to join. A State in which political opinions are formed on such
a foundation is bound to collapse one day. I believe that when
I say No to this question I am even giving the purely secular-
minded better advice as well. Joining a party to keep one's position leads to no good in any life. I am a foreigner here, and am
returning to Switzerland, but even if I were a Hungarian my
reply would be just the same. This is a case where the saying
'We ought to obey God rather than men' has to be put to the
test. Men and women who stand on their own feet: 'Here I
stand, I can do no other'—will be good people for the new
State to have. Every State, including the new Hungarian State,
needs just that kind of men and women.

My dear friends, will you allow me to ask you a question
now?—Have I put my foot in it enough? Can we turn to other
questions? You will have noticed that I had no intention of
dodging awkward questions, and we really have been coming
to grips with real, concrete life. But may we now consider some
questions from the spiritual and theological sphere?

6. THE REFORMED CHURCH BEHIND THE 'IRON CURTAIN'

First published in the Basle 'Kirchenbote' and the 'Kirchenblatt für die reformierte Schweiz'.

Having returned from a journey to and through Hungary, I
have been asked to write a short report for the readers of the
Kirchenbote.

My colleague Charlotte von Kirschbaum and I were invited to
undertake this journey by the Hungarian Reformed Church. My
task was to give lectures to pastors, professors, senior parishioners,

students and other parochial and public groups in six towns. In Debrecen I preached on Good Friday in the 'Great Church', which had just been restored after sustaining heavy bomb damage, and in Budapest I tried to answer questions (some of them tremendously concrete questions!) in public for a whole morning. I met once again or in some cases for the first time most of the leading personalities in Church and theological circles, and I was able to discuss their problems with them more or less thoroughly. President Tildy also received me amiably and sincerely. The Swiss Ambassador, Dr. Feisst, reminded us of our own country in a most charming way. A Hungarian pastor whose mother was born in Basle acted as my faithful interpreter.

The decisive impression with which I have returned is a good, an illuminating and an encouraging one. It is also one that puts me somewhat to shame. I am of course not referring to the political situation. Obviously that is anything but pleasant. And no one expected me to call it pleasant. What I regard as more important than what I saw and heard in this respect is the positive impression made on me by the attitude and the convictions, the work, external and internal, of the Reformed Hungarians who are having to put up with these political conditions with the rest of the nation (they constitute twenty per cent. of the population) without having been consulted. It is not easy and it is not pleasant to have to live behind the 'Iron Curtain'. Curiously enough, however, I came across more calm and serene people there than in Basle. I found them preoccupied with genuine, serious and burning questions. But I discovered that they did not share that nervousness about the Russians, the 'peoples' democracies' and the whole problem of Eastern Europe which some people in our own country apparently regard as inevitable. I came across much impressive humility and patience, alertness and bravery, a faith that holds out and a closeness to the eternal things such as one does not meet here. The ancestors of these people endured Turkish rule and then the Hapsburgs for centuries. They are not so frightened and despairing as one might imagine from a distance. It impressed itself on me—I thought not without sadness of what most Germans lack today—that a real Calvinism can still prove itself a virile, solid and practical affair today.

In 1936, when I last visited Hungary, I found the same people and groups with whom I was concerned this time, in a state of nationalistic fever, compared with which even what I had just experienced at first-hand in Germany seemed pale and artificial. The Hungarian Reformed Christians were also raging furiously against the Treaty of Trianon, they were enthusing about the speedy restoration of the one thousand-year-old Crown of St. Stephen and foaming with hatred for the Czechs and Rumanians, who were then (as now) the lucky winners. All that is now a thing of the past: national pride, national hatred, national aspirations are gone. I cannot judge how far they are a thing of the past among the Reformed population. But certainly their responsible leaders are no longer following this tradition. It now appears to be the sole affair, or perhaps one should say, the tactics of the Roman Catholics to cultivate this rabidly nationalistic tradition. I was struck almost without exception by the decidedly realistic thinking of the leading figures on the Reformed side. They do not need to be lectured about the errors and omissions of the past—the thing that makes discussion so difficult in Germany!— what there was to be learned has been learnt. The 'guilt problem' is superfluous since everything has been acknowledged and admitted. They are trying to see in the national disaster which set in with Hungary's unfortunate entry into the war on the side of Germany, which culminated in the Russian invasion and was sealed by the incorporation of Hungary into the Eastern block (which the Western allies recognised!) with all the consequences that flow from that incorporation—they are trying to see the judgment of God in all this. For the moment they are determined to endure it as such, without grumbling and resentment, and in any case they intend to take it as the basis from which they look out into the future.

This does not mean that the Hungarian Reformed Church will recognise the present political régime as such. If it did so, it could place itself in a favourable position vis-à-vis the Roman Catholics. Tempting invitations to throw in its lot with the new system are not lacking from the government. But it refuses. It has sincerely and explicitly welcomed certain measures taken by the new State, in particular the agrarian reforms which will have important results for the Reformed Church. But it reserves to itself the freedom not to assent to certain other measures if the need arises. I did not meet a single absolute believer in the new system among the Reformed Christians. The naïve enthusiasm of the fiery Red Dean of Canterbury—who had been visiting the country shortly before me—only succeeded in arousing their astonishment. The Reformed Church is taking the risk of not complying with the demand of the ruling power and party that it should decide once and for all to support the new régime. My impression is that it is if anything only too anxious (particularly in questions of personnel) to avoid any possible misunderstanding in this direction.

But the Reformed Church is also resisting the still more obvious and even stronger temptation of following the lead of the Romans and entering into opposition as a matter of principle. It would make many friends that way too. It cannot be easy for it to hear the reproach coming from its own ranks that it is 'lukewarm', and that the only genuine Calvinist in Hungary today is—the Roman Catholic Archbishop! I realised clearly how far from being well-disposed to the new régime the young people are when I unleashed a quite unintended but very clear storm of applause with a quotation from Kant ('Have the courage to use your own intelligence!'). But I met no responsible Reformed Hungarian who considered it right from a Christian point of view to take the line of fundamental, out and out political resistance. My impression is that they will not be silent when they are forced to speak. But they are too well aware of the mistakes of the past and the consequences that flowed from them to want to launch out in the opposite direction. They are now too open to new ideas, particularly in the social sphere, to be able to commit themselves to a complete rejection of Communism. They know the weaknesses of the West at any rate well enough not to feel themselves obliged to throw in their lot with that side.

This Reformed Church behind the 'Iron Curtain' is treading a narrow path. Perhaps I may interpolate here that from a conversation I had with some Czech friends at the airport in Prague on our return journey I gathered that the problems are very similar there. The possibility of accidents on right and left alike cannot be excluded. It may very well be that the Reformed Church will still have to make many painful sacrifices, undertake many easily misunderstood withdrawals, risk the loss of even more popularity. They are determined to face all these possibilities. According to the New Testament the path of the Christian Church is bound to be a narrow one. And if one cannot see the situation from that angle, one might usefully consider the Swiss neutrality which we have found well worth preserving even in the midst of the conflicts of the present age, and which shows that an attitude of 'Neither—nor!' may, if properly grounded, be a sign of moral strength, not, as is usually assumed, lack of character.

To my mind, the decisive proof that the Reformed Church in Hungary is on the right road is not merely the fact that with few exceptions I found them all in a frame of mind not normally typical of the waverer. What convinced me most of all was rather that I found them occupied not primarily with the problem of East and West, with memories of the Russian atrocities and the rights and wrongs of their present government, but with the positive tasks of their own Church, and again, not with the denominational, constitutional and liturgical questions which are the subject of so much laborious enquiry in Germany, but with a new preaching of the old Word of God which cannot be undertaken without thorough theological preparation and reflection; and occupied with the evangelisation of their own congregations as the presupposition of all further work that is to be fruitful. If only the Church had started with all its forces concentrated on this primary task in Germany! The work is not without problems, since the Church and the new political régime, both movements with their own strong points and weaknesses, have still to come to terms with one another. What does seem to be happening in Hungary, however, is a religious revival and an activity in which Church and society are not inevitably opposed, but can work together on a serious and genuine basis. The common starting point is clear, and if they succeed in holding on to it and making it bear fruit, then the narrow path of the Hungarian Church, however it may be shaped by outward oppression, will become the way to a freedom in which its witness will be a tower of strength.

7. A Correspondence

(A) *An Open Letter to Karl Barth*

Many will no doubt have read your report on Hungary with as great an interest as I have done. But not a few, including some of your own theological associates, have been extremely surprised by your attitude to the political problems of the Church under Soviet rule. Those who were familiar with the pronouncements on current events which you have issued since the end of the war were aware that your attitude to the great Communist power in the East was, if not friendly, at any rate emphatically sympathetic, and deliberately avoided any harsh outright rejection of Communist pretensions. I myself have only been able to interpret your approach as an after-effect of the satisfaction you felt at the overpowering of the brown monster in which Communist Russia played such a leading part. I had hoped that this mildness would automatically disappear and give way to a more fundamental judgment as soon as the true character of that power had emerged more clearly. I imagined you would undergo the same change of outlook as Reinhold Niebuhr, who only two years ago was expressing doubts about my fundamental rejection of Communist totalitarianism at an important ecumenical conference, but who has since joined the absolute opponents of Communism, particularly since seeing the monster at close quarters in Berlin. What I cannot understand—and it is this that prompts me to write an open letter to you—is why a similar change has not occurred in your attitude—even after the recent events in Prague.

Not only after the end of the war and during the last two years, but even now, you are passing on the watchword that the Church must not allow itself to be dragged into a clear-cut, fundamental opposition to 'Communism'. You praise the Reformed Hungarians for not 'sharing that nervousness about the Russians, the peoples' democracies and the whole problem of Eastern Europe which some people in our own country apparently regard as inevitable'. You evidently agree with your pupil Hermann Diem that in its first encounter with the 'Communism' of the East the Evangelical Church should not reject it out of hand but wait and see, and be ready to co-operate. I don't know if you even approve of the attitude of your friend Hromadka in Prague, who belongs to the Communist Action Committee and who, although he prophesied only a short time ago in England that there would be no *coup d'état* in Prague, since Czech Communism was different from Russian Communism, was, when the crisis came, ready to co-operate.

All this is inexplicable to those who can see no fundamental difference between Communist and any other brand of totalitarianism, for example Nazism. Naturally we who have taken this line for many years realise that the origins and original motivation of Russian Communism were quite different from those of Nazism. We know too that certain postulates of social justice appear to be fulfilled in Communist totalitarianism. In brief, we know that the red variety of totalitarianism is different from the brown.

The question we want to ask you, however—and when I say 'we' I mean not only the Swiss, but also many of your theological friends in Germany, Britain and America—is whether, whatever the differences between the several varieties, totalitarianism as such is a quantity to which the Christian Church can only issue an absolute, unmistakable and passionate 'No!', just as you said 'No!' to Hitlerism and summoned the Church to say an absolute 'No!'. Let me make a few observations to establish and explain the question:

1. I was always struck, and probably others were too, by the fact that even at the height of your struggle against Nazism you always evaded the problem of totalitarianism. Passionate and absolute as was your hostility to that incarnation of social injustice, if I am not mistaken, you hardly ever attacked the fundamental illegality and inhumanity inherent in the very nature of totalitarianism as such. This may have struck me more than others, since as far back as the spring of 1934 I became involved in a sharp exchange with some German theologians at an ecumenical conference in Paris because they refused to swallow my thesis that the totalitarian State is *eo ipso* an unjust, inhuman and godless State. Since then I have repeatedly defended that position, and was therefore never able wholly to agree with the thesis

you put forward in Wipkingen in 1938, that National Socialism was 'the' political problem of the Church in our time, whole-heartedly as I agreed with you that it was the primary and most urgent problem from a purely political and military point of view.

2. I have been equally struck by the fact that in your utterances and those of your closest friends the problem of the totalitarian State is displaced by two other problems, which I can only regard as concealing the real problem. You talk about 'the problem of East and West' and the problem of 'Communism'.

If the only issue was a 'problem of East and West' the Church would certainly do well not to join too ostentatiously in the con-versations of the politicians. For 'East and West' is undoubtedly not a problem in which the Church as such has anything authori-tative to say. But what one must not forget is that there are nations in Eastern Europe today which have been violated and regard themselves as having been violated by a political despotism in the same way as non-German nations did under Hitler. Nazism did not become an 'Eastern' problem because Hitler occupied large territories in Eastern Europe. Because a political system subjugates and controls by means of puppet governments the peoples of Russia, the Baltic, Poland and the Balkans, the con-flict today has certainly not become one between East and West. That would be the case only if the nations involved had given their consent to the Communist system, and if such consent could be explained on the grounds of traditional modes of think-ing in Eastern Europe. Today everyone with eyes to see knows that that is not so. We churchmen really ought not to associate ourselves with such a camouflaging of the truth.

3. The other shift of emphasis is rather better founded, though no less dangerous. People—including yourself—talk simply about the 'Communism' which the Church should not reject outright. Certainly the Christian who believes in the Communion of Saints and celebrates Holy Communion, cannot be against 'Com-munism' as such. Among the many possible forms of Commun-ism there are some with thoroughly Christian potentialities. One can indeed argue, as I have often done, that the system that calls itself Communism today would not have become possible if the Church had been more communistic on the lines of the com-munism we find in the Acts of the Apostles which is inherent

in the very nature of the Christian society. What we are dealing with today, however, is a manifestation of the totalitarian State, a totalitarian Communism. This so-called Communism is the logical consequence of totalitarianism. If Hitler did not get as far as total nationalisation, total political and military control until the last years of the war, it only shows what an amateur he was. The 'fully matured', the consistent totalitarian State must be 'communistic', since one of its essential foundations is the subjugation to the State of the whole of life and the whole of man. And the nationalisation of the whole economic life of the country is the indispensable first step towards the totalitarian State. The question which confronts the Church today is therefore not whether or not it should adopt a fundamentally negative attitude towards 'Communism', but whether it can say anything but a passionately fundamental No to the totalitarian State which, to be consistent, must also be communistic.

4. You justify the rejection of a fundamentally negative answer to 'Communism' by referring to the social injustice of which there is certainly no lack in the nations of the West. The alternative as it is usually put sounds more imposing: Communism or Capitalism? Of course, the Church cannot and should not deny that there is a great deal of scandalous social injustice in the West. Of course it must fight against all social wrongs with the utmost earnestness and passion. Whether it does well to adopt the slogan of 'capitalism' as the embodiment of social evil will depend on whether it knows what it means by capitalism. If it only means an economy which is not nationalised, I would resist the war-cry vigorously. The crucial point, however, is that we must never forget that in the countries not under totalitarian control it is still possible to fight against social injustice, that the fight is being waged and has already achieved a great deal, though nothing like enough.

5. If I am correctly informed, you are still a Socialist. However you interpret the Socialism in which you believe—the English interpretation, for example, is very different from that of our 'socialist' Press, and the current German version is quite different from the one in fashion there twenty years ago—one thing cannot be denied: Socialism is engaged in a life and death struggle against 'Communism' because and in so far as it is

fundamentally and passionately anti-totalitarian. Is it therefore a good thing that this anti-totalitarian Socialism should be attacked in the rear—by churchmen of all people—in its defensive fight against totalitarian Communism? This is the effect of your statement that the well-advised Christian cannot be anti-Communist. Do you mean that Christians must not participate in the common struggle which the bourgeoisie and Socialism are waging against totalitarian Communism? I believe that would amount to a denial of principles which the Christian must never deny. Why not? Well, what is at stake in the struggle against totalitarianism? What is totalitarianism?

6. The totalitarian State is based on, is in fact identical with, the denial of those rights of the person vis-à-vis the State which are usually called human rights. That was the situation in Hitler's State, and it is the same now in the Communist totalitarian State. The individual has no original rights conferred on him as a creature of God. Only the State can establish rights, and the individual only has the rights the State gives him and can take away from him at any time.

The totalitarian State is therefore a State of basic injustice. It is therefore also fundamentally inhuman and a fundamental denial of personal dignity. It is therefore intrinsically godless even though it may, like the Nazi State, tolerate the Church within certain narrow limits, or like Communist totalitarianism, for reasons of expediency keep its openly declared war on religion within certain bounds which just make it possible for the Church to exist.

The totalitarian State is intrinsically atheistic and anti-theistic since, by definition, it claims the total allegiance of man. From this intrinsic nature of totalitarianism all the familiar, ghastly phenomena have resulted which we got to know from the Russian State from 1917–1948, and from the Nazi State from 1933–1945: the G.P.U. and the Gestapo; the concentration camp without legal proceedings; the slave labour of millions; the utter uncertainty of the law, and so on. My question is: can the Church possibly say anything but a passionate and absolute No to totalitarianism? Must it not take its stand just as definitely against 'Communism', i.e. against the consistently totalitarian State as against the amateurish Nazi State?

7. You assert that the Communist State realises certain social

postulates which the Christian cannot oppose, but must on the contrary welcome. We heard exactly the same argument in the Hitler State—how often they tried to hoodwink us with the marvellous social achievements of the Nazi régime—things which it was impossible flatly to deny and which persuaded the naïve to believe that, in spite of all the horrors, 'at bottom' National Socialism was a good thing. It cannot be denied that the Communist State has achieved and is achieving all kinds of valuable things—how else could it continue to exist at all? But as Christians we surely know it is always the devil's way to mix elements of truth in the system of lies and to endue a system of injustice with certain splendid appearances of justice. Are we no longer to fight the system of injustice, which is what the totalitarian State is fundamentally, because it also contains a number of valuable achievements? The dividing up of large estates was certainly a long overdue measure, in the interests of a healthy economy and a free peasantry. And it is also open to debate how far the nationalising of certain branches of economic life is not in the interest of justice and the common weal. Regarding the last point, I am more sceptical than my Socialist friends; but it is a matter that is certainly worth discussing amongst Christians. What is not open to discussion, however, is whether, because of measures such as these, which may be justified in themselves, the system of injustice and inhumanity which totalitarianism is, may be considered a feasible system for Christians.

8. Your friend Hromadka defends the strange view that Communism—meaning the totalitarian Communism which is the only variety we are concerned with today—is a historical necessity, since democracy has proved its inability to survive: therefore the Christian Church must welcome Communism. We heard just the same argument in Switzerland during the worst years of the Hitler régime. I regard it as an utterly dangerous aberration of which a Protestant theologian ought to be thoroughly ashamed. A doubtful piece of historical determinism, shaky in relation to facts and principles alike, is used to confer the status of a normative principle on what amounts to an abdication of ethics and a surrender to the brute force of reality. Since when has the Christian capitulated in the face of 'historical necessities'? Certainly there are situations in which the Christian or the

Church is powerless to do anything, in which they cannot prevent disasters, in which they cannot redress even the most flagrant
injustice, in which they may not even be able to protest publicly
without endangering their very existence. All the more reason,
surely, why the Church should beware of giving an ethical sanction to something it is powerless to prevent—but that is precisely
what Hromadka is doing. What will he, what will his friends
have to say for themselves when this totalitarian system that has
been forced on their people collapses and is brought to judgment,
as the Nazi system was brought to judgment in the Nuremberg
Trials? They will stand convicted as collaborators, who not
merely co-operated with the power of tyranny and injustice but
even set themselves up as its champions!

9. There is one final argument which we find in your utterances and those of your friends: this fundamental attack on
'Communism' is something the Catholic Church is engaged in
—therefore we Protestants should not join in. I do not feel
called upon to defend Catholic politics. I know perfectly well
how much the Catholics always pursue their own power-political
ends, how much, especially in Hungary, the Catholic Church is
defending its former privileges in its struggle against Communism. But when the Catholic Church declares that the totalitarian
State, red or brown, is irreconcilable with the Christian faith,
why should the Evangelical Church have to stand aside merely
because the truth is spoken by the Catholic Church? Did not
Catholics and Protestants stand together in the struggle against
the Hitler régime, and did you yourself not rejoice in the brave
utterances of individual Catholic leaders and heartily agree with
them when they condemned the totalitarian State passionately
and unconditionally? A doctrine does not become false simply
because it is expressed by the Catholic Church even if we always
have good reason to reserve to ourselves the right to deviate from
the Catholics and interpret and justify the doctrine more closely.

10. One further word about Hungary. I have not visited post-
war Hungary, but I am fairly well-informed about what is going
on, and I know how many different interpretations of the situation are current there. I know that very many good members
of the Reformed Church view with the utmost consternation
these new collaborationist slogans, these tendencies towards a

'positive evaluation' which are inspired by Pétain-Tildy, himself a member of the Reformed Church. The Reformed collaborators, even the Reformed fellow-travellers, will have to atone bitterly one day, I was told by someone who has suffered severely under the Communists. And even now many are turning away disillusioned from these members of the Reformed Church, because they feel they are betraying the cause of freedom, human rights, justice and humanity.

I simply cannot grasp why you, of all people, who condemned so severely even a semblance of collaborationism on the part of the Church under Hitler, should now be making yourself the spokesman of those who condemn not merely outward but even inward spiritual resistance, and why you should deride as 'nervousness' what is really a horror-struck revulsion from a truly diabolical system of injustice and inhumanity; why you, who were only recently condemning in the most unsparing terms those Germans who withdrew to a purely inward line in the struggle against Hitlerism, and maintained that the Christian duty was simply to proclaim the Word of God under whatever political system, why you now suddenly advocate the very same line and commend the theologians in Hungary who 'are occupied not with the rights and wrongs of their present government but simply with the positive tasks of their own Church'. Have you now returned, after a fifteen years' intermezzo of theologically political activism, to that attitude of passive unconcern in which, in the first number of *Theologische Existenz heute*, you summoned the Church to apply itself simply to its task of preaching the gospel, 'as if nothing had happened'?

I have felt bound to submit this question to you in my own name and in that of many of those who listen to you who are equally disturbed. Mindful of the great influence of whatever you say, you will surely regard it as a duty to give the question a clear answer.

Your EMIL BRUNNER

(B) *Karl Barth's Reply*

DEAR EMIL BRUNNER,—You do not seem to understand. At the moment I am not rousing the Church to oppose Communism and to witness against it, in the same way as I did

H

between 1933 and 1945 in the case of National Socialism; you demand a 'clear reply' to the question of how this is to be construed. I will come straight to the point.

Let us begin with a general statement. A certain binding spiritual and theological viewpoint in accordance with its creed is demanded of the Church in the political realm in certain times of need, i.e. when it is called upon to vindicate its faith in the carrying out of its duty according to God's Word, or when it is called upon to give an explanation regarding a definite occurrence. The Church must not concern itself eternally with various 'isms' and systems, but with historical realities as seen in the light of the Word of God and of the Faith. Its obligations lie, not in the direction of any fulfilling of the law of nature, but towards its living Lord. Therefore, the Church never thinks, speaks or acts 'on principle'. Rather it judges spiritually and by individual cases. For that reason it rejects every attempt to systematise political history and its own part in that history. Therefore, it preserves the freedom to judge each new event afresh. If yesterday it travelled along one path, it is not bound to keep to the same path today. If yesterday it spoke from its position of responsibility, then today it should be silent if in this position it considers silence to be the better course. The unity and continuity of theology will best be preserved if the Church does not let itself be discouraged from being up-to-date theologically.

I ask this question: Was it not true that in the years after 1933 up till the end of the war there really was this need? The Central and Western European peoples—first Germany, then the others —had succumbed to Hitler's spell. He had become a spiritual and, almost everywhere, a political source of temptation. He had English, French and American admirers. Did not even Churchill have a few friendly words to say for him? And in Switzerland there were more than two hundred sympathisers, there was a Rudolf Grob, there were innumerable people who were impressed and influenced, though also very many who were frightened and despondent. One of the most important aims of our political authorities was to preserve correct and friendly relations with our powerful neighbour. In the Swiss Zofinger Society there was a serious discussion as to whether it was not time to subject our democratic system, established in 1848 (which event we are triumphantly celebrating today) to a thorough revision. Of the state of the Press one can read in the edifying book by Karl Weber, *Switzerland in the War of Nerves*. How great were the cares of our military directors can be seen from the account of our General, and from the fine book by Lt.-Col. Barbey about the five years he spent in the General's entourage. It was at that time that I made my various attempts to make the Church ready for action against the temptations of National Socialism, in Germany obviously spiritual, in Switzerland obviously political. At that time it had to warn men against tempters, to recall those who had strayed, to rouse the careless, to 'confirm the feeble knees', to comfort sorrowing hearts.

Whether the essence of National Socialism consisted in its 'totalitarianism' or, according to other views, in its 'nihilism', or again in its barbarism, or anti-semitism, or whether it was a final, concluding outburst of the militarism which had taken hold on Germany like a madness since 1870—what made it interesting from the Christian point of view was that it was a spell which notoriously revealed its power to overwhelm our souls, to persuade us to believe in its lies and to join in its evil-doings. It could and would take us captive with 'strong mail of craft and power'. We were hypnotised by it as a rabbit by a giant snake. We were in danger of bringing, first incense, and then the complete sacrifice to it as to a false god. That ought not to have been done. We had to object with all our pro-testantism as though against *the* evil. It was not a matter of declaiming against some mischief, distant and easily seen through. It was a matter of life and death, of resistance against a godless-ness which was in fact attacking body and soul, and was there-fore effectively masked to many thousands of Christian eyes. For that very reason I spoke then and was not silent. For that very reason I could not forgive the collaborators, least of all those among them who were cultured, decent and well-meaning. In that way I consider that I acted as befits a churchman.

Now a second question: Is it not true that today there is again a state of emergency, this time in the shape of Communism? Has history already repeated itself, in that today we only need to take the remedy (which at that time took long enough to learn) from out of our pockets and to make immediate use of it? In the last few years I have become acquainted with Western Germany and also with the non-Russian sectors of Berlin. Fear, distrust and hatred for the 'Eastern monster', as you call it, I met there in abundance, but apart from the German Communists I met no man of whom I received the impression (as one did with almost everybody in 1933) that he felt that this 'monster' was a vexation, a temptation, an enticement, or that he was in danger of liking it or of condoning its deeds and of co-operating with it. On the contrary, it was quite clear to everyone, and it was universally agreed that for many reasons there was nothing in it. Is the situation any different here in Switzerland? in France, England or America? Are we not all convinced, whether we have read *I Chose Freedom* or not, that we cannot consider the way of life of the people in Soviet territory and in the Soviet-controlled 'peoples' democracies' to be worthy, acceptable or of advantage to us, because it does not conform to our standards of justice and freedom? Who can contradict this? A few Western European Communists! Yet are we in danger of letting ourselves be overwhelmed by this power merely on account of the existence and the activities of these latter? Is there not freedom for every man—and who would not take advantage of this freedom?—to vent his anger against this 'monster' to his heart's content, and again and again to bring to light its evils as 'thoroughly' and as 'passionately' as he wishes? Anyone who would like from me a political disclaimer of its system and its methods may have it at once. However, what is given cheaply can be had cheaply. Surely it would cost no one anything—not even a little thought—certainly nothing more, to add his bundle of faggots to the bonfire? I cannot admit that this is a repetition of the situation and of the tasks during the years 1933-45. For I cannot admit that it is the duty of Christians or of the Church to give theological backing to what every citizen can, with much shaking of his head, read in his daily paper and what is so admirably expressed by Mr. Truman and by the Pope. Has the 'East' or whatever we may call it, really such a hold over us that we must needs oppose it with our last breath when the last but one would suffice? No, when the Church witnesses it moves in fear and trembling, not with the stream but against it. Today it certainly has no cause to move against the stream and thus to witness to Communism because it could never be worthy of it, either in its Marxist or its imperialist, or let us say, in its Asiatic aspects. Must the Church then move with the stream and thus side with America and the Vatican, merely because somewhere in the text-books of its professors—ever since 1934 —it has rightly been said that 'totalitarianism' is a dreadful thing? Where is the spiritual danger and need which the Church would meet if it witnessed to this truth, where is its commission to do so? Whom would it teach, enlighten, rouse, set on the right path, comfort and lead to repentance and a new way of life? Surely not the 'Christian' peoples of the West, nor the Americans! Are they not already sure enough of the justice of their cause against Russia without this truth and our Christian support? Surely not the poor Russians and even the poor Communists? For how should they be able to understand what the Western Church, which in the old days and even today has accepted so much 'totalitarianism' and has co-operated with it without witnessing against it, claims to have against their Church? Surely not the Christian Churches behind the Iron Curtain? In their struggle with the 'monster' it would be no help at all to them if we were to proclaim those well-known truths as energetically as possible, since we are not asked for them anyway, nor would they cost us anything. As it is not possible to give satisfactory answers to these questions, I am of the opinion that the Church today—contrary to its action between 1933 and 1945—ought to stand quietly aloof from the present conflict and not let off all its guns before it is necessary but wait calmly to see whether and in what sense the situation will grow serious again and call for speech. If a definite spiritual crisis were again to develop as it did during the years 1933-45—though we do not yet know from what direction it is likely to come—then a concrete answer would be demanded from us, for which we ourselves should have to pay: then it would be obvious against whom and for whom we should have to witness, and whether and how far we should be prepared for this new emergency. Then something would be at stake other than these eternal truths which you wish me to proclaim. According to my view, we shall then profit more from the first article of the Declaration of Barmen than from your knowledge of the objectionableness of 'totalitarianism.'

But, however that may be, with this problem in view I met responsible members of the Reformed Church in Hungary and thought that I could encourage them in their attempt to walk along the narrow path midway between Moscow and Rome. I did not take a ruler with me to draw this dividing line, so I could not leave one behind for their use. Their past history, their present situation and their task do not resemble ours, nor those of the Evangelical Church in Germany which is joining in the battle. They have come to an agreement with the new régime and are directing all their energies towards the positive tasks of their Church, and this is not the same as what the central parties, which you esteem so highly, or even the 'German Christians', are doing in the battle for the Church in Germany. Incidentally, it is a legend without historical foundation that in 1933 I recommended 'passive resistance' when I urged the Germans to fulfil their duties of Christian witness 'as though nothing had happened', i.e. ignoring Adolf Hitler's alleged divine revelation. If they had consequently done so, they would have built up against National Socialism a political factor of the first order.

For Hungary, though not only for this country, everything depends on whether the Church, not bound to abstract principles but to its living Lord, will seek and find its own way and also learn to choose freely the time for speech and the time for silence and all the various other times mentioned in Ecclesiastes, Chapter 3, without thereby becoming confused by any law other than that of the gospel.

Your KARL BARTH

Basel,
 June 6th, 1948

8. TO MY FRIENDS
IN THE REFORMED CHURCH IN HUNGARY

After the fortnight I was able to spend with you in the spring of this year my thoughts have often returned to your country, your Church and to all of you. Everywhere you gave me a welcome the affection of which made the deepest impression on me. And thus the problems, worries and hopes of your present and your future, and your special situation, have constantly been on

my mind. I am particularly glad to hear that the reports on my
visit which I published here in Switzerland have been acknowledged to be mainly accurate and have been kindly received by
those of you who have read them. In recent days I have had
the pleasant surprise of a visit from Pastor Janos Peter. He has
informed me of the important events which have taken place
in the meantime; of the beginning of the negotiations for a
Concordat between your Church and the new Hungarian State
and the discussions on the election of a successor to the much
revered Dr. Ravasz as Bishop of the Church province on the
Danube. He allowed me to examine an extract from the minutes
of your Synodal Council of April 30, 1948, which include
amongst other things the Ten Points in which this body has
expressed the basic attitude of your Church to the new State—
and also the final section of the twenty-seventh and last episcopal
report of Dr. Ravasz. Finally, after a detailed discussion, he asked
me to put my views on these matters in a few words addressed
to you all.

My dear fathers and brothers, it is not entirely easy for me to
comply with this request. After having, in the last days of my
visit to Budapest, joined somewhat vivaciously in the discussion
about your affairs, it may savour of unwarranted interference if
I now take the liberty of sending you the following comments.
Please forgive me and please take them as a quite unofficial
expression of my serious and brotherly interest in the life of your
Church. They are not intended to be binding on anyone.

If my picture of the present relationship of your Church to
your new State is correct it may be stated in its main outlines
as follows: Your Church is faced with the task of having to find
its bearings again as a free Church, that is, in its relationship to
a State that is also free, and it has to do so while remaining true
and becoming still more true to its essential character as a Church
of Jesus Christ.

Your Church suffers from a twofold liability. First, in the past
it did not, to its own knowledge, preserve its freedom vis-à-vis
the State and the society it represented, so that it cannot now
feel justified in referring to its attitude in the past in its dealings
with the new State. Secondly, since the political revolution is
not yet complete, it cannot be foreseen to what extent and to

what end the present Hungarian State will make use of its freedom both in relation to the Church and in other respects. The
first consideration rightly prevents your Church from following
the Roman Catholics and adopting an attitude of resistance
towards the new State. The second consideration again rightly
prevents it from going beyond *de facto* and *de jure* recognition
of the new State, prevents it from identifying itself, for instance,
with the new ideology and sanctioning in advance developments
of which it is not yet possible to see the nature and extent.

The situation may also be described in positive terms: the
new Hungarian State has so far used its sovereignty in a way
that, as you understand it, allows and even impels you, in contra-
distinction to the attitude of the Roman Catholics and whatever
your misgivings over particular details, to affirm the main lines
of its structure and policy, as has happened already in the Ten
Points I have mentioned; and to look forward to your future
relationship with the new State and in particular to the conclusion of a Concordat at any rate not without reasonable confidence. But you are deeply aware of the need to use the freedom
of the Church in a more serious, more fundamental and thorough-
going way than in the past. You face the urgent task of evangelising
and rebuilding your congregations on the basis of a better knowledge of the Bible and therefore of a renewed faith in our Lord
Jesus Christ as the sole Head of your Church as of all others.
In the use of this freedom the new State cannot help you any
more than the old one, but you must not on any account allow
it to hinder you either. This will mean that you must allow yourself plenty of room to move in your relations with the new
State and also that none of the well-considered and voluntary
concessions you have already made and may yet make must be
allowed to imply that the Reformed Church has been 'brought
into line' with the new State, that it has become an 'established
Church' again. Or to put it in military terms: The Reformed
Church cannot and does not intend to attack the new State. It
also sees no need to defend itself against it. But it also does not
think for a moment of capitulating to it! In more peaceful
phraseology: the Reformed Church is determined to tread a
path that runs parallel to the path of the new Hungarian State
as far as may be (point No. 1 in the Declaration of the Synod).

But it realises even more clearly that this path can only be its own path, that is, the path prescribed by the Word of God.

If I have understood you aright in all this, the path on which you are setting out is a very narrow, a very difficult and dangerous but also a very promising path. The way you tread it will be decisive not only for the future of your own Church, but also of exemplary importance for all the other Churches in the East—and in the West too.

Perhaps you will let me draw your very special attention to one last consideration. If you can really make it your own, you will understand even better than you do already why I am so interested in the course of events in Hungary. The vitally important thing for you now is to be quite sure of your own cause as a Reformed Church in a situation that has changed so completely, and to be determined to base your position strictly on your own cause and to allow political and diplomatic considerations only second place in your thoughts. Let me put it a different way: everything will now depend on your being inspired with a joyful confidence in the possibility of thinking, judging and deciding spiritually, instead of strategically and tactically, in the practical problems that confront you. The Churches of the whole world—or at any rate, the responsible personalities, groups and bodies—are making, as far as one can see, far too little use of this possibility. One of them, the Roman Catholic, does not even appear to be aware of the possibility. If I understand the situation aright, the sole possibility that remains open to you in Hungary today is the simplest of all. The only possible course that still lies open to you is to live, with your backs to the wall, for the gospel of God's free grace and to act as conscientiously as you can with that gospel as your sole guide. This means that by the mercy of God you have been offered a unique opportunity. When do the good days of a Church begin if not in moments when, both theoretically and practically, the gospel is its only source of comfort? Such opportunities pass away. The Evangelical Church in Germany had them and has let them slip by for three years now. Such opportunities can slip by irrevocably. Let me appeal to you, not merely for your own sake but with all the other Churches in mind: Do not let the opportunity that is now being offered to you slip by!

If you now intend to act with the gospel as your sole guide, you will not be troubled by the great amount of misunderstanding and head-shaking which you will encounter in your own country and to left and right abroad. Faith is after all not everyone's affair. You will also not be troubled to find yourself in a state of penance and restriction from which you cannot liberate yourselves, from which only God can lead you further on your road. You will not be troubled because you have to re-establish the trustworthiness and authority of your Church vis-à-vis your people and your new Government by dint of simple, faithful and brave work on your own ground. If you act with the gospel as your guide, whatever you do will never be a retreat to interior lines. I admit that the word 'retreat' is the only one that alarmed me a little in Dr. Ravasz's beautiful, wise and dignified report. When the Church resolutely betakes itself to its own ground, renouncing all kinds of fundamentally unimportant and ambiguous strongholds and spheres of influence, it is in fact not retreating at all, but advancing. From the pure preaching of the gospel and the proper celebration of the Holy Communion it will acquire the commission and the authority to carry out circumspectly, justly and courageously the guardianship in the political and social sphere which it cannot possibly neglect even in the new Hungarian State, without becoming a dumb dog instead of a true Church.

I will take the liberty of saying, moreover, that if you act from the gospel, you will make it a rule in the difficulties, great and small, which lie before you:

1. always to meet the difficulties directly, striving to find a way out as far forward as possible, in the direction of the most authentic and the most audacious Christian solution and not on some by-way or other or in some half-solution.
2. always to meet the other party, in this case, the new Hungarian State and its government, with all your cards on the table, since your intention is not to make war or apply warlike stratagems but to bring home to the other party that at least when the Church says Yes it means Yes, and when it says No it means No—and nothing else but No.
3. On no account to allow the other party to dictate your path,

your thoughts, your words, your attitude—either positively or negatively, because you want to avoid pleasing or hurting the other side. May I add a special word on this last point?

Among the Ten Points in your Synodal Council's Declaration there were a few of which the tone and the wording made me a little uneasy, in spite of the fact that I fully understood the authors' intentions. It seemed to me that what was said went too far in the direction of deference to the new order. In my opinion you will fare best in your relations with your government and the ruling party if you face them with a completely straight back: if only because you will then find it much easier to look these men in the face as men. On the other hand, however, I would make one further comment on the problem of electing a new Bishop of Budapest. You seem to be agreed that from a purely ecclesiastical and theological point of view Pastor Bereczky is just the man you need in this position. But there seems to be some doubt about his candidature because he is thought to stand too close to the present régime ideologically and personally, and his election might therefore suggest that you were adapting yourselves or even capitulating to the new régime. You will know that Pastor Bereczky himself withdrew his nomination for a long time with the same argument in mind. Quite rightly, however, he has now agreed to be put forward again. That argument is in fact just the kind of argument you should avoid at present. If you have a good conscience and are certain of your cause and consider it spiritually, ecclesiastically and theologically right to give the office to this man, then it would surely be thinking after the flesh not to give it to him because you were afraid it might make people at home and abroad think you were toeing the official party line. If you have no fear of the ill will of your government—and why should you?—whether you stand or fall rests in the hands not of your government but of your Master who is Lord of all—then you need not fear a decision which may please or at any rate not displease the new régime. I would venture to say that if you get rid of this second fear it will prove that you have no fear at all, and therefore not even that first fear I mentioned either.

But let me close now with this particular application of my general message, which suggested itself because your forthcoming election of a bishop played an outstanding part in my conversation with Pastor Peter. I greet you all with the words of Matt. 10.16: 'Be ye therefore wise as serpents and harmless as doves', and with I Cor. 15.58: 'Be ye stedfast, unmoveable, always abounding in the work of the Lord.'

Your KARL BARTH

Basel,
May 23rd, 1948

III

THE CHURCH BETWEEN
EAST AND WEST

This article first appeared in *Unterwegs*, the lively post-war Berlin journal, and in *World Review* in June and July 1949 (to whom acknowledgments are gladly made for friendly permission to reprint Mr. Godman's translation in the present volume). It is a development of the thoughts prompted by the disagreement with Emil Brunner about the proper Christian response to the present political conflict.

THE CHURCH BETWEEN
EAST AND WEST

I

THIS problem of the situation of the Church between East and West is a real one; if on the surface it is merely a cloud of much wise, but even more foolish, talk and writing, in the depths it is a real difficulty and a task which concerns us all today. As it affects us so nearly, it certainly is also the concern of the God who became the brother of man—of all men in all ages—in His Son. And if it is His concern, then it must also be the concern of His Church which is His witness on earth. The Church must seek an answer to the problem. And this answer must be an honest and authentic answer.

The Church is the community of Christian people, the living congregation of the living Lord Jesus Christ. In the Church, therefore, no one can, as it were, stand outside and merely look at what others are doing, listen to what others are saying. In the Church all are under question and all responsible. When one voice speaks in the Church, that is merely an invitation and a call to all to co-operate as Christians. Therefore we can seek for the answer to this problem only in this community of Christians. By that I mean that we must all bring what stirs and concerns us in this problem before the judgment seat of Him in whose name we are all baptised, in whom we trust that He alone will judge aright in this matter, as in all others. We must all ask for His Holy Spirit that He may illuminate us in this matter and make us to speak and to hear what is right. We cannot take it for granted that that will happen. For, besides being Christians, we are all rather a lot of other things as well—for instance, representatives of this or that economic interest, readers of this or that newspaper, perhaps members of this or that Party, and in addition to all that, under the compulsion of old or new intellectual habits and traditions—and do not let us forget that

we are all provided with our own greater or lesser hardheaded-
ness and our own greater or lesser softheartedness. But let us
approach this present problem as Christians. If we do that, we
shall certainly not fail to come at least a step nearer to an answer.
I say this also as a warning to those who may hear what I have
to say merely as lookers-on, who may be passionately interested
in the problem of East and West, but only slightly or not at all
interested in the Church. To them I should like to say: 'Do not
be surprised if what I shall say annoys you!' I am concerned
with where we stand as *Christians* in this problem.

2

First there is a more simple form of the present conflict of
East and West—and the Christian answer to that conflict can
also be a more simple answer. The conflict is in its simplest terms
a form of the world-political struggle for power. We do not
wish to spend too much time on that, for the question only
becomes really burning in reference to another quite different
form of the conflict. But it will help us to prepare our minds
for the more difficult problem if we look at it for a moment.
    What do we mean by East and West? First of all certainly
quite simply the two world powers: Russia and the United
States of America. Whatever else one may, and must, understand by East and West, the problem acquires its present com-
plexion and weight from the fact that it is incorporated in these
two world powers: each in its natural and historical individuality,
each with its special interests and aspirations, each with its special
political, social, economic and also military potentialities. That
the present world-political power conflict is a conflict between
Russia and America is something peculiar to our time. What
would a Bismarck or Gladstone, or even a Metternich and a
Richelieu, have said if they had lived to see it? But the fact is
that the former 'great powers' of the little peninsula called Europe
have almost ceased to exist as such, have ceased to compete in
the struggle for world dominion, or are at any rate passing
through a grave crisis in this respect—I am thinking of what we
still call the 'British Empire'. Japan has fallen out altogether.
China will perhaps become a power to be reckoned with one
day, but not yet awhile. All that remains are Russia and America.

They were the decisive factors in the late war. These two powers face each other today, eye to eye, ignoring their fellow-victors as well as the defeated. On the one hand, Russia asserts a claim which has been announced and prepared by her Czars since Peter the Great. And, as the incorporation of the Slavonic world, which for a thousand years was driven back to the East from the West, she is now powerfully pressing and striking back from East to West. On the other hand, America enjoys the advantage of having been able to keep her country intact during two world wars in which she did not participate at close quarters. In both wars she became rich and powerful on land and sea and in the air. And out of these she has made a completely new discovery, of which she is now making the fullest use: she has discovered her own importance in the world.

Russia and America are both, though in different ways, children of old Europe. They are children who have run away from their mother or, to put it more pleasantly perhaps, children who have come of age, who, at first quietly and then very suddenly, have grown into giants. They are giant rivals who agree in this (for each says it of himself), that each, in his own way, would like to be teacher, patron, protector, benefactor—or, to put it more frankly, the master of their old mother, Europe, and with that of the rest of the world as well. Both have this, too, in common—that they are each surrounded by a safety-zone of other greater and smaller states which, though formally independent, are, to put it impolitely, vassals of one or the other, linked up more or less closely in a so-called bloc. Then between these safety-zones we have the famous Iron Curtain, through whose openings each of these two great powers proclaims its dislike of the other in abusive language and hurtful pin-pricks. Both are very fond of phrases like 'the free community of the nations' and 'peace'. It is not very clear what either of them means by 'freedom', but for the present there is no reason to suppose that either of them is seeking war, and to that extent is in fact seeking peace. What they have in common is, finally, this: that they are both afraid of the other, because they both feel encircled and threatened by the other. And since the earth is spherical, both may be right in a way. One must concede to the Eastern partner, however, that his anxiety may be somewhat

I

better founded than that of his opponent, if one observes from
a map in how many places America—directly, or indirectly through
her British ally—has blocked Russia's access to the open sea.
That, then, is the more simple form of the present conflict between
East and West.

3

The answer of the Christian attitude to this conflict can also
be put in a comparatively simple form:

We must remember, above all, that, as Christians, we may be
startled by an event like this, but we must under no circumstances
take fright. Such happenings belong to a certain extent to the
natural history of the world, in which the Kingdom of God,
the glory of Jesus Christ, has been proclaimed but has not yet
appeared, has not yet been revealed. There have been such mighty
lords with their fear, one of the other, and with their quarrels;
there have been such concentrations and conflicts of secular power
before in history. They are probably one form of the travail in
which the creature is waiting for the great Revelation, one form
of that bondage of the transient life, from which the creature
will one day be freed into the glorious liberty of the children
of God.

They are part of the shadow of the judgments passed on man
on the Cross of Calvary and in which God revealed Himself to
man as a God of mercy. They cannot shake the secret dominion
of Jesus Christ, let alone overthrow it, and therefore they can
neither shake nor overthrow the Hope for the whole Creation
in which we, as we look up to Him, look towards the end of
the ways of God. They can put the belief in His promise to the
test, but they cannot endanger it. One thinks instinctively of the
situation of Israel between Egypt on the one hand, and Assyria
on the other. One thinks of those great wild animals which are
spoken of in the Book of Daniel. There is no reason why one
should not take that as a starting point and think of all the great
movements and crises of world history from the appearance of
Jesus Christ right up to our own day. They came and they went.
There was always a community of Christian people there in the
midst of them, suffering and enduring, but surviving them. At
least, their Christian witness joyfully outlasted the roaring of the

animals again and again. The extent of the contemporary conflict does not make it any more difficult for us than smaller
conflicts of this kind have been for the men of other ages. So
far as the conflict between Russia and America is concerned, one
single hymn by Paul Gerhardt is stronger than the worst that
we have read in the papers or will ever read or experience ourselves. It would be a great gain for the whole discussion of the
East-West problem if we were to become quite clear as Christians, at any rate, that fear must not be allowed to be our coun-
sellor in this matter. That is one thing which we have to tell
ourselves and our fellows today.

The other is: not to take part in the conflict. As Christians it is
not our concern at all. It is not a genuine, not a necessary, not an
interesting conflict. It is a mere power-conflict. We can only
warn against the still greater crime of wanting to decide the issue
in a third world war. We can only speak in favour and support
of every relaxation of the tension, and do what we can to increase
the remaining fund of reason which may still be at the disposal
of notoriously unreasonable humanity. With the gospel in our
hearts and on our lips, we can only go through the midst of
these two quarrelling giants with the prayer: 'Deliver us from
evil! . . .' What we can do in the midst of the conflict can only
consist in the wholehearted, sincere and helpful sympathy which
we are in duty bound to extend to all its victims as far as lies within
our power. What we Swiss would have to defend if it came to
the worst could never be anything but our Swiss neutrality and
our Christian freedom: only the forgotten cause of God and
man in international life and never the cause of Russian or
American imperialism.

4

The third thing that has to be mentioned is what I have called
the Christian 'disillusionment', which we can gain from this
first aspect of the matter. We shall have to look at that under
a different aspect shortly. We shall see that the antithesis of East
and West does not consist only in a world-political power conflict. But we must not forget the first aspect of the matter for
a single moment. We shall have to look at the ostensibly higher
conflict with which we now have to deal very closely to see

whether it is not, in fact, so closely related to the very unholy battle between the two giants which we have been discussing as to make it impossible to see good on the one side, and evil on the other, here an Angel of Light, there the incarnation of Satan. Whatever we now have to consider, the first aspect of the matter should have been a warning to us, forcing us to ask ourselves whether it can be Christian from *any* point of view to take sides, as the conflict between East and West is primarily simply this quarrel between two giants. Will not the way of the community of Jesus Christ have to be another, a *third* way, its *own* way?

What is the meaning of 'East and West'? It is true that it is, among other things—and it is already becoming more difficult to describe it—the conflict which has become so acute today between two different conceptions of man, and especially of the social and politico-economic ordering of his life, between two powerful intellectual principles and systems, two 'ideologies', to use the term of which the Russians are particularly fond. This conflict is, moreover, not merely a quite interesting but harmless 'academic' quarrel between the adherents of two different schools of thought, but a conflict between two modes of living, applied quite consistently to all the details of daily life, a conflict between two sets of facts, two textures of life, in which not merely America and Russia, but under their leadership a great part of the world is involved, co-responsibly and as co-sufferers. What are the issues? As it is a quarrel, let us simply listen to the accusations which East and West hold out against each other.

This is what the West says, what it complains of: what you want and what you are putting into practice in the East is based on a completely wrong, one-sidedly materialistic conception of man. You act as if man were merely an economic being, as if production and consumption were the only problem in life, and their organisation the task to which all others must be subordinated. You have the absurd belief that man will be good once this organisation is properly established. You have the absurd belief that man is already at any rate good enough to create the perfect organisation for which you imagine, absurdly, that you have the recipe in your pocket, the recipe of radical socialism. And precisely in order to bring about this perfect organisation of economic relationships of yours, you allow the individual

only enough freedom to produce and consume, enough freedom
to take part in the fight for this perfect order—and woe to any
one who claims for himself any other freedom in his actions and
words or even in his thoughts, in so far as they can be guessed
from outside! Thus you make man a mere component of a collective whole, of a machine; you make him into mass-man.
And in carrying through the struggle for this socialism of yours,
you know and respect no higher law and make use of any available means: whether it is the most transparent propaganda, or
the most reckless agitation or, even worse, the most calculatingly
cruel and brutal police methods imaginable. In fighting this
struggle, you sacrifice ruthlessly not merely thousands, but millions, of human lives. We charge you with inhumanity. But this
is not surprising, for it is obvious and you even say so yourselves,
that you have either never known Christian civilisation or you
have cast it wantonly away. You live by a faith in which the
barren demon of your idea of social progress has taken the place
of God. This false faith is the other charge we bring against you.
This is how the West speaks to, and about, the East. But as
Christians it is right that we should hear what the other side has
to say as well.

This is what the East says; this is the burden of its complaint
against the West: what you in the West want and what you
put into practice is based on a completely wrong, because hypocritical, spiritual and moral conception of man. You know as
well as we do that man is primarily an economic being, and that,
in fact, his life really revolves around production and consumption in the West just as much as it does with us in the East. But
you will simply not admit it because things are not what they
should be with you. You criticise our materialism and you talk
so much about spiritual things and morality because you have
something to hide: namely, the fact that you are ruled by money,
by blind, anonymous capital, and the yield of interest; some few
of you are the wheels, but most of you, the overwhelming
majority, whether you know it or not, are under the wheels of
the cart on which your real god sits enthroned. *You* are breeding
the real mass-man, not *we*! Do not come along to us with your
merely formal democracy as if that made you free, because you
pay an occasional visit to the polling-station, are allowed to have

and express your own opinions and have independent papers and parties and all the rest of the bag of tricks. To whom do they all owe allegiance in the last resort—your papers and parties and unions from which you get your supposedly free opinions, and your democratically elected councils, and even your courts of law? Where else but in the great banks are the wires pulled on which you dance in your imagined freedom; who else but the banks decide in the last resort whether you are able to work or not, to earn or not to earn, and therefore to live or not to live? Is not any means good enough for you when you are carrying on your partly wilful, partly deluded fight for the dominion of this god of yours; any kind of war, and in peace-time any civilised brutality and fraud, any machination and pro-fiteering, any lying about inconvenient facts and persons? Your whole so-called democracy is dust thrown in the eyes of the masses to which, above all, your so-called intellectuals belong as well. Your pretended esteem for spiritual things and morality and, above all, your pretended Christianity in which you speak of God, so that the real life of man shall not be discussed and revealed, in which you refer man to heaven so that everything shall remain as it is on earth, in which you talk about cultivating the inner life as if there could be any inner life worth speaking of when the outer life is so corrupt—all this is dust thrown in the eyes of the people, a deliberate deception. What charges do we bring against you? Inhumanity in the first place and a false, because absolutely hypocritical, faith in the second! So there we have the two choruses to whose alternating song we have to listen today.

5

And now what about the Church? What about us Christians? If we speak of ourselves, of our Church and of ourselves as Chris-tians, then it will be as well to be quite clear in the first place that we are not disinterested, nor impartial in this matter. Geo-graphical and natural circumstances inevitably lead us to take sides with America and the Western hemisphere. And therefore we are influenced in our judgment of the issue. We hear the voice of the Western chorus; we hear its battle-hymn against the East much more strongly, much more clearly than that of the East against the West. Furthermore, something inside us instinctively joins in the battle-hymn of the West, whilst it goes against the grain for us to listen to the chorus of the East at all. Now, it has pleased God to bring us into the world as men of the West. But it does not follow by any means that it pleases Him that we should simply give way to Western prejudices and especially to the pressure of our Western environment. It follows rather that we must be all the more on our guard against regarding our Western judgment as the right and Christian judgment. We have, precisely because we are here in the midst of the Western world, every reason to remember our duty and our freedom as Christians.

6

Now it is certainly merely a Western opinion, and by no means simply on that account a Christian opinion, that the political attitude which it is incumbent on the Church to take up today should consist in a choice between the two opposing and quarrelling world systems. Your money or your life! Clearly defined words! Clear decision! Open partisanship! Such are the cries that go up today from every street in the West, and it is taken for granted which party it is intended the Church should support. How the Amsterdam Church Conference was criticised for not coming to the clear-cut partisan decision on this issue that was expected of it! Curiously enough, the West has not always cried thus to the Church. In other cases it has not always showed the same interest in being confronted by the Church with a clear-cut either-or. The same West has, in fact, blamed us, either in certain or uncertain language, for taking sides, when we regarded it as our duty to do so, and has spared no effort in reminding us that the Church should stand above all conflicts and parties. Why this eagerness today? We are not going to pursue the question, but simply want, first of all, to state quite clearly that the Church is *not* identical with the West, that the Western conscience and judgment is not necessarily the Christian judgment. Just as the Christian judgment and the Christian conscience are not necessarily the Eastern conscience and judgment either. That is precisely what they are trying to ram into the Eastern Church today with the same eagerness, that the conscience and judgment of the Eastern Church must be identical with that of the East. And how can we see exactly from this distance whether the Christians in Prague and Budapest would prefer to remain 'firm' rather than tread the path of collaboration? Would *we* be remaining firm, would we not rather already be treading the path of collaboration with the West if we were to succumb to that cry 'Your money or your life!'? We have *no* Christian reason to meddle with that at all. We have rather every Christian reason, simply to say quite clearly and decisively: neither money nor life!— no partisanship! That is the first element in our Christian political attitude: our refusal to fight one way or the other in this conflict. We are not saying that merely as an edifying truth in the quietness of the study; we are saying it to the West, to all of you: The cause of the West may be our cause because we happen to live in the West, happen to inherit Western traditions, but it is not therefore necessarily God's cause—just as the cause of the East is certainly not God's cause either. Therefore, as far as we are concerned, what we have to say is, first of all: Away with the knives! No more oil on this fire! For, if we simply go on cursing each other until there is nothing left to do but have another war, then nothing will improve in any case, no one will be helped and no problem solved. The only possible way is a third way. Let the Church in the East see to it that it says the same thing there! It is all we have to say, we of the Church in the West.

7

Ten years ago one single and absolutely clear-cut political and spiritual menace stood on the horizon, and to turn against the wild boar then was not to commit the folly of exposing one's rear to the wolf. Ten years ago it was a question of National Socialism, and that was not a movement which had a single serious question to put to us, but it was quite simply a mixture of madness and crime in which there was no trace of reason. At that time it was still impossible for anyone to realise the full depth and extent of its madness and criminality. But, with a bit of instinct, it was not difficult to make a fairly accurate guess! The whole business was complicated by the fact that National Socialism tried to represent and recommend itself in the guise of a falsified Christianity. Ten years ago it was one's simple duty to call the world to order. And ten years ago, and during the first years of the war, it was necessary to warn people to keep alert and watchful, because, in spite of everything, there was a certain magical quality in Nazism, and it was a long time before the enemy was recognised as such, and he had stupid supporters and advocates even in the very Church itself. There was a curious softness and adaptability in the whole European attitude towards the Nazi movement and above all, even at that time, a great and trembling fear of it. Incidentally, ten years ago it cost something to say the one-sided, unequivocal 'No' that it was necessary and imperative to say at that time. For anyone who said that 'No' was not able to whistle it with all the sparrows from the rooftops. At that time he saw himself surrounded by the careful silence of most of the fine people who are so excited today, saw himself criticised, by the same papers that shout so loudly today, as a prejudiced fanatic, saw himself accused of infringing the law of Christian love with his speeches, and of endangering Swiss neutrality. The situation ten years ago was wonderfully simple: with a good conscience and clear understanding one could only say 'No' and it only needed a bit of intrepidity really to say 'No'. It was good that the Church, or at any rate one or two voices in the Church, really did say this simple 'No' at that time.

And so everybody is rushing about today crying that the same 'No' must be said again, with the same intonation, by the Church, or at least by those in the Church who spoke out ten years ago, against the East, against Soviet Russia and the satellite 'peoples' democracies'. As if such simple repetitions ever occurred in history! And as if the Church were an automatic machine producing the same goods today as yesterday as soon as you put your penny in the slot! It may be remembered, however, that people became receptive to these same goods at that time only very hesitantly, slowly and after much resistance! In all friendliness I must say that the whole campaign really is a feverish agitation. Ten years ago we said that the Church is, and remains, the Church, and must not therefore keep an un-Christian silence. Today we say that the Church is, and remains, the Church, and must not therefore speak an un-Christian word. We have reason to say precisely that today and for the same reason as ten years ago.

Red is just as bad as brown; one totalitarianism is as bad as another—so what! this is what people are crying out at us today. Now at least none of the many contemporaries and fellow-Christians are justified in joining in this cry who were rather glad to see brown at one time because brown was so much against red: none of those, that is, who thought the good thing about National Socialism was that it seemed to form such a strong dam against Communism. Neither are those entitled to join in—and certain circles in the Allied Military Governments in Germany seem to belong to them—who consider it right to play off the newly awakened nationalistic instincts of the Germans against the Russians. Neither are any of those entitled to join in who do not find anything amiss in the fact that the West has so far not hurt a hair of the head of the Spanish dictator Franco, but that it is by no means averse to including this totalitarianism, of which the Spanish Protestants can tell us a good deal, in the planning of its future eastern front. And why was so remarkably little said here when shortly before Christmas last the Dutch with whom, generally speaking, we have so much in common, attacked their Indonesians with a *Blitzkrieg* which inevitably reminded one to a quite remarkable degree of certain proceedings in May 1940? This is what we want to ask: is it really totalitarianism and its methods which we are being called upon to fight? For if that is really a Christian call to battle, then it ought to be directed against every totalitarian system. The battle-cry which we are being asked to join today is, in fact, not a Christian battle-cry because it is only directed against the East. It is, in a word, not quite honest. Therefore we must refuse to make it our own.

8

If we compare Russian Communism with the National Socialism of ten years ago, quite calmly, we shall see that at any rate the Christian Church has no cause to repeat itself quite so simply as is so much desired, in its attitude to the Russian Communist East. One can have much on one's heart and say much too against the East on account of its totalitarianism and its methods. All that Asiatic despotism, cunning and ruthlessness in the Near and Far East, and especially in Russia, has been and has meant from time immemorial, has certainly become abominably and horrifyingly aggressive today in the guise of Russian Communism, and we are terribly conscious of it. In the past we have probably not taken sufficient notice of the fact that that kind of thing has always been active—even without Communism—in that part of the world. Our memory of the atrocities of the French Revolution (on the 'achievements' of which, incidentally, our whole Western system is based) and of the atrocities of the preceding allegedly Christian era in Europe (including certain outrages committed by the old Swiss!) is also not as lively as it might be. Those atrocities are no excuse for the disgusting methods of the East today. We are right to be indignant. But if we have learned to discriminate by taking a glance at the French Revolution and at our so-called 'Christian era', if, as I hope, we do not condemn the Asiatic world outright simply because some form or other of despotism has always been, and very largely still is, the accepted form of public life, then it is pertinent not to omit to discriminate in our view of contemporary Communism between its totalitarian atrocities as such and the positive intention behind them. And if one tries to do that, one cannot say of Communism what one was forced to say of Nazism ten years ago—that what it means and intends is pure unreason, the product of madness and crime. It would be quite absurd to mention in the same breath the philosophy of Marxism and the 'ideology' of the Third Reich, to mention a man of the stature of Joseph Stalin in the same breath as such charlatans as Hitler, Göring, Hess, Goebbels, Himmler, Ribbentrop, Rosenberg, Streicher, etc. What has been tackled in Soviet Russia—albeit with very dirty and bloody hands and in a way that rightly shocks us—is, after all, a constructive idea, the solution of a problem which is a serious and burning problem for us as well, and which we with our clean hands have not yet tackled anything like energetically enough: the social problem.

9

Our Western 'No' to the solution of this question in Russia could only be a Christian 'No' if we had a better conscience with regard to what we mean and intend with our Western freedom, if we, too, were attempting a more humane but no less energetic solution to this problem. As long as one cannot say that of that West—with all due recognition of the good intentions of the British Labour Party for example—as long as there is still a 'freedom' in the West to organise economic crises, a 'freedom' to dump our corn into the sea here whilst people are starving there, so long as these things can happen, we Christians, at any rate, must refuse to hurl an absolute 'No' at the East. We are not wrong to accuse the East of inhumanity in its methods. But do not let us forget that the East, as we have already heard, also accuses us of inhumanity, the inhumanity of our intentions, and charges us with a mode of thinking and feeling basically corrupted by our appalling respect for material values; charges us not only with hard deeds, but also with hard-heartedness. So long as the East can do that even with the slightest semblance of truth—and there is indeed more than a semblance of truth in these charges—we have, at any rate seeing and judging the matter as Christians, reason to regard and to treat the very existence of the charges as a thorn in our flesh, of which no noisy declamations against the wrongs of the East can rid us.

The other important difference as compared with the situation ten years ago is this: the cause of the Russian-Communist East is doubtless a decidedly godless business: the cause of a false belief in accordance with which Christianity is seen and treated as an inconvenience from a pedagogical-tactical standpoint: tolerated for the moment, but in the expectation that in the process of development, that is, with the dawn of the great kingdom of socialist justice, it will vanish of its own accord, which does not, of course, exclude the possibility of a little coaxing if necessary. But please note that, in its relationship to Christianity, Communism, as distinguished from Nazism, has not done, and by its very nature cannot do, one thing: it has never made the slightest attempt to reinterpret or to falsify Christianity, or to shroud itself in a Christian garment. It has never committed the basic crime of the Nazis, the removal and replacement of the real Christ by a national Jesus, and it has never committed the crime of anti-Semitism. There is nothing of the false prophet about it. It is not anti-Christian. It is coldly non-Christian. It does not seem to have encountered the gospel as yet. It is brutally, but at least honestly, godless. What should the Church do? Protest?

Join in a general Eastern front as the representative of the special interests of the Divine? This is the first I have heard of its being the duty of Christendom to react against the oppressions and persecutions perpetrated by the godless with protests and a summons to political warfare. Something quite different is required here, namely the 'patience and faith of the saints', joyful perseverance and fearless profession. If the Church achieves that, it stands on a rock; it can laugh at the whole godless movement, and whether they hear it or not—one day they will hear it— it has something positive to say to the godless. In fact, if it has the gospel to confess, it has not merely the philosophy and morality of the West, not a religious disguise in the place of real life, not a mere injunction to escape into the inner life of the spirit or into heaven, no imaginary, but the living God and His Kingdom, the crucified and risen Jesus Christ as the Lord and Saviour of the whole man. Therefore, not that which the East, in returning the false accusations of the West, can call a false belief! Is there no truth at all in the East's counter-accusation? We shall not dismiss it merely by reproaching those in the East for their false belief. We are being asked about our own faith: where, then, is the Christian West that could look straight into the eyes of the obviously un-Christian East even with a modicum of good conscience? Whence has the East derived its godlessness if not from the West, from our philosophy? Is its cold non-Christianity something so completely different from the wisdom that is allowed to swagger about even here in the West in every street and in every newspaper and (naturally toned down a little) even in our churches to a very large extent? Whence does it draw its sustenance, this non-Christianity, if not from the offence that has been given to it by the fragility of Orthodox, of Roman and of Protestant Christianity? And are we Christians in the West being asked not to notice that, or to act as though we had not noticed it? Where is our justification for talking about a 'Christian West' and all of a sudden wanting to come to the aid of this 'Christian West' with a summons to an intellectual, political and one day even a military crusade? What fools or hypocrites we should have to be to stoop to that!

10

Against the false belief of the East, only the true, the clear, Christian faith can hold its ground. If we fail to participate in it completely afresh, then we shall also lack its steadfastness. But it is precisely this Christian steadfastness which will have nothing to do with a partisan attitude to the East, with the agitation, the propaganda and other machinations which such partisanship involves, with any kind of crusade in fact. Not a crusade but the Word of the Cross is what the Church in the West owes to the godless East, but above all to the West itself, the Word through which the Church itself must allow itself to be rebuilt completely afresh.

The third important difference between today and the situation ten years ago is this: so far no one has told us in what the desired Christian attitude against the East is really to consist. In a kind of new Confession, like that of Barmen in 1934? But the Church declares Confessions when it has to defend itself against a temptation. But for which of us is Communism a temptation? Or should it consist in a call to prayer for the destruction of the bulwarks of the false prophet, such as we made in 1938? But Communism is not even a false prophecy, and if it were, then we should have to pray in the same breath for the destruction of the bulwarks of the Western Anti-Christ as well. No, in actual practice, what is demanded of the Church in the way of a partisan attitude to the East-West conflict could consist, in great contrast to the earlier episode of the Nazi period, merely in cheap, idle and useless talk: cheap because it needs no kind of intellectual effort and demands no self-sacrifice today, to keep on repeating here in the security of the West what we all have it in our hearts to say against Eastern Communism—idle, because the profoundly unsatisfactory nature of the whole Eastern set-up is so obvious that it is really not worth while repeating again in Christian terms what is being said *ad nauseam* in every newspaper in secular terms—and useless, because with such protests we definitely make not the slightest impression on the wild man of the East and would be helping no single man or woman suffering out there under the wild man, and because such partisanship is the last thing that the Christian churches in the East expect of

us. If the worst were to come to the worst again, as happened
ten years ago, then we should see who would then be standing
in the front ranks: those who are calling for some kind of
'definite' word from the Church or those who are of the opinion
that our only political strength now lies in quietness and hope.
Let me sum up: the partisanship of ten years ago was a matter
of a good Christian-political Confession. Today, if we were to
become guilty of the kind of partisanship which is desired of us,
it could only be a matter of merely dabbling in politics and expressing badly certain completely unclarified and imperfectly
grounded Western feelings. The Christian-political Confession
today must consist precisely in the renunciation of such partisanship.

Only therein? No, not only therein! Just as Swiss neutrality
is not merely something negative, not merely renunciation, but
in so far as it is a genuine neutrality, a positive contribution to
the life of the European community of nations: a contribution
which, for all its modesty, has proved itself more solid and more
valuable than the old League of Nations and the new U.N.O.
put together. The Church is freer in this matter than Switzerland,
in that it is not pledged to any 'eternal neutrality'. It can, if
need be, take sides. If, in contrast to the situation of ten years
ago, it has reasons for not doing so, then this 'No' is also a
quite definite 'Yes', just as Swiss neutrality is positive and
affirmative and not merely negative.

II

This does not mean that the Church is uninterested in political
events today. It does not mean that its responsibility in the State
and for a good State, the responsibility of the Christian community for the civil community, the connexion between the
justification which God alone can give and the law which we
honour, love and should continuously confirm and protect, that
all these things are suspended or should to a certain extent be
allowed to rest. Everything that had to be said about this connexion between Church and politics ten years ago is still absolutely valid today—and especially today.

But today it is not a question of struggle, but of reconstruction. That is the basic idea for which we Christians have to be

responsible in the political world today. It is not easy to judge
from here in what measure and to what purpose, serious, solid
and promising reconstruction work is being carried on in the
East. But let us see to it that all our thoughts are based on reconstruction in the West, at any rate! If we are concerned with
reconstruction in the West, then we need have no fear of the
East. If we are not concerned with that, then there may well be
cause for anxiety! All these choruses of hate and anger, the
Western just as much as the Eastern, are going to lead to further
destruction—as if enough had not been destroyed already! The
result is that the more important thing which should be happening on both sides—to remove the mutual fear—is being neglected.
That is why we cannot join in these choruses of hate and anger.
But we do not ignore the fact that something like reconstruction
seems to be intended on both sides of the quarrel.

Both sides seem to be concerned with 'humanity', since each
side accuses the other so violently of 'inhumanity'. In any case,
it is striking that both sides make enormous use of the same
words: democracy, freedom, justice and peace. Only the justice
of which the East speaks still seems to be a long way from finding a right relationship to justice. And the peace of which both
sides speak, in all sincerity no doubt, is full of secret threats and
the danger of war. The Christian Church stands for reconstruction. It cannot therefore agree with one side and disagree with
the other. It can only take both sides at their word. It believes
in, and it proclaims, the justice of God which does not cancel
out human freedom.but establishes it in its inviolable dignity and
sacredness. But it also believes in, and proclaims, the freedom
of God, namely the majestic freedom of His grace which does
not make human justice superfluous, but which in fact im-
petuously demands the rule of human justice. It believes in,
and proclaims, the peace of God, which is beyond all understanding and therefore comprehends all human understanding,
and keeps it intact, and which sees to it that we do not fall upon
one another on the pretext of unreasonable reasonings, and which
therefore cares for human peace. The Christian Church can therefore stand neither against the West nor the East. It can only
walk between the two—which only means that here in the West
—may our brothers in the East do their share too—we must

stand all the more emphatically for those things which might
be overlooked and forgotten in the West, for those things, therefore, which it is necessary to say and to hear in the West. Its
task must be to call men back to humanity, and that is its contribution to reconstruction. The Church can only be the Church
in this particular time if it remains free to fulfil that task. It
can only stand for Europe: not for a Europe controlled by the
West or the East, but for a free Europe going its own way,
a third way. A free Church is perhaps the last chance for such
a free Europe today.

Now both East and West seem to be concerned with something else besides, with faith. Both sides accuse each other of a
false belief. Our beliefs seem hypocritical to the East and theirs
seem demonic and godless to us in the West. Very well, we
hear what both sides have to say, and as Christians we shall
hardly be able to deny that there is something in what both of
them say about each other.

12

What can be done about it? May I tell you a little story: in
the summer of 1947 I sat in Berlin for a whole afternoon with
a group of real, flesh-and-blood German Communists: please
believe me when I say I did sometimes contradict what they
had to say! Towards the end of the discussion they complained
vigorously enough in their own way about the attitude of the
Western Church. 'Allow me to inform you of something in the
Bible!' I said to them at the end, and recited to them these words
from Ecclesiastes: 'Be not righteous over much; neither make
thyself over wise; why shouldst thou destroy thyself?' (adding
that that could be truly said to the Western Church as well!),
and then continuing: 'Be not over much wicked, neither be
thou foolish; why shouldst thou die before thy time?' (adding
that that might well be said against or rather for you men of
the Eastern persuasion!). Curiously enough, these Communists
put up with this without a murmur and allowed it to be the
final word in our discussion, and presumably to be recorded in
the minutes too. I think that is precisely what the Church must
say to both sides today. It can only stand for the right faith,
which has just as little to do with the hypocrisy, which might well

be hidden behind our all too boastful Western justice and wisdom, as it has to do with the admittedly all too great godlessness of the Eastern persuasion. It stands for reconstruction. It can only take both sides at their word: both sides are, in fact, aiming at something like a right faith, if one disregards their mutual invective. What shall the Church do? It must exercise itself in the true faith in order to be able to proclaim it to both sides with a good conscience. Here in the West—and may our brothers in the East do their part in this respect as well—it must say the more urgently that the truth of the Faith which comes from the Lord in whom we believe cannot be sufficiently thoroughly cleansed of the hypocrisy and unreality which creep into our faith all too easily. Let the Church in the West see to it that it keeps itself in and through the Word of God so that it may proclaim it to West and East alike with a joyful conscience. If it stands and lives and speaks in the faith, then it will be serving the cause of reconstruction.

So the Church looks out over the conflict between East and West in which it now stands and suffers with the whole of humanity, but in which it can participate only believing, loving and hoping and thinking of the word of promise, the Word of God through the prophet Isaiah:

'In that day shall Israel be the third with Egypt and with Assyria, even a blessing in the midst of the land: whom the Lord of Hosts shall bless, saying, Blessed be Egypt, my people, and Assyria the work of my hands, and Israel mine inheritance.'

IV

POLITICAL DECISIONS IN THE UNITY OF THE FAITH

This is No. 34 of the new series of *Theologische Existenz Heute*.

POLITICAL DECISIONS
IN THE UNITY OF
THE FAITH

UNTIL recently we had reached—had we not?—a large measure
of agreement in recognising in principle the political responsibility of the Christian and the political mission of the Church.
It had become no longer possible to claim or to distrust that
Christian mission and responsibility as a specific of Calvinist
theology. There was not yet any agreement perhaps as to whether
(and if so, in what sense?) this recognition of the Christian
responsibility could be established 'christologically' or according
to the widely traditional theology of a more or less abstractly
conceived first article. In fact, those who now found themselves
in substantial agreement had started from the most varied points
of departure. The marketable doctrine of the separation of the
'two kingdoms' was hardly any longer being defended with the
old inflexibility even on the Lutheran side—the small but tough
Hessian 'rebels', with their special doctrine of the regal dominion
of Christ, had been opposing it for eighty years—and there was
no lack of instructive attempts to clarify and correct it in the
light of Luther's own writings. The Fifth Thesis of the Barmen
Declaration of 1934 not only protested in due and proper form
against the doctrine of the totalitarian State that was then officially
valid, but it reminded men in positive terms 'of God's Kingdom,
God's commandment and righteousness and of the responsibility
of governors and governed'. The 'public claims' of the Church,
its 'guardianship', its active relationship to the State, the obliga-
tion of every single Christian to seek the best interests of the civil
community—all these things were discussed clearly and loudly
(almost too loudly at times). Efforts—some of them bold and
dangerous efforts—to put all this theory into effect were made
in Germany even during the Nazi régime. And a number of
attempts have also been made since then with more or less

determination and adroitness. Particularly in the West today people are rather fond of reconnoitring behind the Iron Curtain with the question: whether and how Christians there intend and are able to master this problem of political responsibility. Anything that is said to the Soviet Zone on this matter at any rate from West Berlin is welcomed. And probably only a few people would now want consciously and seriously to dispute the fundamental point that in this matter a different answer must be given today from the one that was given under the Weimar Republic or even in Imperial Germany.

In practice, however, the matter seems to have reached a curious deadlock in the West today. A political problem of the first order—incalculable in its consequences for the whole of Germany and the whole of Europe, and for every German and every European—has now come on the agenda: the question of the remilitarisation of the German people within the framework of a defensive organisation directed against the East by the West under American leadership, which is desired by the Allies who previously demilitarised the Germans so thoroughly and so solemnly. Alongside other more or less determined opponents of the scheme, many Evangelical Christians have protested against it—in conscious and deliberate fulfilment of their political responsibility as Christians, and as a practical expression of their faith. Curiously enough, however, they have been contradicted by still more Evangelical Christians (including most of the bishops) —not only, and at any rate in theory not primarily, because their political decision is challenged on objective grounds, but precisely because they have intimated that the motive behind their protest is obedience to the gospel and its commandment, and that their decision was therefore made in the freedom and commitment of Christian faith. For this reason they are encompassed by deep groans and strong criticism—I am assuming that the groaners and critics are sincere. What has happened, then? May it be that the fundamentally new perception of the Christian's political responsibility has not yet been discussed widely and thoroughly enough for it not to fail in the first test of any severity? I would prefer not to assume that, or at least not to take it into account at present. There is another possibility. This episode has shown that the acknowledgment of the principle of

Christian political responsibility is one thing and recognition of its practical bearing and significance another: ethics one thing —ethos another. The way leading from the one to the other seems to be hidden from many people.

I should like to be allowed to say a word here, not about the question of German remilitarisation as such, but about the discussion on the subject that is going on inside the Church, since it is an important discussion for Protestant Christians outside Germany as well.

How then can the Church do justice to its political mission? No doubt only in rare, and not the most difficult and important, cases by agreeing on the political decision to be taken, as an organised body, speaking for a tangible majority of its members and backed by the votes of its official representatives and therefore with a certain unanimity and authority. Admittedly, that is how it ought to be. But to have to wait for such unanimity and its public expression in synodal resolutions and the like would mean—not only in our ponderous national churches—that in the most burning questions of the day the Church would never have anything to say until it was too late. It would come out with some possibly ingenious but quite useless, because belated, afterthought, when everything was over, the baby drowned, the house burnt down. There is an outstanding current example of this, but I won't mention it. If the political mission of the Church is to be turned to practical account at all and in good time, it can only take the form of comments and declarations by individual members of the Church, made in the freedom and commitment of their personal responsibility as Christians. Thus it was in apostolic times, and thus it always was: whilst the majority and the authorities temporised, silently or articulately, the Church spoke and acted primarily through the daring service of a few enterprising individuals. It is the same with the political service of God. Dietrich Bonhoeffer lived and died at the end of the Hitler period in that kind of individually accepted responsibility: for once, the Church, in his person, did not arrive too late. And the campaign which Heinemann, Niemoeller, Mochalski and their friends are running today is another instance of personal Christian responsibility in action. They thought it right not to wait for the decisions of majorities in a German Evangelical

Church which is dawdling towards another 1945 and only partly articulate; nor did they consider they ought to wait for the pronouncements of the Church's official representatives. They thought it their primary duty to exercise and demonstrate the political responsibility of the Christian in their own words and deeds. That is what they did and what they are still doing.

There is a question which suggests itself and which demands an answer: how does it come about that such individual Evangelical Christians feel themselves constrained and called to take a definite political decision and to defend it publicly? The question applies no less to those who for the moment are unable to approve and support the decision of these few individuals, perhaps because they 'regard the Federal Chancellor's policy as the right one on the whole', and therefore prefer to let German remilitarisation take its course. And it is a question that must be put to those who for the moment think—in itself a political decision—that the political problem of the day can be regarded as irrelevant by the Christian believer.

The way a Christian comes to adopt a political position, pro or contra, is by bearing in mind, conscientiously, soberly and as fully as possible, all the arguments and counter-arguments that have to be considered in the matter under discussion (in relation to which he is in just the same position as all his fellow-citizens), balancing them one against the other, giving both sides of the case their full weight—exactly as he would in making any other decision in his life, including purely 'private' decisions. He will try to 'assess' the respective weight and value of the arguments. But—and this is where he will differ from his fellow-citizens— he will do so not in a space apart from his Christian faith, but before God—and not before any god, but before the God who speaks to the world, to the Christian community and therefore to the individual Christian, in the gospel of Jesus Christ. He will look for a decision which is not arbitrary or just clever in a human sense, but which is made in the freedom of obedience to God's command.

In the present situation, for example, he will listen to all the arguments for and against German remilitarisation: on the one hand, the need to meet a military threat to Western Europe from the East with comprehensive military countermeasures, to which the West Germans must make a concrete contribution—West Germany's dependence on being integrated into the Western community, and in particular its dependence on the interest and goodwill of the Americans who are demanding its participation in Western defence—the prospect of West Germany's future equality of rights (and possibly European leadership) on the basis of this military contribution—the prospect of a peaceful discussion about Eastern Germany and its future frontiers (or the future frontiers of Germany as a whole) which might be successful if Western Germany had a hand strong enough to be a potential threat to Eastern Germany. On the other side of the argument: the provocation, which might lead to a third world war and would in any case not serve the cause of peace, of a Russia which has not so far been guilty of any military move against the West—the extreme probability that German remilitarisation will involve the sacrifice of democratic developments in Western Germany and the return of German militarism—the provisional surrender of the East Germans which remilitarisation will involve and the possibility of a permanent consolidation of a divided Germany—the certainty that West German remilitarisation will make practically impossible the one effective defence against Communism, that is, the establishment of a higher degree of social justice. All these arguments—I have not attempted to give a complete list of them here—are political arguments, based on rational considerations, and they are answers to questions of judgment. None of them will be found in the Bible or the Catechism. Again, it must not be forgotten that each series of arguments represents a definite train of thought, a tendency, a vision, a spirit. The Christian who is aware of his political responsibility will, like his fellow-citizens, take the individual political arguments as such with the utmost seriousness. He will realise that the questions he has to answer are questions of judgment and—in the words of Kant—he must have 'the courage to use his own mind'. But he will differ from his non-Christian fellow-citizens inasmuch as he will give heed to the spirits that speak in the two series of arguments and to the trains of thought, trends and visions that are to be perceived in them. The Bible does say at least that in the events of the age, small and great, the Christian has to reckon with the dominion of spirits, different spirits, good and evil spirits, and that, led by the Holy Spirit of the Word of God and measuring them by His standard, he has to discern the spirits and adjust his own attitude to this spiritual discernment: not in one way. or another but in one way and *not* another. As he looks at the backgrounds of the two sets of arguments the Christian confronts the mystery of history and of his own life, in the conflict between the God who rules the world and the chaos that resists Him. This is a case where it becomes impossible to say: 'Perhaps—or perhaps not!' He has to listen to God's commandment; he has to choose aright not only between a better and a worse, but in accordance with his Christian faith ('as far as the measure of his faith will let him': Rom. 12.6), and therefore, in the meaning of Deuteronomy, he has to choose between life and death, God and idols. In the midst of problems of reason and evaluation, the Christian faces the problem of obedience. Since (and the salvation of his soul is at stake!) he can only do justice to the problem in one absolutely definite direction and can answer it in one way only and in no other, he finds himself called and constrained to make a concrete political decision and to stand by his decision, to defend it publicly and to summon other Christians (and non-Christians!) at all costs to take the same decision (since God, known or unknown, is the God of them all).

The first thing that must follow from this is clear: to begin with, all Christians will not be willing and ready to follow his decision. Many of them may—as opposed to him—see only the conflict of political arguments as such, the conflict of the mere words, and may be quite unaware of the backgrounds, the conflicting trends and attitudes behind the words; they may consider that the question of obedience does not arise at all, that the *status confessionis* is not in question, and that they themselves are free to remain neutral in the conflict or to join one side or the other *libero arbitrio*. Many other Christians may see the backgrounds and the trains of thought but, to begin with, quite differently. They too may consider it their duty to make a choice —a different choice from his—in accordance with their faith. The result will be that, in any given political situation, for the time being Christians will be opposed to one another: on the one side there will be those for whom the hour of decision in faith and obedience does not yet seem to have struck—on the other there will be those who believe their faith calls them to make a decision in one way and those who, apparently in the same faith, believe they must make it in quite a different way. A critical moment! The unity of the faith and its profession, the unity of the Church, is undoubtedly in question. Much previously existing and well-tried fellowship may fall to pieces— irrevocably perhaps, if it has really had its day. This will be regretted, and not unjustly. Understandably, the blame will be put on those who have made their political decision most definitely as a decision of faith and have defended it as such to others, who have therefore signified that (ignoring the neutrality and opposition of the other Christians) they have deemed it their duty to act and speak proleptically for the whole Church and that, as Christians, this was the only way they could act and speak. The neutral Christians and the Christians who differ from them may then work up the quite understandable grievance against them into the accusation that they are trying to impose a law on their fellow-Christians, to bind their consciences, to question their faith, to exclude ('excommunicate') them from the Church and therefore tear the Church to pieces.

The resolute opponents of remilitarisation among the Evangelical Christians face this charge today. But why not the Christian advocates of remilitarisation as well? As far as I can see, they have never stood up for it with the same determination as the others have stood against it. They have hardly ever pleaded the Word of God as the ground of their decision; they have hardly ever resorted to the obedience of faith. They have therefore hardly called the unity of the faith into question. Their decision has not made them a nuisance to Christendom. From a spiritual, not a moral point of view, does that necessarily confirm the rightness of their cause? Why is not the Niemoeller who is anti-Adenauer not confronted by a Niemoeller who is pro-Adenauer? Let us leave that question undecided, however!

What is certain is that the charge is founded on a serious theological misconception. In a Church that is alive, and not dead, it must be not only possible but necessary for its insights to be questioned, only to be rediscovered on a higher level, in a later hour of its history. In the sphere of preaching, the creeds and theology it has long been obvious that a statement of any originality or pungency always implies a questioning of the unity of the faith which no sensible person would dream of belittling, as such, even in the Roman Catholic Church. After all, in the sphere of Christian thought and word the *one* Truth is never merely something given but also a task to be performed, something that cannot simply be repeated over and over again by the Church as a whole, but has constantly to be sought and found afresh. And even in the purely theological sphere this can come about in the first instance only in the daring enterprise of pioneering individuals. The enterprise may always lead to what may be sometimes a very acute threat to the Christian fellowship. Even the simple but determined repetition of a familiar sentence in the Christian creed may have an uncanny explosive power in certain situations and provoke some who hear or read it to complain most bitterly about the exclusiveness, intolerance and so on of some of their fellow-Christians. But because some Christians take offence, is that any reason why such enterprises should be forbidden?[1]

In a live Church which is not neglecting its political responsibilities the same thing is bound to happen in the political sphere. Here too individual decisions are a risky undertaking, but no more so than in the theological sphere. Certainly, the man who thinks his faith calls him to make an absolutely clear-cut choice and decision and to defend it before his fellow-Christians, calls himself into question under the judgment of God. He calls into question the purity of his own heart; the quality of his thought; his ability to see the problems and discern the spirits behind the arguments; to weigh the arguments for and against; and he calls into question the strictness of the obedience to the faith in which he makes his decision. But where is the Christian not subject to the sovereign divine Judge of his own will and decision and yet aware that this does not exempt him from the necessity of making up his own mind? Certainly, with these divergent words and

---

[1] If in 1934 we had had to wait for the unanimity of all the groups and circles in the Church which were not even adherents of the 'German Christian' school—or even merely for the understanding and agreement of the wise men of Erlangen and Tuebingen, etc., either nothing at all would have been said in Barmen or only a lot of vague mumbling.

deeds he is bound to hurt the feelings of his fellow-Christians who, though sharing the same faith, feel themselves called to no such definite decision or to quite a different one. But does not the same thing happen in the case of any Christian action or attitude which transgresses the usual, generally accepted standards? No doubt the very existence of anyone who risks taking an unconventional line does compel all the others to ask themselves whether, sharing the same faith as they do, they ought not to share in his decision. And they may certainly feel themselves disturbed and even challenged in respect of the rightness of their own faith and their position in the unity of the faith, if they cannot bring themselves to the same decision straight away. But what sort of a Christian fellowship would it be where such things were not feasible and bearable? Indeed, how could it be a Christian fellowship living in expectation of its Lord, journeying on its way towards Him, if such things did not in fact take place— hard as they may be for all concerned? It is through such happenings that the Christian fellowship grows. How could it be the communion of saints, how could it stand in the service and the battle of the spirit against the flesh, in the conflict of belief with heresy, superstition and unbelief if such things did not happen, if it were spared these worries? The decision of individual Christians—including the political decisions under discussion to-day—can and must take place, with all their consequences, within the unity of the faith, which can only be the unity of the Christian and the Evangelical faith if it has a dynamic character.

Why should such political decisions of individual Christians, instead of provoking groans and criticisms, not be taken as a call and a summons *in* the Church *to* the Church—as an invitation to all the members of the Church, possibly, first of all to realise that neutrality is out of the question, that it is a matter of obedience or disobedience—or, possibly, if they realise that already, as an invitation 'to prove what is that good, and acceptable, and perfect, will of God' (Rom. 12.2), to consider whether the will of God may not after all lie in the direction of the decision that these few individuals have already made? Why should anyone, simply because he sees others taking a resolute line or one different from his own, need to feel troubled in conscience, or threatened by a possible charge of heresy and exclusion from

the fellowship of the faith? And however the self-examination
may turn out which is induced by the decision taken by the
few individuals, even those who reject the decision must concede that such self-examination cannot be carried out too often,
too strictly or too exactly. And instead of groaning and criti-
cising, instead of being so supersensitive about their troubled
consciences, they might in any case be grateful for this invitation
to examine themselves—even if in the end they decide to per-
sist in their neutrality or their own contrary decision. And if it
should turn out after all that the decision made by the few individuals (fallible, like all human beings)—was in fact made in an
erroneous interpretation of the faith, then those who were unable to follow them will be all the more assured of the rightness
of their own faith as they make their own self-examination. But,
to begin with, they will also have to reckon with the possibility
that that decision may have been reached in a right interpretation of the faith and a proper inquiry into the will of God in its
relation to the various spirits and tendencies which both sides
of the argument reveal, and that the decision may therefore turn
out to be a true witness to the Word of God, which those who
at first dissent from it will have no right to evade. No one can
believe in another's place or allow anyone else to do his believing for him. Therefore no choice and decision made in obedience
to the faith can be taken over unexamined by anyone else and
turned into his own choice and decision. On the other hand,
no one can consider himself exempt from the duty of testifying
openly and earnestly to his faith and the choices and decisions
made in accordance with that faith, nor can anyone consider
himself exempt from the duty of listening in all freedom but with
a humble and open heart and mind to the testimony of a fellow-
Christian. Instead of complaining about a troubled conscience,
let him take the risk of finding out whether he really is able
and under a compulsion to evade the witness of his fellow-
Christians or whether it may not prove itself a testimony to the
Word of God in his own conscience.

Anyone who knows he is on firm ground will have no need
to be afraid of putting this question to the test. But anyone who
really knows that he is not on firm ground at all, should not
give vent to his fear by making noisy complaints about those

who bear this challenging witness. Otherwise he will be the one not only to call the unity of the faith into question, but to tear it to pieces. The unity of the faith can maintain its spiritual truth and reality only by constant renewal. It can and will be renewed only if Christians do not try to avoid crises in their fellowship with one another, but are determined, whatever the outcome, to see them through. And let us not forget our point of departure: in practice the Church can choose only between using its political responsibility and thereby exposing itself to the risk of crises, and sparing itself the crises and thus failing to do justice to its political mission. And there is no simpler and easier way than that of bringing about a positive relationship between the Church and the State and its problems. Anyone who knows and acknowledges the political responsibility of the Church in principle, must be ready to risk some deed of bravery for the sake of God, or at any rate not to be angry if, for the moment, others do the brave deeds for him. It may be that, in spite of all the theoretical progress that has been made in this matter, this inevitable consequence of the Church's political mission is still not clearly appreciated.

I now wish to say one or two more things about these crises in the life of the Christian fellowship, of which I have spoken, and the way they can be mastered.

If political decisions made in the unity of the faith are to be genuine and fruitful, they will make a number of supreme demands on all those involved. They will demand from those who make them and commend them to others an extreme degree of political sobriety and theological insight: sobriety in considering the material factors to be taken into account—and insight in judging them and viewing them as a whole; and also a spiritual instinct for the relative values of each side of the case, an acute perception of the sense or non-sense, the good or the harm, which lie behind the different evaluations of the conflicting factors in the situation. A political decision is unlikely to be successful without a good deal of simple common sense and a spark of prophecy—or rather, without something of the urgent and all-seeing love of Christ.

The advocates of political decision may lack one or other of these qualities and, in that case, they have no right to be surprised if even the best of their causes fails to make the powerful impression they expected. Again, however, the words and deeds of the few individuals who lead the way with their political decisions call for an extreme degree of open-mindedness from their fellow-Christians. If they are loyal, these others will regard themselves as no more entitled to find fault with the few individuals for arguing politically—even to the extent of dropping all religious vocabulary and theological reasoning (as if they had thereby already abandoned the 'eschatological' sphere of Christian thought and speech!) than to blame them for the apparent opposite: forcing them to note how, in the very midst of political discussion, these few individuals—whether they actually quote from the Bible or not—nevertheless speak with the accents of an extreme earnestness and a supreme joyfulness and resolution which, in that sphere, may well shine as lights from a fourth dimension. (To blame them for this would be tantamount to assuming that they had already committed the crime of a fanatical invasion of a foreign field and a foreign authority.) Must the others not see that if political decisions in the unity of the faith are to occur at all, they can become a reality only when they take place on the extremely narrow frontier that divides the world from the Kingdom of God: where common sense speaks the language of the Holy Spirit and the Holy Spirit the language of common sense?

In addition, genuine and fruitful political decisions demand from those who make them an extreme degree of courage and humility: courage for the dangerous but necessary enterprise of seeing an earthly hope entirely in the light of the heavenly hope, of finding and uttering a human Yes or No in obedience to God, and of taking a limited step in utter trust and certainty—and humility in the knowledge of the profound questionableness and feebleness, temporariness and relativity of even the best that man can strive for and achieve with all his desires and accomplishments—humility which accepts this knowledge and yet does not cease, in and with this knowledge, to be courageous, to speak and act with definiteness and resolution. As a testimony by Christians to Christians (and non-Christians!), political decisions can speak an intelligible language only in so far as they make this dialectic clear. Neither the hearts, words and deeds of the despondent, the doubting and the weary, nor the hearts and words and deeds of the puffed up, the conceited and the proud are any use as a testimony to the will of God. The others, those who hesitate or have made a different decision, are, however, also summoned just as strictly, to understand and respect this dialectic of courage and humility. It would not be loyal and it would not be in accordance with the common faith if, instead of reckoning with the possibility that in this very unity of apparent contradictions the few may be bearing a valid witness to God, these others tried to find fault with the few for the curious tension of courage and humility, resolution and modesty in which they can alone defend their cause, as Christians.

The more concretely they encounter this tension of opposites in the political decisions which seem so strange to them, the more thoughtfully they will have to ask themselves whether what they are confronted with may not be the human form of a divine commission and instruction which calls for their obedience too. They will know, from other situations in their own lives as Christians, that thought, speech and action which are obedient to God always proceed in the unity of that apparent contradiction, uniting great courage and great humility for their mutual limitation, but also for their mutual confirmation. If, on the other hand, they first experience this in the political decisions of their fellow-Christians which they cannot at first accept, this can only redound to the credit of these fellow-Christians.

Finally, real decisions in the unity of the faith demand, from those who take the risk, an extreme degree of New Testament joyfulness and Old Testament severity: a joyfulness radiating from within, because political decisions, as the testimony of Christians to Christians (and non-Christians!) can be full of light and power only if they are grounded in the gospel, in the liberated and liberating belief in the perfectly accomplished reconciliation of the world with God which has already taken place in Jesus Christ—and severity, towards themselves and others, because such decisions are a practical confirmation of God's Covenant with His people, and flow from knowledge and practice of His commandment. If those who advocate such decisions lack the New Testament joyfulness of the free children of God who, because they are free themselves, must call others to freedom,

L

it will show that they have become enslaved to an ideology, a system, and to the supremely mistaken absolutism of a logic and ethic of a purely human development and trend. If they lack the Old Testament strictness of the committed and committing servant of God, whence can they derive the determination and constraining power with which, if a Yes or a No are to be heard, Yes or No must be said? How could the Yes or No then make that absolute claim on them which is necessary if they are really to make a claim on others? If they lack the one or the other (if they lack one they will certainly lack the other!), they will be useless as witnesses to the will of God, however much they may be right objectively. And the others, who hesitate to follow or who oppose the decision of the minority? They ought to realise above all how difficult it is in practice to be a New Testament and an Old Testament witness at the same time, a biblical, and therefore at the same time both a joyful and a strict witness, as the political witness (particularly the political witness, though not only he) must be at all costs if his words and deeds are to be strong—and as they themselves ought to be at least in other spheres. Wherever he stands, as a political witness the Christian will probably always be, in the world and the Church alike, the afflicted member of a tiny minority or even almost entirely isolated, and gravely oppressed within and without, a man who will often enough lack the very air in which to enjoy the Word of God and the strength to meet the severity of its demands. He will probably not always be successful with the weapons of righteousness. It will be difficult for his words and deeds not to be lacking in charm. If the others stand by their faith—for the time being a differently orientated faith—they will see his affliction; and his incapacity—they are bound to have come across both in another form—will be, if not forgivable, at least understandable. They will not point at him and bewail his obstinate adherence to the mere letter of the law if it should happen that the strict, sharp, challenging, warlike aspect of his testimony threatens to hide the other aspect, the peace and joy and freedom of the Gospel—nor will they bewail his light-heartedness, if sometimes he appears to lack the severity, the discipline and the consistency which should be characteristic of his witness. They will not make these failings an excuse for evading the question and the challenge which he represents. And they will not reassure themselves by imagining they have a religious and moral advantage over him because they are more balanced themselves. They will be prepared, without saying a word, to make the necessary additions and amendments which his witness may need, and then listen to and consider it all the more earnestly.

He himself will be called to account for the 'provocativeness' of his testimony, for which he has only himself to blame, for the untrustworthiness which that may imply, and for the weakness of the call and summons he makes to others. But for ignoring his testimony altogether the Church itself will be called to account in quite a different way, since, as the community of the faith, it should know how to receive in the faith whatever is said in the faith, even when it is said provocatively.

It must on no account be said that there is no way out of the crisis in which the unity of the faith is involved by the political decisions which take place within it. It is true that the conditions on which the crisis can be overcome, and on which the unity of the faith can be regained and improved, may not be easy for either side. Where the Church is a live fellowship, however, they cannot be beyond fulfilment. The crisis can be mastered even in the Evangelical Church in Germany today, and a solution there would be of exemplary significance for the Evangelical Churches everywhere.

What a curious Church it would be which, instead of living in the unity of its faith, lived in fear of this crisis, even though it had been promised the power to fulfil the conditions on which it could be overcome.

What a curious policy the Church would be pursuing if those whose very existence is quite indispensable, not only to bring the crisis into being, but also to overcome it and to create a new and better unity of the faith, were treated as tiresome mischief makers!

What a curious ethics it would be in which validity was granted to the ethos of the political *status confessionis*, and therefore to the emergency which should be the reason for its existence, only in exceptional cases (as Wolfgang Schweitzer says in *Evangelische Theologie*, 1952, p. 144: 'It is to be hoped this is the exceptional case').

What a curious preaching of the gospel it would be which, out of sheer anxiety not to make forbidden anticipations of the Eschaton ('Roman ecclesiocracy and the Basel theocracy of the preaching of the Word', W. Schweitzer, *loc. cit.*, p. 142), had nothing better to offer the living, erring, and suffering men and women of today than the weary 'reference to the ambiguity and provisionalness of all political activity' (p. 133)!

In this case, what interpretation could be put on the invitation to 'Choose Life!' (as the Stuttgart *Kirchentag* chose for its theme) if the individual were not to be left free to decide for himself what 'life' and 'death' mean in this context?

What a strange kind of responsibility before God it would be which was only allowed to take place in the form of an empty recognition of the principle of responsibility, but never—or only in the 'exceptional case'—in the shape of concretely responsible political decisions!

What a strange unity of the faith it would be in which Christendom condemned itself to such impotence!

No, under this law the crisis certainly cannot be overcome. If this was the only practical way, should not we do better to take some different theoretical point of departure from the one I presupposed at the beginning of this paper? But after all, the practical way to overcome the crisis is not bound to be the one we have just been describing.

V

THE CHRISTIAN MESSAGE
IN EUROPE TODAY

Based on a lecture given in the
summer of 1946 in Düsseldorf,
Cologne, Bonn and other German
centres.

THE CHRISTIAN MESSAGE
IN EUROPE TODAY

EUROPE is the place where we all, Germans and Swiss, French and English, Swedes and Italians, live together and belong together as a family, a community united by a long and full history. As far as the situation today is concerned, many things seem to point to the fact that Europe has lost its former position as the political, cultural and religious centre of the world. That fact need not mean the end of the whole world; yet it would seem to mean the end of that little world which was governed and determined by the Europe we know, and the end of the heyday of the European.

Europe was once the Roman Empire—its most important part being for a long time called the Holy Roman Empire (of the German nation)—founded by the classical age and by Christianity, to be a great, vigorous and shining unity, political, cultural and religious. Its outward form began to disintegrate quite early on; but while still in possession of this inheritance, Europe achieved world importance, and for centuries the European was left to believe that his idea of might and right, science and education, religion and the moral code must necessarily be the right one, and that the great spirits of humanity must of course be those whom we hold to be such, and honour accordingly, and that spirit and form must be what we understand by them.

This idea seems to have lost its power today. Probably it had already been losing it secretly for a long time. But in these days—after what happened in the two world wars, both of which had their starting point and conclusion in the centre of Europe—in these days, so it appears, Europe has ceased to be what it was formerly. The great German mistake and the resulting terrible German ruin seem also to have made negative the claim of all the old Europe; the glory of this our whole sphere, and its domination over all other spheres, seem to have vanished. A different spirit, a different way of life, one that is not European and one that either differed originally from, or has long been emancipated from all that is European, seems now to determine the course of the world, and Europe and its inhabitants appear now on the contrary to have come under its influence and power. Once everybody cried out: 'Europe needs peace', and today that seems to mean that it needs peace in order to become accustomed to the position and the role of a queen, now dethroned, who has become more or less a servant or even a beggar. It is most likely that here is to be found the great secret wound which aggravates all the other ills from which we suffer today.

What has happened in our day to bring about this great change? It can be explained in a few words: it came about that at the height of European development, here in the heart of Europe, an unparalleled revolutionary movement arose—called the revolution of nihilism; it was, however, in reality also the revolution of barbarism, quite simply the revolution of mediocrity. From the Christian point of view it was in its most critical aspect, under the name of anti-semitism, a revolution against Israel and thereby against the mystery of the incarnation of the Word of God. At all events, it amounted to the taking up of arms, the revolt against everything in Europe that till then had been given the names of justice, order and faith, against everything that had made the European community a great and honoured leader of the world.

There was no lack of opposition to this movement. Throughout Europe, and even in Germany, this opposition was going on, and we have every reason to think gratefully and reverently of all those still living who fought on its behalf, and of those who gave their lives for it. Above all, we should think of those nameless ones who wittingly or unwittingly have suffered or died for the cause of the old Europe; in the concentration camps of Germany, and in the resistance movements in France, Holland, Norway and elsewhere. We think with respect how in 1940 Britain stood firm through that hour of mortal danger, and I think in all modesty of how, during those years, we Swiss kept within our frontiers, believing that in so doing we were acting in everybody's interests.

It was right, and indeed necessary, that the opposition to this revolution should take place. This was then perhaps the last stand of the real, old Europe. In history, however, there is always the irrevocable; events which cannot be recalled. Perhaps among these irrevocable things for which there is no atoning belongs the fact that here in the centre of Europe, here in the land of Meister Eckhart and Luther, of Kant, Goethe and Beethoven, it has come about that million upon million of hands have been raised in salutation before a man who after all was nothing more than the personified negation of all justice, faith and culture. I do not wish to speak of everything that resulted from this salutation, voluntary, enthusiastic and coming from the heart. European resistance had, perhaps, come too late, and was perhaps even too weak to be of any great significance. 'The great mistake' began and was allowed to rage itself out. We cannot forget that at the Olympic Games in 1936 the flags of all nations were gathered round the swastika. We cannot forget that in 1938, during the days of the Munich crisis when the evil began for the first time to reach out over the frontiers of Germany, the bells of the Christian Churches throughout Europe were ringing as though the approaching evil had not already been decided upon definitely, and the death warrant of million upon million of people signed and sealed. And we cannot forget either that in every country there were quislings, traitors, collaborators, sympathisers and fainthearts; they were to be found even in my country of Switzerland. All this was evidence that the great German mistake was fundamentally a European mistake. And now it may be that with this great German mistake not only Germany but Europe as well has for ever lost its clear conscience, and thereby its trustworthiness, and its position and significance in the world. It may be that the ruins of Germany mean the end not only of the Germany that has existed till now, but also of a whole European epoch.

The forces of the opposition did in fact finally triumph. It was, and is, right that this should be so, and whoever wishes that things had turned out differently can hardly be called sensible. The final and decisive victory was, however, won by other than European forces. Europe could not free itself but had to be freed. 'What a disgrace', someone wrote recently, 'that men had to come thousands of miles over land and sea to liberate the

Germans from the power of certain other Germans, and to deliver Europe from certain of its inhabitants!' On account of this very fact, Europe came under the tutelage of others, and now, full of care though perhaps also full of hope, it looks to the East and to the West, asking what its liberators—themselves considerably oppressed by their differences and by many other troubles—will be able to do to its advantage or disadvantage. What has become of European initiative and leadership? We have become a land whose future is decided and determined by outsiders.

Shall we, must we, let ourselves be rehabilitated by America? Can you imagine what would have happened if that question had been asked at the end of the fifteenth century when America was discovered! Today it is, however, a very serious question, for there can be no doubt that we have good cause to envy America for its material wealth and potentiality and for its unbounded vitality. Nor is there any doubt that we need America's money and technical skill, and that spiritually and economically we are within its sphere of influence. Will that mean that we must conform to American standards of democracy, of economy, psychology and sociology, of ethics and Christianity? If for various reasons this does not seem desirable, another very serious question arises, namely, whether we are still capable of a genuine and therefore fruitful understanding with this mighty Western country. Or do we wish to console ourselves with the fact that up till now the Americans in Europe have not turned out to be as conceited, nor have they exhibited as much interest and missionary zeal as we might have expected? But supposing that they and we were no longer consulted? Supposing that our destiny and our future were simply to be an Americanised Europe?

Or must we let ourselves be rehabilitated by Russia? That too would have been a strange question, had it been asked in 1905! This today has become a very serious problem too. Russia nowadays stands essentially for Communism, and Communism means, whatever view of the matter one takes up, a radical solution of the social problem which we in Europe have for a long time kept putting aside. It is a last challenge, maybe, in the face of which the closest attention would be more in place than an over-hasty alarm-cry, and the consciences of us Europeans should really be clear as far as this problem is concerned. But is there any hope there? Evidently only if Europe still has the power to take up the challenge, and so make good the delay by instituting a form of socialism of its own. Shall we be able to raise the necessary enthusiasm, the necessary spirit of renunciation, and also the necessary firmness of purpose?

Now, Russia signifies not only Communism, but quite simply the resurgence, now visible and effective, of the Slavonic races, who had for almost a thousand years been thrust back by German pressure towards the East (*Drang nach Osten*). It was as the result of a fateful wantonness that in June 1941 these very floodwaters were let loose! However, that is all past history, and we cannot put the clock back. The Russia of today is merely the new shape of the imperialism of the Tsars, and is perhaps in the final count quite simply the awakening of Asia. Perhaps we are not even asked whether we approve or not, and surely it is true that there is only one last question open to us: whether we have the power to protect and preserve at least the remnant of the Western spirit in the face of this attack?

I will sum up: Europe today is being ground between two millstones. It has become the country of a people seriously threatened from the West and from the East. Have we really refused and thrown away our birthright—in a final *salto mortale* —just like the Prodigal Son, so that we cannot wonder if we find ourselves in a strange land, all of a sudden? Must we then really pay for our sins by ceasing to be ourselves in our own home, but have our way of life determined for us by others?

I take into account that England and the Scandinavian countries are perhaps still healthy and strong enough to find their way out of this difficulty. And I also bear in mind that in Switzerland we will in no wise accept this change without a fight, but will do our utmost to counteract it. These possible and even probable conceptions will in the end merely serve to prove the rule. *The Decline of the West* is the title of a book that was read a great deal after the end of the First World War. 'Decline?' This strong expression should perhaps not be used so readily. Yet we cannot deny that for the present the situation in Europe is steadily deteriorating.

Now, in spite of this deterioration, there are in Europe *Christian Churches* having the task of *Christian evangelism*. In speaking of this matter, I should like, at first quite simply, as it were objectively, to point to certain historical facts, which portray the life of the Christian Church in Europe today. If I am right, there are four essential points to be noted here.

1. We can and must state that the Christian Churches do still exist in the Europe of today. The fact is not always obvious, but is true nevertheless, that they have up till now survived 'the great mistake', the terrible destruction, the decline of Europe, in spite of the threats, in spite of the oppression, in spite even of the persecution to which they were subjected in many places. They have survived all that, and we may say that they have survived better than many other institutions in Europe. We may add that the Church today in many places stands in far greater esteem than it did before the approach of this great catastrophe. We may thus draw the following conclusion: even in the present state of affairs in Europe, the message of the Christian Church seems to have been kept alive. And in spite of the crisis before us at the moment, the offer, which for so many centuries has been made to humanity through the existence of the Christian Church, still lies open today.

2. It is obvious that the Christian Churches here in Germany and in other lands have sided whole-heartedly with that just and necessary resistance against the great revolutionary danger. At least, they took the side of those forces which remained more or less steadfast in the face of this threat. There can be no doubt that whatever sense of justice and culture is alive in Europe at the moment is in the final count founded upon the Christian faith as expounded by the Church, a faith which still, directly or indirectly, determines the life of many in Europe today. Above all, there can be no doubt that during those years, thanks to the existence and the effective working of the Church, it has been possible for countless individuals to walk through the darkness of the age as men who have found salvation and protection, or at least comfort, as men who have never lacked a light to guide them during that difficult time. That is true, and it is also true that during those years there grew up between the various churches, even between those with widely differing views, a

spirit of co-operation and an understanding never before realised.

3. While we grant all this, we must both see and state equally clearly that up till now the errors, the ruin and the decline of Europe have been halted neither by Christian Rome, where, according to Roman Catholic teaching, the Vicar of Christ, the successor to St. Peter, speaks infallibly, nor by the existence of Wittenberg, from whence proceeded the pure teaching of Luther and his reformation, nor by the existence of the old Calvinist Geneva, nor by the new Geneva of the ecumenical movement These Christian Churches—let us say in all fairness, any one of these Churches—have not yet been able to give us the right word at the right time, a prophetic word giving leadership, pointing a way or calling to order. Pious words, clever words, yes! but at all events no such words as could have been effective and powerful enough to put a stop to the evil. It is a simple fact that the Christian Churches have not achieved this, nor has this been the meaning of their existence. Hitherto no great light has proceeded forth from them to pierce the gloom of a Europe on the decline.

4. With all the terrible afflictions oppressing mankind, in these times when events have taken place comparable only with what were described in the Revelation of St. John the Divine, as the final torments, there has been no sign of any remarkable Christian revival in Europe, nor any noticeable change of heart in its inhabitants who were so hard hit and downtrodden. The blows came, the bombs fell, judgments were let loose in all their horror, and men ducked, stood up again and went on their way as before. I am speaking not only of those people with a non-Christian outlook, but also, and above all, of those with a Christian outlook. For even in the Christian Church and in Christian circles, there are, among theologians and non-theologians, more men who lay greater stress on restoring rather than on reforming the Christian way of life; the followers and heralds of a neutral Christianity, which can at all times be had cheaply, are more numerous than those who would like to make a stand against the bitter reality of the times because they have heard the call, and would themselves like to proclaim aloud the message that now, in the preaching, the teaching, the cure of souls, the theology and the directing of the Church, something new must be created

out of the ABC of faith, love and hope, and sown in the world.
No, the cry for a building up again and a return of Christian
faith in Europe is not noticeable when viewed from afar. How
then can it make itself felt in the world? Can Christians wonder
if the material and technical interests which lie outside the province of the Church govern man more strongly than ever, and
that the saying, 'He who pays the piper calls the tune', is more
than ever indicative of the material conditions of the average man?

It must be stated quite simply that catastrophes, evil and want,
such as have fallen to our lot, have obviously no power of themselves to enlighten or convert. They have not the power of
themselves to rouse the Churches and to revivify them, nor the
power to make the world alive to the Church's message. Catastrophes alone cannot achieve this. Nor will they achieve it in
the future even if they break over us with ten or a hundred
times the force. The saying, 'Necessity leads to prayer', is not
to be found in the Bible, and it is not even true. Necessity can
teach us to curse and can deaden our sensibilities. Man is an
inflexible creature, fundamentally obstinate and unteachable, and
when we say this we as Christians are not thinking primarily of
the worldly or of the so-called secular man but of that most
inflexible of all human beings, namely the pious churchman.

Thus—we have tried to see and to weigh both sides of the
question conscientiously—that is the position with regard to the
Christian message in Europe today, looked at from the historical
point of view and therefore to a certain extent from an objective
point of view as well.

Now, however, let us consider the same subject, namely, the
Christian message in Europe today, from a different standpoint.
Let us try to think about it, not as clear-sighted and impartial
onlookers but as Christians. Let us then look at it, not from the
outside, but from the inside, not in the light of history but as it
must appear to those who believe in the Christian message and
who recognise their responsibility to proclaim it and carry out
this task really well. As a Protestant Christian and theologian
I am thinking, as is only proper, in the first place of the message
of my own Church, the Evangelical Church. What does it expect, what is expected of it in the light of the Word of God,
which, it claims, is its source and substance?

If we once again approach the subject from that direction, then we must say plainly that the Christian message cannot and may not rely upon the fact that it is surrounded and sustained, as it was previously, by the glory and the pathos of the culture and the politics of a Europe rapidly rising to prominence and power. Its future will have to be enacted in a modest, even sadly small sphere in which it will have to do without many important and useful points of contact upon which it could formerly rely. The Church will have to learn afresh to walk towards its Lord as Peter did, not along smooth paths and up fine staircases with handsome balustrades, but on the water. It will have to learn to live on the edge of a precipice, as it did of necessity in its beginnings. It must learn again how to fulfil its duty none the less—simply in the impetus and magnetism of its own beginning and its own aim.

This means that the Church cannot allow itself to be hindered by the question of whether and to what extent the European of to-day, with his particular hopes and fears, will come to meet it, will take an interest in it, favour it and take pleasure in it. Indeed, it ought always to have regarded this question as 'taboo'. And if its view and understanding of the present-day European is correct, it will in future cease to solicit or beg for his interest.

Is it not true that this modern European, here in Germany and also in other lands, is sick and tired of all these words, since he feels that they are uttered merely in order to agree with him, that after all they only repeat what he himself knows, and that they are determined by and dependent upon those of his opinions and wishes which formerly held sway? What he needs and what he is searching for fundamentally, is a sign from above, since nothing is more certain than that he himself is living in the depths.

The Christian message in Europe today must once more be free and independent—not blown about by each prevailing wind, not dependent on the alternatives of revolution or tradition, optimism or pessimism, West or East. The Christian message can be free because its source is the freely-given grace of God, which everybody—in every conceivable and possible situation—needs because it is the only thing that can help him, and which is in fact bestowed on him in every conceivable situation although he has done nothing to deserve it. The Christian message must derive from this source. It should speak of the grace of God, freely given to all sinners and to all in misery whom God has remembered and will always remember, and then only will it be the right message for Europe today.

Further, it is essential that the Christian message should on no account become entangled with the problem of whether the future of Europe will somehow lead us upwards again or whether it will carry us further downwards. Particularly if it genuinely wishes to reach and help the inhabitants of Europe today, it will have to remember that they have already heard so many wonderful promises, and on the other hand so many terrible threats, that their feelings towards both have grown numb.

The Christian message must neither make promises nor make threats. It must proclaim eternal truths, such as are applicable to every age and to men of every epoch in history, whether it be an epoch of rise or decline. The hope of a rebirth—also the hope of a Christian rebirth in Germany and in the West—is an admirable but human hope which the Christian Church has no authority to proclaim. Thus the fear of a definite collapse of Europe is today very much with us, yet it is no more than a human fear, and the Christian Church has no authority to give it room either. The Church's objective is the Kingdom of God, the revelation of which we may approach from the heights or from the depths, since while yet veiled from our eyes, it has become a reality in our midst and in the heart of time; the Kingdom which, whatever the circumstances, means for all men, living or dead, peace, joy and freedom. It may be that the future will hold for us some kind of restoration, though possibly in an unexpected form. It may also be that the future has in store for us much the same as in olden times it had in store for the land, the people and the Church in North Africa, in Asia Minor and Syria, where once life was rich and culture flourished and where for centuries afterwards there was nothing but pasture for sheep! It could be either, and we do not know which of these two destinies will be ours. It is not this which is important, however, but rather the fact that at the last day the Kingdom of God will be revealed, God will be justified, and we mortals, living and dead, will receive our deserts. Let the Christian message proclaim this future! Let

it comfort and counsel men to go to meet this future in confidence. Let it teach mankind today, with all its fearful questioning and in the face of a hazy future, to pray with a new urgency
yet with a new sense of peace: Thy Kingdom come. Now is
the accepted time to proclaim this goal—even in Europe today,
whatever the circumstances.

The grace of God and the Kingdom of God, and thus the
source and the end of Christian teaching, bear a name, the name
of Jesus Christ. Thus in Europe today this teaching can only consist in proclaiming this name, in proclaiming the true divinity
of Him who bears the name, and His dominion in heaven and
on earth, and in proclaiming His true manhood, i.e. the yoke
which He took upon Himself for our sakes by becoming the
humblest and most despised of men. Christian teaching must
proclaim His death as bringing salvation and redemption to all
men, and His resurrection as being the revelation and the working out of this salvation and redemption. Jesus Christ is Himself
free grace, is Himself the Kingdom of God. He it is who is the
same yesterday, today and for ever. He is the substance of the
Christian message. The Europe of today is waiting for Him to
be proclaimed anew as the eternal truth bringing freedom to
mankind.

Whoever believes in this Christian teaching and knows that it
is his responsibility—and let us charge ourselves with the fact
that this is indeed the case with us—will put on one side all unnecessary questions, because he is stirred and concerned but at
the same time inspired by certain definite and serious questions
relating to his life and work, questions which arise from these
very subjects.

I suggest that we can formulate the questions regarding our
life and work, which are put to us by the Christian message in
Europe today, as follows:

1. The question of *understanding*. Do we realise that nowadays,
as in every age, there is a school in which we all, great and small,
educated and uneducated, may easily learn to know Jesus Christ
and thereby the free grace and the Kingdom of God, and in so
doing learn the essentials of the Christian faith? I mean the school
of the prophets and apostles, the school of the Bible, which is
and must remain the most important and decisive school for the

M

Church in Europe today, even while Europe is on the downward path. Do we realise that we may enter and stay in this school, and that we are invited to attend it all the days of our life?

2. The question of *faith*. Do we realise that the gospel of Jesus Christ, and thus of free grace and of the Kingdom of God, cannot be the subject of voluntary weighing-up and communication, nor merely a matter of the expression of emotions or of opinions, but rather that this gospel deals only with the proclamation of a direct, unshakable and absolute certainty? It is this certainty that we mean when we speak of faith. Is it clear that this certainty, this faith, which alone can give meaning and power to Christian teaching, is not a thing which we can take and create for ourselves, but which must always be given to us by God? Is it clear that we are bidden to pray continually for this certainty, this faith—today, tomorrow, all our life?

3. The question of *obedience*. Do we realise that Jesus Christ forces us and every Christian to a decision, and sets our feet upon a road? Do we realise that while we travel along this road our faith cannot remain hidden, cannot be merely the private concern of our own hearts, can no longer be the subject of impartial thoughts in the silence of our own rooms, but we must, on the contrary, set up, by means of our words, our actions, our behaviour, our decisions, certain visible signs—signs of our understanding, our witness, our joy and gratitude, of the origins of our life and of the goal towards which we press? Is it clear that we as Christians are bound to these practical forms of obedience, and that it is incumbent upon us to make these signs visible?

4. The question of *sincerity*. Do we agree that obedience to Jesus Christ must of necessity induce in us a completely sober frame of mind? And that today this means that He commands us to acknowledge—soberly, openly, calmly and avoiding all intellectual arts of evasion or efforts to escape—not only the present state of our life, but also the conditions and events which contributed to it and the whole system of guilt and atonement of which we are a part, and finally our own responsibilities. Do we agree that we must cease to make excuses—which are recognisable as such because they have no connection with Jesus Christ, 'the Author and Finisher of our faith'—and must leave ourselves

free really to think, say and be what in truth we ought to think, say and be—in the truth of Jesus Christ, of free grace and of the Kingdom of God?

5. The question of *love*. Have we learnt that obedience to Jesus Christ necessarily leads us to believe, without any reservations, that our fellow-men belong to God, not only those who think as we do, and who are recognisable as fellow-Christians, but our fellow-men whoever and whatever they may be, whatever their names? That means in effect that in obedience to Jesus Christ we must not first think the worst of every one of those frightened, miserable, erring, misled and perhaps really godless creatures around us, but rather the best, just as we like to think well of ourselves. We must impute to them good, not any human good but the good which consists in the fact that Jesus Christ died and rose again for us all, including those who are outside the fold, those who no longer acknowledge Him or who do not yet know Him. Have we learnt that we are capable of loving—perhaps austerely and jealously, but at any rate fundamentally—and that therefore, especially in these days, we must not lose our sense of humour?

6. The question of *loyalty*. Are we determined not to waver between God and man, yet neither—let it be clearly understood—to take God's part against man and to wage a holy war against him as though we were some kind of crusaders, as indeed we Christians love to do from the fortresses of our churches? Are we determined to be faithful to God and therefore to men, to the Church, to the world, to heaven, and also, my friends, to earth? Are we determined not to be men only—certainly not! nor to be Christians only, but rather to be Christian men, i.e. to mediate between God and man through our intercessions and our thoughts, and indeed also with the right words, the right actions and in the right frame of mind?

7. The question of *hope*. Shall we be able, while always looking to Jesus Christ, who has overcome the power of death and opened to us the gate of everlasting life, to live in spite of everything somewhat more positively rather than negatively, somewhat more joyfully than sadly, patiently rather than impatiently, and, in spite of all the decline in Europe, to live with thankful rather than with sorrowful hearts, and in confidence rather than in

despair? Anything other than 'somewhat more' is scarcely possible, and indeed is not required of us. 'Somewhat more' is asked for, however, because we have this hope. When it is a case of being Christians in earnest, then it must be possible for us—and we are in fact enabled—to live a little more positively, joyfully, patiently, thankfully and confidently rather than the reverse.

I am coming to the end. The interesting question with regard to the Christian message of the grace and the Kingdom of God and the gospel of Jesus Christ in Europe today, can only be whether those who believe in this gospel and who know that it is their responsibility, really are intimately concerned with the above questions? We—whose concern they are—must answer them, and how shall we do so? Let us remember that Christians are never, not even in these days, men who themselves have to set questions, but men who are commanded simply to give the answers. Whether we carry out this command and whether we are genuine Christians depends upon whether, in the Europe of today, be it on the downward or on the upward path, be it an Americanised or a Russianised or any other kind of Europe, there is at least one completely clear, certain and consoling factor, one 'safe stronghold' amid the 'changes and chances of this fleeting world'. The outpouring of the Holy Spirit as the answer to the prayer which is laid upon our lips: *Veni Creator Spiritus*! Come, Creator Spirit! can only consist in God's arousing of a few people who will let themselves be stirred, concerned and inspired by these questions regarding the life and the activities of the Christian message—and who *cannot* and *will not* evade the true answer which lies ready and waiting and which is promised to us.

VI

THE CHRISTIAN MESSAGE AND THE NEW HUMANISM

A lecture given in Geneva at the Rencontres Internationales, 1st September 1949. The present version has been made not from the original French but from the German text of the author.

THE CHRISTIAN MESSAGE
AND THE
NEW HUMANISM

A 'new humanism' is the subject under discussion in our society during this session. We are an assembly of intellectuals of widely differing capabilities and interests. This evening two theologians are going to speak about the 'actuality' of the Christian message in the light of our general theme: the Reverend P. Maydieu from the Roman Catholic point of view, and I as a Protestant.

The situation is not self-explanatory. Forty or fifty years ago nobody would have thought of calling upon theologians on such an occasion, perhaps a representative of the so-called science of religion, but certainly not a theologian confessing the faith of a particular Church, let alone two such men. I will leave open the question of how a situation has come about today which would never have arisen in the past. I should like, however, to draw your attention to the fact that our presence and participation here implies a certain risk.

Why should we theologians not be open to all the various points of view from which the theme of a new humanism in these days is to be developed and discussed? We shall, however, have to regard the subject from our own standpoint, i.e. from the standpoint of the Christian Church, or rather of Him whom the Christian Church has to thank for its existence, and whom it wishes to serve. The other members of these *Rencontres* will certainly not expect us to be ashamed of our theology. They will surely give us the benefit of *sint ut sunt aut non sint*. Here, however, there arises for them a certain risk. If the Christian message is not veiled and not diluted but is proclaimed in all its truth, if its 'actuality' is spoken of as is right and proper, then this might cause embarrassment, even distress, in such a gathering as ours. Neither the Roman Catholic nor the Protestant theologian will be able to conceal the fact that the Christian message would be misunderstood today as it always has been, if it were presented as one of many theoretical, moral, or aesthetic principles or systems, as one 'ism' in agreement, in harmony or in conflict with other 'isms'. Nor will it be able to conceal the fact that today as at all times its intention is to make known to man the will, the works and the revelation of God, in the face of all men and of all human opinions and strivings. We shall not be able to conceal the fact that with the Christian message it is not a case of a classical humanism nor of a new humanism which is to be rediscovered today, but rather of the humanism of God. Further, we shall not be able to conceal the fact that this divine humanism on the one hand only exists and can only be comprehended in a definite historical form, and yet in this form it is the same yesterday and today, and thus has not only a temporal but also an eternal validity.

Above all, we shall not be able to conceal the fact that this very question of the 'actuality' of the Christian message of the humanism of God is one which has this paradoxical quality: that positively or negatively it can be answered only in the form of a highly comprehensive personal and responsible decision. Now, I cannot guarantee what effect it will have on you if we really do not conceal all this, but declare it openly. I can imagine that the presence and the participation of Christian theologians here will be felt to be as disturbing as perhaps the presence of Communists. And I can imagine, too, that Communists and non-Communists could be united in seeing that the very presence of Christian theologians in this society would seriously hamper a profitable discussion on the question of the new humanism. There were maybe very good reasons why forty or fifty years ago, on occasions of this sort, one kept the 'parson' at a distance. I did not wish to begin without first having warned you expressly about the risk that you are now running.

Coming now to my subject, I should like to state that the time which I have been allotted is too short for me to do more than give you the barest outline of what Protestant theology has to say, such being my special task here.

The Christian message is the message of the humanism of God, as I have just said. I have chosen the formula with an eye to the general theme of this conference. The substance of the Christian message could well be expressed in other words. It has many aspects and manifold tongues. Two words will, however, suffice: The Christian message deals with the humanism of God. And these very words are a paraphrase of the idea which is decisive for the Christian conception of man: the idea of the Incarnation. 'The Lord was made flesh and dwelt among us.' That is the work and the revelation of God—the ontological and noölogical premise—in the light of which, according to the Christian viewpoint, man is regarded. For the Christian message is the gospel of Jesus Christ. He is the Word which became flesh, and thereby the Word spoken about men. From the Christian point of view man is no higher, no lower, no other than what this Word declares him to be. He is the creature made visible in the mirror of Jesus Christ. Later I shall try to paraphrase this. Let me first of all, however, dwell for a moment on my first statement.

1. Inherent in the Christian knowledge about the humanism of God, about the Incarnation of Jesus Christ, is the definite knowledge of God Himself. The word 'God' cannot here be made synonymous with the essence of reason or of life or of power, nor with the more popular modern conceptions of limits or of transcendence or of the future. God is not—as gnostics and agnostics assert—what we think that He might or might not be, or perhaps ought or ought not to be. God is what He wills Himself to be, in His works and in His revelation of Himself to man. He is the living God who exists in and through and out of Himself, omnipotent in His own freedom and in His own life. I cannot spare you from the glorious but hard statement: He is God the Three in One, who of His very nature is Father, Son and Holy Ghost. This is the God of the Christian message, a God of loving kindness towards man. When we as Christians speak of the humanism of God and thus of Jesus Christ—and through Him of man—the basis of our thought is His revelation of Himself.

2. The loving kindness of God is free grace bestowed by God on whom He will: being that fundamental relationship between God and man, which is, according to the Christian message, to be found in the humanism of God or in Jesus Christ—a relationship corresponding to our knowledge of God. That is to say, the fact that God through Jesus Christ declares Himself to be the God of

mankind is not inherent in the nature of God, nor does it consist in the necessity imposed upon Him, but it is rather His sovereign, creative, merciful decision and act. It is not inherent in the nature of man, nor is it included among those things possible to man, nor is it man himself who (in and by his very existence) has brought it about that out of all creatures he, particularly, should belong to God. By this sovereign act, by this divine message and gift, and to a great extent by this free grace, God and man are one in Jesus Christ and Jesus is perfect God and perfect man. It is from this point of view that we regard man. Any idea about God and man, according to which their relations with one another, self-explanatory by their very definition, might be grasped through an analysis of the conceptions of God or of man, would here be unbearable and would distort everything. We must have the free grace of God before our eyes if we wish to speak of God and man from the Christian point of view.

3. If the Christian message speaks of the humanism of God and thus of Jesus Christ, then it means by this—because it is concerned with God's free grace—an event which took place once and for all: an event fulfilled in the Jewish race and in the land of the Jews, at the time of Caesar Augustus and of Tiberius, for all time and on behalf of the men of all lands. Whoever speaks of Jesus Christ must think of Him as an effective regent or else the words will not apply to Him. We neither were nor are what He is. He is no mere image or symbol of the general reality of man, of man's life and death, suffering and triumph. That the Word became flesh is an event which cannot be repeated, a single event, finite yet eternal. What Jesus Christ is, what He suffers, what He does, is all for us. He is Emmanuel, that is, God with us, that living God who in His sovereign grace comes to meet us, to give us the good news that we belong to Him. Thus this particular man Jesus Christ is not to be seen and judged from the point of view of a general reality, ostensibly human, but rather every man on earth must be regarded from the point of view of this one particular man.

What is man? I will now attempt to sum up under four headings what Christian teaching has to say on this question.

1. Man is from God and belongs wholly to God: purely and

simply the object of His creative love and equally a subject devoted to God, His creature, yet a creature possessing free will. That is the description of a movement—a history. It takes place in the appointed time allotted to each individual and to mankind in general. From the point of view of God the Creator it is a history of the proofs of His mercy. From man's point of view it can only be the history of his gratitude, his obedience, his adoration. The essential man exists while this history is being enacted. This is the Word that is spoken about him by Jesus Christ. The assertions of human understanding need not on that account be false. The old as well as the modern natural sciences, or rather natural philosophy, teach that man is a very special and strange element in the cosmic-terrestrial, in the physico-chemical, in the organic-biotic processes of universal existence. Idealism throughout the ages has taught that he is a man because, as an understanding and moral creature of reason, he has the freedom to make himself felt and assert himself amid, and in opposition to, the forces of nature. In our day existentialism teaches that man exists in that he, the one who in his natural and spiritual totality is limited, threatened and imprisoned by an overpowerful unknown, is in fact able to transcend himself continually through his own existence, i.e. *de facto* to pierce the future which is really closed to him. All this may be true according to the Christian view, but only if included in it is the fact to which it is subordinated and in connection with which it is understood, that man is from God and belongs wholly to God, that as His creature man is hastening towards Him and towards eternal life with Him. Everything else can only be surmise. Man's understanding of himself embraces, not the real man but merely his possibilities. The real man exists in the living God being for him and with him as his own beginning and end. The real man exists in that history. That is the fundamental fact, on which the Christian message can agree peaceably with the classical as with any other type of humanism, though it may on the other hand be a source of conflict.

2. Man exists in the free communication with his fellow men, in the living relationship between one man and his neighbour, between 'I' and 'Thou', between man and woman. An isolated man on his own is not a man. 'I' without 'thou' is nothing,

neither is the man without the woman nor woman without the man. Human being is being with others. Without this relationship there can be no human being. We are human because we live together, see and hear each other, speak to each other, stand by one another, and, let it be understood, because we enjoy doing that and do it freely.

Reflected in the mirror of Jesus Christ—of the one who exists for everyone else—is human existence, since, seen vertically, it is only real in the relationship between God and man, and, seen horizontally, in the relationship between man and man. Here we stand before a question, which, from the point of view of the Christian message, is to be put to mankind, individually or collectively, in every age. It does not exclude individualism or collectivism. It is directed to both the individual and the community, but always to one particular individual as opposed to the other, and to that community which is founded on free reciprocal responsibility. Thus it defends discipline against the teaching of Nietzsche and freedom against the teaching of Marx. Or rather, in these days it defends social freedom against the attacks of the West, and personal freedom against the attacks of the East. It is the inexorable protest against both the man who rules and the man who is ruled. It recognises and acknowledges human dignity, human duty, human rights, but only within the framework of the knowledge that the real man exists because of his free relationship with his fellow-men.

3. Still regarding him from the Christian point of view, man does not exist in the reality with which he ought to exist in his relations with God and his neighbour. He does not exist in the freedom in which he was created. I am speaking of a fact for which there is no explanation because it is absurd; yet it is a fact that man has strayed from the right way, to one where he cannot stand and walk but where he can only stumble and fall. He did not want to thank, obey and call upon God as God, and he wanted to exist as a man without his fellow men. He wanted to be like God, and thereby he sinned. Thereby he was fully guilty, both towards God who is his source and end, and towards his neighbour. Thereby he broke the circuit by which he was bound to God and to his neighbour. His two-fold life-history faltered. Thus human reality has disintegrated and

fallen a prey to nothingness and to eternal death. That, however, is not man's destiny. He himself wanted it to be so and
continues to want it. That is the reason for the accusation made
against man in the death of Jesus Christ, and for the judgment
pronounced on him by that death. There is no doubt that God's
humanism includes this accusation and this judgment. Classical
humanism believed that it could afford to ignore this accusation and this judgment. Many illusions about the goodness
of man and his good fortune in being alive have been taken
from us. But when I read Heidegger and Sartre I ask myself
whether that spirit of defiance in man which despises grace and
therefore lacks grace, is not perhaps just as unteachably sure of
itself as it ever was. While the defiance remains, surely these
illusions must and will return one day? The Church will at any
rate not be able to shirk the unpopular task, set it by the Christian
message, of pointing to the fact that the danger to human existence is greater, very much greater, than one wishes to believe.
Tu non considerasti, quanti ponderis sit peccatum. The real man is
endlessly and incurably endangered by himself.

4. The decisive point in the Christian message is as follows:
this man estranged from his own reality, this man endlessly and
incurably endangered, this man who is quite simply wicked and
lost is sustained by God—by the God who is the one true God
and as such true man. Man is faithless, but God is faithful. The
death of Jesus Christ is not only God's accusation against man,
not only His judgment. It is also—indeed, first and foremost—
the victory and the setting up of the complete dominion of His
grace. God is just; He is not mocked. That which man sows he
must also reap. But God has taken it upon Himself to reap this
fatal harvest, and God Himself has, in man's stead, sown for man
new seed. God Himself has placed Himself under this accusation
and under the judgment on the godless Adam and on the fratri-
cide Cain. And God Himself (in their stead and ours) became the
true man from whose way we have strayed. God Himself has
thereby spoken the word of forgiveness, the word of the new
commandment, the word of the resurrection of the body and
the life everlasting. There is no doubt whatever that His grace
is free and unmerited. More important, however, is this other
statement: that here is the foundation, the revelation of the fact

that God's grace is permanent, triumphant, glorious and of great price. The humanism of God is just that free and precious grace. The Church is the place where it is recognised and proclaimed. However, it concerns all men, it concerns the whole world. It is the truth on which live, unknowingly, the Jew and the Gentile, and even the indifferent, the atheist, the misanthropist. It is not merely a religious but also a universal truth. It is that 'condition humaine' which takes pre-eminence over all others. Classical humanism has never really attained this truth, in spite of its well-known link with so-called Christianity. It remains to be seen whether a new humanism will really be new. In the form in which it has made itself known so far, it reveals a strangely doubting and sad face—although, and perhaps because, it still knows too little about the sin, guilt and destruction of man. However that may be, nothing can be clearer than the fact that the Christian message, by reason of this definite assertion, is the gospel—the good news. This message starts from the assumption that the Kingdom is not yet visible, although it has come, and that everything is accomplished. On the basis of that supposition it protests against pessimism, tragedy and scepticism. It forbids all those who hear it to wear such a doubting and sad expression. It is the message of hope, a hope which the wicked lost man may set, not on himself, but on God, in which he may love his neighbour—and this is the premise of all ethics.

What can I say finally about the 'actuality' of the Christian message? I have already given you some idea of the meaning of this word in its more limited sense by describing the Christian message specifically in its anthropological aspect, and by indicating point by point its significance regarding the question of humanism. But the idea of 'actuality' says that a thing is not only significant but also living, practical and effective. Now the Christian message is such, that, besides its source and substance, Jesus Christ Himself—in Him it is eternally 'actual'—it can and it will become living, practical and effective, and therefore 'actual' only through its own strength, i.e. through the Holy Ghost, only in faith, love and hope. At the beginning I spoke of the paradoxical quality of this message whereby it comes to us in the form of a decision, itself demanding a decision on our part. Thus I could not show you the 'actuality' of the Christian message by telling you anything about the present state and life of the Christian Church, about its greater or lesser influence, or about its correct or less correct view-points. I cannot in fact show you the 'actuality' of the Christian message at all, I cannot hand it to you on a plate. And with every attempt of this kind I should only succeed in leading you away from its true 'actuality'. If I had to preach a sermon, I should have to continue with the exhortation: 'Repent and believe the gospel.' But I am not here to preach but to bring this lecture to a close.

Thus there remains nothing more for me to do but to look at this subject with you to a certain extent from outside, and to say that if the Christian message should become 'actual' as far as the question of the new humanism is concerned, then it would indeed be a case of repentance and faith—in fact, of conversion. If discussion on this subject were to become 'actual' in its turn, it would have to begin with our saying together the Lord's Prayer, and celebrating the Lord's Supper, in order that we might always think and speak, first and last, and from every aspect, from that position—and then to arrive at the sure conclusion that the new humanism, in order to be genuinely new, can be nothing more than the humanism of God. I need not say here that I am refraining from making that suggestion, but that rather I am conscious that this would be asking too much. I only say it so that calmly and cheerfully I may make it clear what would happen if the Christian message here or elsewhere should suddenly become 'actual'.

VII

THE JEWISH PROBLEM
AND THE
CHRISTIAN ANSWER

A Radio Talk given 13th December 1949.

THE JEWISH PROBLEM
AND THE
CHRISTIAN ANSWER

THE Jewish problem has existed for over one thousand nine hundred years, and we must accept the fact that during the last few decades it has become more pressing than ever before.

Anyone who, from the Christian point of view, has studied the answers given to this problem during these decades, has usually heard something like this:

The Jews are a people distinguished, like others, by their race, religion and customs, a group in the human family, a part of the population, and citizens of our States. Thus, to the Jewish problem must be applied the commandment, 'Thou shalt love thy neighbour'. The Christian has to bear in mind, when thinking of the Jews, the great Christian conception of the fatherhood of God and the brotherhood of man, which in fact has its origin in the Jewish religion. Therefore, he will, with regard to the Jews, be particularly insistent that they too should be granted full enjoyment of civil and human equality, and that they should be met with tolerance and above all, with an unprejudiced understanding and a positive esteem. Therefore, he complains of and condemns anti-semitism in any form as a barbaric insult to our culture and our civilisation, which have been moulded by Christianity, and as a breakdown of Christian values, which have become confused and lacking in humanity. He will do his utmost for the victims of anti-semitism. He welcomes the Jewish bid for independence now being made in Palestine. He hopes and demands to see in future a wider interchange of ideas and a new brotherly co-operation between Christians and Jews.

It is possible to agree with all this and yet to be of the opinion that herein justice is not done to the Jewish problem, nor has any decisive Christian answer been given. I should like to stimulate further consideration of the matter by making four points.

1. Surely the problem begins with the fact that the Jews as a race are still in existence, a fact which the above statement takes no account of and which is yet fundamental to the Christian solution. By all analogies of world history, the Jews as a race should no longer have existed after the Fall of Jerusalem in A.D. 70. Why have they not, like so many of the peoples of antiquity, both great and small—not excluding the Romans, at that time victorious—been absorbed into the sea of other newer races? Throughout the centuries, however, they have in fact always been recognisable as Jews, despite the fact that they were not favoured by their circumstances, but scattered, unloved, persecuted and oppressed, some of them even completely exterminated, and combined with the most varied and differing races. And today, even after the greatest catastrophe in their history, they seem to be in process of founding a new state in Palestine, in order that in future they may be more than ever a Jewish nation. Should it not be said that at that very time of their downfall as a nation, they came out of their corner and found a place in world events? How have they, all things considered, attained this surprising position of historical permanence, a permanence which increases rather than decreases?

The Christian answer to this preliminary question arises simply from the fact that forty years before the event mentioned above something else happened which also found a permanent place in world history—namely, the crucifixion of a Jew—Jesus of Nazareth. Is the Bible right? Is it true that from the beginning of time there has existed a faithfulness in which God has revealed Himself to man? Is it true that the people of Israel, later called the Jews, are the chosen people of God? That God is faithful to this people, although according to their own scriptures they were continually unfaithful to Him; faithful to them even in spite of all the evil which came as a result of their unfaithfulness? Finally, is it true that God's faithfulness reached its climax because He Himself, in the person and by the death of one of these Jews, put an end to the unfaithfulness of His people and to that of all mankind, and gave them a fresh start? If all this is true, then the permanence of the Jews in history is a mystery of faith, yet as such not entirely inexplicable. They could and can disappear just as little as God's faithfulness can come to an end, just as little as we can cancel out what happened to that one Jew while He was on the earth. This continued existence of the Jews which is so puzzling is a sign which cannot be ignored, a sign of what the one true God has done for us all, once and for all, in this one Jewish person. That is the first, the fundamental Christian answer which can be given.

2. Now, however, we are talking of the Jews as though we knew just to whom and to what this designation refers. Are they a people? They are not what is usually meant by the word 'people'. For nobody has been able to say what is understood by the term 'the Jewish race' and what are supposed to be their national characteristics. Some other people, for example the Arabs, who today are the bitterest enemies of the Jews, are also Semites. The Jews do not even possess a language of their own, for Hebrew has long since become a learned theological language known only to a few, and if in the present State of Israel it is cultivated again as a kind of Esperanto, this only goes to prove that the Jews who have come to live together really speak other, foreign languages. Since the year A.D. 70 there has certainly also been a good deal of Jewish co-operation in the formation as well as in the destruction of various foreign cultures, but there has been no specifically Jewish culture. It is also impossible to speak of a common Jewish religion, for the orthodox and liberal synagogues comprise only a small number of Jews. A Jew may very well be a pantheist, an atheist, or a sceptic, indeed even a good or bad Christian, Roman Catholic or Protestant, and yet he may remain a Jew at heart. Finally, there remains the very serious question of whether since A.D. 70 there has been a common history of the Jewish race. There has certainly been a history of various Jewish groups, movements and individuals, but apparently not of the Jewish people as a whole.

Are the Jews a people or not? The Christian answer will take up just this strange paradox, that, quite unaccountably, they are a people quite unlike any other, whose special characteristics lie in their ability to exist so anonymously, lacking in glory and having no national character of their own. They must have lost their national character! No doubt once upon a time they had their own characteristics by reason of which they stood head and shoulders above all other races. They did not recognise them, but cast them away. Doubtless this took place when that Jew died on the Cross outside the gates of Jerusalem. However, God's choice has not been withdrawn from them because of this, nor has His grace been withheld. The fact that this very mercy of God has sustained and upheld them from age to age, is surely so obvious that it can literally be grasped with the hands. Yet they are no more than the shadow of a nation, the reluctant witnesses of the Son of God and the Son of Man, who came out of their midst, to whom they belong, and whom they rejected, yet who has not ceased to call them, the very Jews themselves, saying, 'Come unto Me, all ye that labour and are heavy laden, and I will refresh you!' They neither know it nor hear it; but He it is, from whose sake they were once a nation and under whose sovereignty they are once more to be united.

3. What are the origins of anti-semitism? I need not say that in all its forms it is the senseless and evil work of man's utter blindness. But where exactly do its roots lie? How is it to be explained that it has broken out again and again like a plague and was able, even in the middle of this enlightened century of ours, to break out again worse than ever? What is our quarrel with the Jews? Every nation has some unpleasant characteristics, yet these do not arouse the antagonism of others in the same way as the Jews bring forth the animosity of other people just because they are Jews. But why do we object to their being Jews? Why are we so hard-hearted, why so unforgiving? Do they not possess good characteristics, too, like other races? Why then are these not taken into account? Why are the moral arguments against anti-semitism of no avail at all? Anti-semitism seems to be just as inexplicable as the very existence and character of the Jews, and there are grounds for the supposition that there is some connexion between the two.

The Christian answer must, in fact, arise from this supposition, and two points in particular must be mentioned here.

We cannot dispute the fact that the Jew is no worse than any other man. But it depresses us—and is the reason for the grudge we bear the Jew—that he is a mirror in which we see ourselves as we are, i.e. we see how bad we all are. The Jew pays for the fact that he is the elect of God. The one Jew on the Cross paid by having laid upon Him the sin and guilt of all mankind.

Wherever the grace of God sheds its light, it reveals the fact that man does not deserve it and that he is a transgressor and a rebel. There is no room for camouflage and 'whitewashing'. The sun shines down—not on the Egyptians and Babylonians, not on the Philistines and Moabites, not on the Greeks and Romans, not on the English nor on the Swiss, but on the chosen people of Israel, the Jews—and thus brings to the light the truth about us all. This we suspect and therefore dislike the Jews. Therefore, we deem it necessary to punish the stranger in our midst, with contempt, scorn and hatred. The most wrong-headed thing we could do! What is the good of turning the mirror to the wall, or even smashing it? That will not alter the fact that we are still what we saw ourselves to be in the mirror. However, the folly of turning the mirror to the wall and smashing it is the only bit of sense in all the nonsense of anti-semitism.

There is, however, another significant thing; we find it uncanny that the Jews live among us and move like shadows through world history with that unheard-of historical permanence, yet without roots, without security; without roots because they are sustained by the free grace of God—so persistent because that grace holds them so firmly. Why do we find that uncanny? Because in this connexion also they are the mirror of our own life and that of all mankind. This people without roots, the Jews, tell us—and we too suspect—that we, who believe ourselves to be secure on the bank, are in fact not so, and that our own roots, our own security, are in rather a bad state. The existence of the Jews tells us that in world history there seems to be neither security nor permanent abiding place for any nation or for any individual. No wonder this idea is repugnant to us! Do we shiver at the thought that we too might be bidden to live on nothing but the grace of God? And how painful is the other question that arises from this thought; that with all its helplessness this race is still so permanent, so enduring! Why do we so dislike to be told that the Jews are the chosen people? Why does Christendom continually search for fresh proof that this is no longer true? In a word, because we do not enjoy being told that the sun of free grace, by which alone we can live, shines not upon us, but upon the Jews, that it is the Jews who are elect and not the Germans, the French or the Swiss, and that in order to be chosen we must, for good or ill, either be Jews or else be heart and soul on the side of the Jews. 'Salvation is of the Jews.' It is in their existence that we non-Jews come up against the rock of divine choice, which first passing over us is primarily made by Another, a choice which can concern us only in that it first concerns Him and cannot affect us except in Him and through Him. In the 'lost-ness' and in the persistence of the Jews that Other One looks down on us; the Jew on the Cross, in whom is salvation for every man. We refuse to accept that and many a man refuses it who yet would not like to be suspected of anti-semitism. Even the Jews refuse to accept it. Yet they should remember that this is just that other bit of sense in all the non-sense, this is just the other root of anti-semitism! Whoever re-fuses to accept this, let him see to it that he does not become an anti-semite; he is already well on the way to becoming one.

4. What conclusions can we draw from all this with regard to the Christian attitude towards the Jews? We can all admit the truth of the fine words on this subject which we heard at the beginning. It is doubtful, however, whether they are speci-fically Christian, whether they give to the Jews the honour due to them, and whether they have the power to accomplish any-thing practical in the matter of the Jewish problem. This problem opens up a gulf which is too wide to be bridged by mere human reason and ethics. And we Christians are too firmly linked with and indebted to the Jews to be able, on those grounds alone, to put them off with a few assurances of goodwill and refusals to countenance anti-semitism.

Without any doubt the Jews are to this very day the chosen people of God in the same sense as they have been so from the beginning, according to the Old and New Testaments. They have the promise of God; and if we Christians from among the Gentiles have it too, then it is only as those chosen with them, as guests in their house, as new wood grafted on to their old tree. The Christian community exists in the same way as the Jews; miraculously sustained throughout the years, it too is a people of strangers; and just as the anti-semites are offended by the Jews, so the Christian community will necessarily arouse the same feelings.

What is the barrier that lies between us? Strangely enough,

it is the same as what unites us, namely the one Jew, on the Cross of Golgotha, whom we acknowledge as the fulfilment of the promise to Israel and as the Saviour of the whole world. The Jews, who ought to be the first to do so, do not acknowledge this one Jew. Therefore, they are not so ready to accept the fact that they can live only by God's grace. That is why the Jews are to this day so defiant a people, and why their defiance is so closely allied to anti-semitism. That is the essence of this permanent and terrible riddle of Jewish existence. We Christians from among the Gentiles cannot, however, acknowledge that one Jew, the Lord Jesus Christ, without knowing that we are one with the Jews. In their defiance we recognise the same emotion as works in us. But we also know Him, who has already overcome all human defiance and thereby healed all divisions among us, and first and foremost the division between the Jews and other nations. He alone can make self-evident what the other nations without doubt owe to the Jews, and just for that reason we Christians greet the Jews this Advent-tide—in the Name of Him, over whose Cross the Gentile Pontius Pilate had the inscription set up, 'Jesus of Nazareth, the King of the Jews'. When the Jews protested against this, Pilate replied, 'What I have written, I have written.'

VIII

THE CHRISTIAN UNDERSTANDING OF REVELATION

Based on a course of open lectures
given at Bonn University in the
summer semester 1947.

THE CHRISTIAN UNDERSTANDING OF REVELATION

I

REVELATION means the publication of something private, something hidden. The Greek concept *Phanerosis* signifies the appearance of something hidden, and the parallel concept *Apokalypsis* the unveiling of something veiled. A closed door is opened; a covering removed. A light shines in the darkness, a question finds its answer, a puzzle its solution. In general terms, this is the process we call 'revelation'. In this general sense the concept covers many things that are not contained in the Christian connotation of revelation. Let us first make a brief survey of this general connotation of the term in ten points.

1. In the general sense of the term there are revelations which man may find good and useful, enriching and deepening his life, but which are not necessary, vital or indispensable. There are many things we do not need to know even if we could know them. Is there also such a thing as a necessary, an indispensable revelation?

2. There are revelations which man may find interesting, stimulating and exciting and possibly useful in some way or other, but which are nevertheless dangerous and therefore of doubtful value. As everyone knows, it has been questioned whether the revelation on the basis of which Prometheus discovered fire, was not rather a curse for man, and the question is all the more pertinent in regard to the invention of gunpowder and certain discoveries which are making our own age so remarkable.—Is there a revelation of which it can be said that it is clearly a good and wholesome revelation for man?

3. There are revelations which occur today and which may be superseded by others tomorrow. There are therefore relative

revelations.—Is there, on the other hand, an absolute revelation, independent of the changes and chances of time?

4. There are revelations which are vouchsafed to possibly only a few, even very few people. There are therefore esoteric and exoteric relations to such revelations.—Is there, in contrast to such special revelations, a general revelation which concerns all mankind?

5. There are revelations which are disclosures of matters of fact which were only temporarily unknown—that is, contingent revelations.—Is there, in contrast to these, something like a necessary revelation?

6. There are revelations which consist in the translation into reality, life and activity of hidden but existing possibilities which are available to and can be realised by man.—Is there, on the other hand, a revelation which cannot be effected by man at all, which does not consist in the realisation of an existing possibility, but can only be interpreted as a gift?

7. There are revelations which, when they take place or have taken place, pass into human possession, so that man can master them and do as he likes with them. Such revelations may be said to be open to exploitation.—Is there, on the other hand, a free revelation, free in the sense that man cannot use it for his own purposes at all?

8. There are revelations which occur in the form of partial and approximate revelations in the course of intellectual inquiries, whether conducted by individuals or groups.—Is there, in contrast to such merely approximate revelations, an original and definitive revelation?

9. There are revelations of which man can establish the existence, constitution and quality, and which he can contemplate with more or less pleasure and insight: we may call such revelations 'speculative' revelations.—Is there, on the other hand, such a thing as a 'practical' revelation?

10. Everything that has been said so far may be summed up as the self-revelation of something that already exists, a self-revelation of man in the cosmos or a revelation of the cosmos in relation to man: in other words, immanent, this-worldly revelation, which occurs in the human and cosmic realm.—Is there, in contrast to this, such a thing as a transcendent, other-worldly revelation?

2

Revelation in the Christian sense is the wholly other revelation which only appears on the brink of all the above-mentioned possibilities.

Revelation in the Christian sense is:

1. A revelation which man needs not relatively, but absolutely, for his very life and being as man, a revelation without which he would not in fact be man at all, a revelation which decides being and non-being: in other words, one which man cannot please himself whether he accepts or not.

2. Revelation in the Christian sense is a revelation which accepts man absolutely, which takes place for his salvation, for his perfect salvation. Revelation in the Christian sense is an affirmation of man, however much it may be bound up with threats and judgments.

3. Revelation in the Christian sense is a revelation which was completely new to man yesterday and the day before yesterday, which is completely new to him today and will be new again tomorrow. It is absolute, not relative.

4. Revelation in the Christian sense is a revelation which comes to all men with equal strangeness from outside, but which concerns all men with equal intimacy. It is not a revelation intended for a few men only, but for all men.

5. Revelation in the Christian sense means the unveiling of certain facts that are fundamentally hidden from man, things no eye has seen, no ear has heard, no human heart conceived. Revelation in the Christian sense is not contingent.

6. Revelation in the Christian sense is the revelation of a reality outside man. It is the realisation of a possibility which lies wholly in the place where the revelation takes place, not in the human realm. It is therefore a revelation which man is powerless to bring about of his own will.

7. Revelation in the Christian sense is a revelation which remains free in its relation to man. It cannot be capitalised.

8. Revelation in the Christian sense is a revelation which is complete and final, which fulfils past, present and future, which fulfils time itself. It is anything but merely approximate.

9. Revelation in the Christian sense is not an object which man

can observe from outside; it is rather one which takes possession of man, seizes hold of him and calls him to action. It is anything but merely speculative.

10. We may sum up what has been said so far by saying that revelation in the Christian sense is the self-revelation of the Creator of all that is, the self-revelation of the Lord of all Being. It is not an immanent, this-worldly revelation, but comes from outside man and the cosmos. It is a transcendent revelation.

This is what is meant by revelation in the Christian sense of the term. It is useful to realise what revelation in this sense connotes, whatever the personal attitude may be that one adopts towards it. In any case it is the question we are to consider in this lecture.

We have seen that there are many kinds of revelation. In the ten points which we started with we tried to indicate the nature of the revelations that occur in all the spheres of human life, art, science, history, nature, and in man's personal life and experience. We contrasted this with the Christian understanding of revelation. You must decide for yourselves whether the two kinds are merely two aspects of the same reality. But is it really feasible to lump together what we call revelation in all the fields of human experience and what the Christian means by the same term? Is it feasible, as happens so often, to derive, explain and justify the Christian interpretation on the basis of what we are in the habit of calling 'revelation' in everyday life? Is it even possible to compare the two realities? Is not revelation in the Christian sense rather a specific reality of its own, a revelation which begins at the very point where all the others end? We shall come back later to the significance, from the Christian point of view, of the existence of other revelations and meanings of revelation. What is certain is that Christian and non-Christian revelations are two quite distinct realities which must not be confused. We are concerned here with the sphere of Christian revelation which cannot be seen or penetrated from the sphere of any other revelation, but which has a special content and constitutes a special order of its own.

Revelation in the Christian sense is the revelation of God. For the Christian there is no need of a special enquiry and a special proof to know and to declare who and what God is.

For the Christian the revelation is itself the proof, the proof furnished by God Himself. The Christian answer to the question as to who and what God is, is a simple one: He is the subject who acts in His revelation. This act of revelation is a token of His Being and the expression of His nature.

3

Keeping to the sequence of our original ten points, we may define the Christian understanding of God as follows:

Who is God?

1. God is He who is absolutely necessary to man. God decides man's being or non-being.
2. God is He who accepts man with the utmost seriousness and in the deepest love. He is his saviour.
3. God is He who was, who is and always will be new to man. He is absolute.
4. God is He who is above all and for all: 'Before Thee none can boast but all must fear.'
5. God is He who meets man as the inherently necessary and fundamentally hidden reality.
6. God is He who is able to come quite close to man, though He is the farthest away from him. Though unknown, He is able to become most intimately known to man.
7. God is He who in revealing Himself to man, is and remains free.
8. God is He who was, is and shall be, the Lord of time, the eternal God, the God of the aeons.
9. God is also the Lord and Master of man, who makes demands on man.
10. God is the Creator and as such acts upon man, without whom no other being, including man, could exist.

God is He who acts in His revelation and thereby describes Himself. The revelation of God, that is, the action of the Subject who reveals Himself in this revelation, is what is meant when Christians speak of revelation. They mean the revelation of this God, the one, the only God. There seem to be many gods, just as there are many revelations. In accordance with this multiplicity of revelations there are many religions, theologies, philosophies, ideologies and, therefore, many and multiform

o

images of God. Sometimes God is said to be that which is most necessary or even most dangerous to man, sometimes He is merely a general ideal or an individual dream, sometimes the embodiment of an historical ideal or a temporary exigency, some-times the essence of the universal cosmic possibilities of man in their known and unknown depths. Sometimes God may be the longed-for opium of a personal or general development, some-times the exponent of some human caprice; ultimately and really all these gods are simply some form of man himself in his rela-tionship to the cosmos. I must leave you to decide for yourselves whether God, in the Christian understanding of revelation, is simply one of these gods, or whether the *Deus non est in genere* (Tertullian) is not true, whether the antithesis between the true God and the false gods, the 'nonentities', as the Old Testament calls them, is not valid and true. God is not an abstract category by which even the Christian understanding of the word has to be measured, but He who is called God here is the One God, the Single God, the Sole God.

4

What is this revelation, what is the subject of the revelation of which we have been speaking? What is the frame of mind which is open to receive what we call revelation? What is the theory of cognition for which revelation in the Christian sense is a valid object of knowledge?

And on the other hand: is there a conception of the world, a basic view of existence which can include what we have called God? If the general conception of the world and the general pattern of human thought are the criteria, can such a thing as revelation in the Christian sense exist at all? Does this God exist, of whom we have spoken as the subject of this revelation? What are we in fact talking about? Are we possibly talking nonsense, talking about a non-ens? There are theories of knowledge which can account for what we have called the self-revelation of that which exists, and there are ontologies which can embrace the gods corresponding to these revelations. But as far as one can see there is no theory of knowledge and no pattern of thought which can embrace revelation in the Christian sense of the term. We can work through the whole history of philosophy from

Thales to Martin Heidegger, and we shall be forced to the same conclusion. There is no room for revelation in the Christian sense in any human inquiry or any human faculty of reason. And the same applies to what we have called God in the Christian sense. There may be conceptions of the world which provide for gods, but the God of Christianity cannot appear in any imaginable human conception of the world. Try to map out a conception of the world in which God, as understood in Christian thought, would have room!—And so we must say that if a purely human conception of the world is the measure of all things, then neither revelation nor God in the Christian sense exist at all. We would in fact have been speaking about 'nothing' when we were speaking about revelation and God.

We have not, however, been speaking about 'nothing', but about a reality, something incomparably more real than anything that can be called real in the sphere of human thought and knowledge. When the Christian language speaks of revelation and God it means a reality which is very insignificant-looking and outwardly most unpromising; it speaks quite simply of a single concrete fact in the midst of the numberless host of facts and the vast stream of historical events; it speaks of a single human person living in the age of the Roman Empire: it speaks of Jesus Christ. When the Christian language speaks of God it does so not on the basis of some speculation or other, but looking at this fact, this story, this person. It cannot place this fact in relationship to any system of principles and ideas which would illuminate its importance and significance; it cannot explain and establish it from any other source; it makes no presuppositions when it points to this event. Its sole concern is with the event itself; all it can do is to refer to the existence, or rather, more precisely, the presence of this fact and the reception of the news of its presence as recorded in a tiny sheaf of news about the existence of this Person.

With its eyes concentrated on this news, Christianity speaks of revelation and of God as the subject of this revelation. Looking at this fact, it speaks with absolute assurance. Here—but only here—it sees revelation (in the sense of the criteria we have stated) and it sees God (again, in the sense of the criteria we have stated). Revelation in the Christian sense takes place and

God in the Christian sense is, in accordance with the news of Jesus Christ, His words and deeds, His death and resurrection. That is what we now have to expound and, once again, we propose, for the sake of clarity, to make ten points. Each point will be based on a certain item of the good news of the gospel.

1. 'And the times of this ignorance God winked at; but now commandeth all men everywhere to repent. Because he hath appointed a day, in the which he will judge the world in righteousness by that man whom he hath ordained' (Acts 17.30ff.).

This is the news: Because judgment is pronounced on all men in the one man, and their being and non-being decided, revelation in the Christian sense takes place, and not as an approximate but an original and final revelation. And He who makes the decision in the Person of this one man is God.

2. 'If any man sin, we have an advocate with the Father, Jesus Christ the righteous. And he is the propitiation for our sins; and not for ours only, but also for the sins of the whole world' (I John 2.1ff.).

Since, in accordance with this news, man in this one Jesus Christ, in this offering of Jesus Christ as a propitiation for our sins, is accepted by God, revelation takes place, and not for the imperilling but for the salvation of man. It is God who does this.

3. 'I am the light of the world'. 'The light shineth in darkness; and the darkness comprehended it not' (John 8.12 and 1.5).

Since, in accordance with this news, Jesus Christ came into the darkness as the light of the world, since, therefore, Jesus Christ is and remains absolutely new for man, revelation takes place in the Christian sense, and not as a relative but as an absolute revelation. And it is God who shines in Jesus Christ.

4. 'For all have sinned, and come short of the glory of God; being justified freely by his grace through the redemption that is in Christ Jesus' (Rom. 3.23f.).

Since, in accordance with this news, the event that is called redemption takes place in Jesus Christ, in this one person, the event that cannot proceed from any man and which no man can bring about, but which has been brought about by this One revelation in the Christian sense takes place. Without all, but for all! And therefore not as a special, but as a general revelation which concerns all and is meant for all. And it is God whose honour is so high and whose grace reaches so deep.

5. 'No man hath seen God at any time; the only begotten Son, which is in the bosom of the Father, he hath declared him' (John 1.18).

Inasmuch as what is hidden from all men is revealed in this One, the one exclusive revelation takes place. And it is God that makes Himself known in the One.

6. 'Ye have not chosen me, but I have chosen you and ordained you that ye should go and bring forth fruit' (John 15.16).

Inasmuch as this happens, inasmuch as this One chooses others and calls them to Himself, revelation in the Christian sense takes place; revelation that man cannot bring about by himself but which he receives as a gift. And it is God that has this freedom of choice in relation to man and exercises it in the One.

7. 'I am the vine, ye are the branches: he that abideth in me, and I in him, the same bringeth forth much fruit; for without me ye can do nothing' (John 15.5).

Inasmuch as this One, Jesus Christ, has and exercises such sovereignty over His own, revelation takes place, revelation that cannot be capitalised, but is and remains free. And the origin and the essence of this sovereignty is God.

8. 'Jesus Christ the same yesterday and today and for ever' (Heb. 13.8).

Revelation as an event that has happened, is happening and will happen in the future, which fulfils time in all its three constituents, is not approximate, but complete and final. And the Lord of this time is the eternal God.

9. 'For we are his workmanship, created in Christ Jesus unto good works, which God hath ordained that we should walk in them' (Eph. 2.10).

Inasmuch as this necessity of a definite change comes into force in this One Jesus Christ, revelation takes place: practical, not speculative revelation. And it is God who thus disposes of the way of man.

10. 'In the beginning was the Word and the Word was with God and the Word was God. The same was in the beginning with God. All things were made by him, and without him was not anything made that was made' (John 1.1f.).

Inasmuch as this creative Word, which is superior to all being, is spoken and heard in Him, revelation takes place: transcendent, not immanent revelation. Revelation from the origin of all being. And it is God who speaks this Word.

The concept of revelation and the concept of God in the Christian sense coincide, therefore, in the contemplation of Jesus Christ, in which they are both related to reality. And in contemplation of Him it is decided that God is and what God is; that God is a person and not a neutral thing. And that revelation is His acting and speaking and not a blind occurrence or an unarticulated sound.

5

When it refers to God's revelation as the Word of God, Christianity means Jesus Christ. What is a word? A word obviously differs from a mere sound in that it is formed with the definite intention of calling on others to make a common cause. When I utter the simple word: 'Look!' I call on others to look at something I think I have seen myself. Or if I say: 'Listen!', I call them to listen to something I think I have heard myself. The primary intention of words is quite simply to be heard by others. Words cannot compel, they can only make an appeal. But every word has in view, in some sense or other, the obedient response of other persons. When I utter words I want to induce others to listen and conform to my wishes. In this sense too revelation is a word: God wants our interest, He wants us to listen, He wants to call us to decision, He wants us to obey His Word.

When we speak about the Word, and particularly this Word of God, a certain uneasiness is liable to come over us. Is what we are discussing really no more than a word? Are words not 'sound and smoke clouding the glow of heaven'? 'In the beginning was the Word? I cannot possibly esteem the Word so highly; I must translate it differently: in the beginning was the Deed', as Goethe says. What have we to say to that? Simply that the argument overlooks the fact that the 'glow of heaven' and the 'Deed' without words are phenomena which may be most impressive, but in relation to which it is possible for man to remain free and aloof and which are in any case something essentially different from what we have discerned as revelation in the Christian sense. Secondly, in contrast to all mere words and all empty words, revelation in the Christian sense is both Word and Deed at one and the same time. It is not merely the 'glow of heaven' but a consuming fire and a blinding light. According to Heb. 1.3 the Word of revelation is 'his enabling word on whom all creation depends for its support' (cf. John 1.3). Jesus Christ is the Word. Inasmuch as what happens in Him, happened and happens and will happen, the word of revelation is spoken. The whole criticism of the concept 'the word' is superfluous as far as this Word is concerned. And thus we might take leave of Dr. Faust by suggesting he might have done better not to have tried to translate the Word differently! Incidentally, it is significant that immediately after the translation the Devil appears!

Revelation in the Christian sense is the Word of God, the Word spoken in divine Majesty. He to whom man belongs, to whom man cannot refuse to listen without calling himself into question, who calls man to decision, summons us to make common cause with Him. Neutrality towards the Word of God is impossible; we cannot say Yes and No at the same time. Obedience to the Word of God is not merely one of several possibilities. We do not confront this Word like Hercules at the crossroads. This is a case where there is only one possibility, the possibility of obedience. Man's genuine freedom does not consist in an ability to evade this Word. If he does not submit to it he chooses the impossible possibility, he chooses *nihil*.

Because revelation in the Christian sense is the Word of God, it is impossible to adopt the attitude of a mere onlooker towards it. The revelation of God can only be searched, understood and judged in the act of obedience, of listening, which leads to decision—or it will not be searched, understood and judged at all. We cannot think and talk *about* the revelation of God; we can only reflect on what the Word itself says to us. We can only speak out of the revelation itself; otherwise we shall be thinking and talking about something else.

Since revelation in the Christian sense is the Word of God, we cannot bring it forward as if it were an object outside ourselves. I cannot demonstrate the revelation of God to you in the way that my colleague in the Chemistry Department demonstrates his objects. Because it is the Word of God, the revelation of God cannot be recommended and defended; it has no advocates and no propagandists. And, finally, one cannot profess one's belief in it by protesting and asserting that it exists. Revelation can only be believed in by becoming worthy of belief. Revelation can only be attested as any other unknown fact is attested by someone who happens to know it. Revelation can only be presupposed in our thinking and our speaking, and in our Christian theology and preaching too, in the way that certain axioms or objective facts are presupposed in every branch of knowledge, when the belief and the testimony and the presupposition are only forms of that one possible decision, the decision of obedience. *Omnis recta cognitio ab obedientia nascitur*, Calvin says. Thus it is with revelation because it is the Word of God.

6

A negative attitude to revelation is also possible. What is the significance of that in view of the fact that what we are concerned with here is the Word of God? A negative attitude to revelation is a perilous undertaking. But one thing is certain: no denial of revelation is capable of upsetting the objective facts. Paganism of all kinds, indifference and error are possible, but cannot be taken seriously in the long run by those who know what revelation really is, since every human denial of revelation is subject from the very outset to the promise of the affirmation of the Word of God. Resistance to the Word of God is bound to fail in the end.

It is in accordance with the character of revelation in the Christian sense that its occurrence and therefore also the existence of God can only be published in the way we have indicated in point 4, that is, by reference to the verbal, literal, written tidings of this event. The news of the revelation of God in Jesus Christ stands in Holy Writ, and therefore any reference to it, any announcement of the event of revelation, must follow the biblical text. To put it quite plainly: what we have come to know as revelation in the Christian sense is to be found in a book, in the book of the Old and New Testaments. God and His existence are to be found in this book. Everything I have said so far and shall say is taken from this book and is to be judged by what is to be found in this book. Seen or unseen, explicitly or implicitly, the hypothesis, 'It is written', must underlie all our thought on this subject. What is the significance of bringing the concept of revelation into this close relationship with the Bible?

First, let me draw two boundary-lines, one on the right and one on the left.

1. The fact that God's revelation is contained in this book does not mean that the texts of this book are a revelation as such. Even today Roman Catholic theology holds that the Bible and the revelation of God are identical, though according to Catholic teaching the Bible is, admittedly, supplemented by a further source of revelation, namely, tradition. Catholic teaching refuses to confine itself to the Bible, in spite of its identification of the Bible and the revelation of God. The Protestant theology of the so-called high orthodoxy of the second half of the seventeenth century embraced the doctrine of so-called verbal inspiration, according to which the writings of the Old and New Testaments were literally inspired by God, so that the Bible gives us not only the Word but the actual words of God. This identification of the Bible and the revelation of God is unacceptable because the authors of the Bible do not themselves attest any such identity between their own words and the Word of God. Even the old formula, 'Thus saith the Lord . . .', was not intended to imply that the prophet was about to utter words he had received from God verbatim, but rather that he was commanded to speak these words by God. No one who reads the Bible carefully will find in it any claim that its texts are as such a revelation of God. It must also be said that such a conception contradicts the interpretation of revelation which we have elaborated here.

2. On the other hand, it cannot be said that the texts of the Bible merely include the revelation of God; that is, that only some parts of this book are pregnant with revelation whilst others must be denied this honour. To say this would be to imply that the Bible is a more or less thick husk enclosing a sweet kernel and that it is up to us to decide, on the strength of our reason (eighteenth century), or our religious experience (nineteenth century), where the revelation is to be found. This conception of modern Protestantism is also unacceptable because the intention

of the authors of the Bible was not to express opinions which we are open to contradict with our own opinions. They speak from a Word that does not allow us to enter into discussion with them.

What are these texts and what is the meaning of this book? The texts of the Bible are the human though authoritative, and authoritative though human, documents of the fact, the story and the Person of Jesus Christ, which we have come to know as the real subject of the revelation. They are an account of His life in the years 1 to 30, and at the same time they tell of the antecedents of His appearance and also the beginnings of His historical influence. The centre of Holy Scripture is the fact of Jesus Christ—*et incarnatus est*. The Word became flesh. This is the event that divides time itself into *ante Christum natum* and *post Christum natum*. This does not mean simply all time before Christ and all time after Him, but it is *qualified* time before Him and after Him.

Before Him time was filled with the history of the people of Israel in its life in the Covenant with God who had chosen and called it, who led and ruled it, to whom it was perpetually unfaithful and with whom God nevertheless kept faith. That is the content of the Old Testament, the old Covenant, the form of the one Covenant before the appearance of Jesus Christ. But the New Testament begins with the appearance of Jesus Christ as the goal of Israel and the basis of the new pattern of the one people of God, the basis of its Church, which brings us to the story of His influence, of which only the beginning is seen in the Acts of the Apostles and the letters of the Apostles. But both parts, the Old and the New Testament, are, for all their differences, alike a testimony to the one revelation of Christ and its immediate context. What is described here is not time in general, not the history of the world, but the time of the Covenant of God which is fulfilled in the appearance of Jesus Christ. The Bible contains the human, but authoritative, the authoritative but human, documents of this fact. To that extent revelation is to be found in the Bible, and the Bible contains this revelation. And to that extent we depend on Holy Scripture for the revelation of God. It is *the* testimony of *the* revelation.

What do we mean by an *authoritative* document, what do we

mean by *Holy* Scripture? We mean that the authors of the Old
and the New Testament are the only direct witnesses of this
revelation known to us, that is, of revelation in the Christian
sense. From the outset we made clear that there are also other
so-called 'revelations'. The history of the world and the history
of the human race teems with 'revelations'. And there is no lack
of witnesses. Every great poet, every great artist is undoubtedly
a witness in this sense. It may not be in very good taste to treat
the word 'revelation' in this way, but in principle there is nothing against it from a theological point of view. The revelation
to which the Bible bears witness is, admittedly, something fundamentally different, so that, however much we may revere Plato,
Socrates and Goethe, we shall not refer to these witnesses in the
same breath as the witnesses of the Bible. There we are confronted by something utterly different.

There also exist indirect witnesses of revelation in the biblical
sense. The biblical witnesses are not exclusive. We are certainly
entitled to apply the words of Jesus, 'Ye are to be my witnesses',
to the life of the whole Church, and to every Christian. The
term 'witnesses' will then be used figuratively, however. We
must be quite clear about that. Luther and Calvin were undoubtedly witnesses of Jesus Christ and therefore witnesses of
the revelation of God. Certainly there exists a vast throng, a
cloud of witnesses, known and unknown. But all these are indirect
witnesses of the revelation, witnesses who presuppose the testimony of the prophets and apostles, who derive from this source
who have been brought to the Faith by their words.

The witnesses of the Bible, on the other hand, are direct, first-
hand witnesses. None of these later witnesses can be compared
with them. Neither the witnesses of other revelations nor the
indirect witnesses of this revelation can compile direct and to
that extent authoritative records of this revelation. Only what
the Old Church called the 'choir of prophets and apostles' was
able to do that. The Bible is Holy Scripture because its authors,
and they alone, this choir of prophets and this choir alone—
though there are many other, beautiful choirs, world choirs and
church choirs!—are able, by dint of first-hand knowledge, to be
the authentic and immediate heralds of this one revelation, the
direct reporters of this event.

The literary form of their writings also corresponds more or less to this unique authority and authenticity. The writings of the Bible are kerygmatic writings, related to the extraneous, new, absolute event that is the goal of the Old Testament and the beginning of the New. Their concern is to make known to the world this story, along with what led up to it and what followed from it. Because the writings of the apostles and prophets were interpreted as kerygmatic writings, because the evidence of the revelation of God was found in their words and through their words in these texts, they were regarded as an official canon in the early Church, as the standard of its life and teaching. In the Bible the Church found its rule of life. It had to decide for itself what it should choose as its canon. It found itself surrounded by many witnesses of every kind. Why did it not take such a fine document as the writings of Plato for its 'canon'? In fact, the Early Fathers did come perilously near canonising them. Why were they not accepted after all? The Early Church did not despise the wisdom of the world. The small difference which made it necessary for such a modest writer as the author of the Epistle of James to be accepted as canonical and not a great writer such as Plato, was simply that the Epistle of James bears direct witness, clearly and simply, to Jesus Christ. Again, whatever the Church decided was the product of a later testimony was not canonised, nor were such texts as seemed problematical, though not of later date. Wherever the Church did not hear the revelation of God in Jesus Christ directly, it was unable to accept such writings into the canon of Holy Scripture.

Thus the knowledge and understanding and the interpretation of the revelation of God is in fact bound up with the knowledge, understanding and interpretation of the texts of the Bible. It would save theological students a lot of work—but there is no easy way to the revelation of God—the Bible cannot be by-passed. The Bible confronts us with many linguistic, historical, and philological problems. Our relationship to the revelation of God is indirect. The Word waits for us in the words of the prophets and apostles. In this sense Holy Scripture is the source and the guiding-principle of all Christian doctrine and exposition which claims to preach the Word of God on the basis of the revelation of God.

Since the Bible is kerygmatic in character, the Church must also necessarily be unconditionally kerygmatic, on the basis of, and guided by, the kerygma of the prophets and apostles. The Bible is the foundation of the Church and also its consolation and its warning. The Church which departs from this foundation ceases to be a Church.

The Bible is a collection of human documents. It was written by men in the language of men, at a definite time in human history and in a definite human situation. It follows that:

1. In our search for an absolute, unconditional, supreme source of divine revelation we inevitably come up against the fact of the human relativity and limitations of the authors of the Bible. Martin Noth rightly says:

'The human and historical limitations of the Old Testament text are real and boundless.'

Real—and therefore not merely apparent; boundless—and therefore not merely partial.

What we call the Bible is a section of the literature of the Semitic world of middle antiquity and of the Hellenism of late antiquity. Why is this literature authoritative? The Bible is not, as used to be said, the oldest literature; there is literature thousands of years older. And if we were to ask whether the Bible is the most interesting piece of traditional literature or the most valuable and impressive from a human point of view, we should be raising topics on which opinion is very divided. The authors of the Bible were human beings with all the limitations of their own individuality and the powers of expression of Hebrew and Hellenistic Greek, both tongues with very remarkable limitations; they were human beings who lived and thought and spoke within the modes of thinking and feeling, the knowledge of nature and history and the intellectual tendencies of their age. And an outstanding feature of that age was a fondness for expressing ideas in the form of myth. Moreover, it is impossible to read the Bible attentively without realising that what the Old and the New Testaments offer is not a consistently sustained outlook on the world nor even a uniform theology. Finally, not a single verse of the Bible has come down to us with such absolute certainty and clarity that alternative versions cannot be suggested. We are therefore on uncertain ground.

To what extent can these texts, behind which all this human relativity is present so 'really and boundlessly', be admitted as authoritative?

2. The same question can be put from a different angle: Let us assume that the reader has discovered in these texts, just as they stand, the reality of the revelation of God in Jesus Christ. This means inevitably that he is confronted by the whole problematical nature of man. He may wonder why the authors of the Bible do not offer a well thought out philosophy as the worthy receptacle for their theme? And why cannot these texts be approached purely scientifically? The more clearly the biblical witnesses of Jesus Christ speak, the more what they say gets lost in what we should today call the realm of pure legend. And finally, what about the humanity of these biblical witnesses? That too appears to be highly problematical. It is as if the theme they have to expound were too big for the vessel that contains it. How many more noble figures meet us in other places! Neither the patriarchs, nor Moses, nor even such a central figure as Paul in the New Testament, are very illuminating as human beings. There is more fear of humanity in the Bible than respect for it. Were these human beings not all somewhat impaired, impaired by the greatness of the cause to which they bear witness? Do we not constantly come across traces of human disturbance in the Bible? Even of Christ Himself we read: 'He is mad.' Or, in the Easter story: 'They thought it was a fairy tale.' Or, in the story of Pentecost: 'They are full of new wine.' The Governor says to Paul: 'Paul, thou art beside thyself; much learning doth make thee mad', and there is the parallel in the Old Testament when Amos is greeted by the 'High Consistory' with the words: 'Go flee thee away into the land of Judah, and there eat bread and prophesy there'—from which one gets the impression that the people would have been delighted if he had gone!

The question does suggest itself: How can all these men speak authoritatively? The dilemma is that if the Bible is a collection of authoritative documents and testimonies, then the human element must either be denied or ignored. The human element in the Bible would then be a *pudendum*, and one would have to make a *sacrificium intellectus* in order to say: The Bible, as it stands, is revelation: it is therefore in reality not a human document at all but a divine document. The Hebrew and Greek letters are merely an outward form: the reality behind them is the Word of God. In that case we should be forced to regard the whole stock of words in the Bible as spoken by God, and we should have to understand and receive it as such. The whole relativity of the Bible would then have to be denied and its problematical character disputed.—This method can be tried—and it has been tried—but it is impossible in the long run because the Bible itself does not conceal its human character: on the contrary, it exposes it to full view.

It is a remarkable contradiction that the very people who make the most extravagant claims for the Bible are thereby being fundamentally unfaithful to it. For without an act of intellectual dishonesty no one can deny the relativity or the problematical nature of the Bible. And the great danger is that the elimination of the human relativity of the Bible may lead to the elimination of the very thing the Bible is intended to bear witness to: the relevation of God. For is it not of the very nature of revelation that the form in which it confronts us is relative and problematical? One may say, on the other hand, of course, if this is so, and if these are purely human documents, how far can they possibly be authoritative? Why not place them alongside the other interesting documents of their time and confer the same degree of authoritativeness on them?

The phenomenon with which the Bible deals is and remains in any case a unique phenomenon. As such it is capable of making a deep impression, so that in great moments a Goethe or a Kant have expressed deep reverence for the Bible. And if we refuse to revere the Bible we shall still not be able to alter the fact that through all ages it has proved itself a phenomenon which has disturbed mankind in a remarkable way. How often it has been said that the Bible has had its day! But whereas some philosophical treatises have died overnight, the Bible continues to live as the absolutely indispensable source of the phenomenon which it reveals. No doubt Plato may be of value for many, and Kant even more so, but as far as this phenomenon is concerned, we shall have to keep to the Bible.

All this is naturally just a provisional answer. The real question which the Bible presents and will always present is twofold:

1. How *do* these men come to speak with authority? and:

2. Assuming they do speak with authority, how do we establish contact with them?

The main answer to this must be:

1. None of the biblical writers claimed that he came to speak of revelation by virtue of some special faculty or aptitude: on the contrary, they all testify that the revelation of God came to them with a supreme authoritativeness of its own. The revelation which we have tried to delineate in our ten points came to these men in all their relative and problematical nature, with all the limitations of their Hebrew and Hellenistic tongues. This humanity of theirs certainly did not qualify them to become the recipients of the revelation. On the other hand, it did not disqualify them. They spoke as these particular human beings within the historical situation of their time, in the language and pattern of human thought that persisted for many centuries—during the period covered by their writings, which embraces more than a thousand years. But—and this is the all-important point—they *answered* something that came *to* them, not from them. 'They spoke', the Bible says, 'in the power and truth of the Holy Spirit.' By the Holy Spirit the Bible means a reality which comes to man. The legitimacy which the biblical witnesses can claim is simply and solely the charge which this answer to the Holy Spirit lays upon them. They do not live by something they can have, see, know, feel and experience, but by the worthiness and the light of the object which they encounter. They live by the revelation which is vouchsafed to them. That is their strength and also their weakness. And that is the light in which they see themselves.

2. How do *we* come to recognise the authoritativeness of their words? We are all in the same position. There is no trick by which the Bible can be made accessible to all. The revelation of God comes to us with a supreme authority of its own. It happens to us as it did to the prophets and apostles. We are given the freedom and the opportunity to perceive the revelation in these texts, but the mystery still confronts us in all its integrity: we cannot dispose of it arbitrarily, but we are put into relation with it. No one has ever found what he thought he would find. One day the door has opened quite unexpectedly. Their human condition is not the qualification of the biblical witnesses; Hebrew

is not a sacred language (though theologians have to know it!). But the human condition is not a disqualification either. It is nothing to be ashamed of. 'We hear every man in our own tongue, wherein we were born. Parthians and Medes and Elamites . . . Cretes and Arabians, we do hear them speak in our tongues the wonderful works of God.' When, and because the Holy Spirit has made them His witnesses, we hear Him speak to us too, we are empowered by the human words of the Bible to hear the Word of God.

To that extent the revelation of God in Jesus Christ is 'in the book': the authors of the book have received its witness and in their words it testifies of itself to other men too. The Bible is the opportunity which the revelation of God has created for itself by the appointment of human witnesses. It is offered to us as the possibility which waits to be realised by revelation; it is offered as the place where we have to seek for revelation, because it offers itself to be found there. Thus Holy Scripture is *the* source of revelation.

7

We have interpreted revelation as the self-revelation of God, that is, as His revelation in Jesus Christ, as the Word that is spoken to us, that is given to us in the witness of Holy Scripture. Wherever revelation in the Christian sense is known and acknowledged, there the Christian Church is. The Church is the reality which arises and continues wherever the revelation of God in Jesus Christ has made itself known, wherever it allows itself to be known of men and succeeds in winning their acknowledgment.

The Church does not exist in any sense at all where revelation is understood merely as the revelation of existence in general. To mention a few trivial examples: a society for chemical research will certainly be concerned with 'revelations', but with revelations of existence in general. Or a society for the preservation and cultivation of folk customs in the Rhineland: it can also speak of 'revelations', but not of revelation in the specifically Christian sense. Or why should not an Art Academy have 'revelations'—that is, revelations of existence in general? The Church, however, is distinguished from all such possibilities in that it is

P

not concerned with a self-revelation of existence but with a relation to existence.

The Church is not to be found when revelation is taken to mean the knowledge of the disclosure of existence. If we were existentialist philosophers like Heidegger, or even Kierkegaard, we could speak of a revelation of the 'limits' of all existence. But such a revelation could not be the foundation of the Church. The Church is not concerned with the revelation of some existence or other, or of its limits, but with the revelation of God.

The Church does not exist where revelation is based on some general idea of God which is thought to manifest itself in various ways, of which Jesus Christ is merely one among many, though He may be conceded the first and highest place. The revelation on which the Church is founded is the revelation of God in Jesus Christ, and it alone. Wherever the exclusiveness of this revelation is not acknowledged, the Church is no longer to be found. And, lastly, the Church is on the point of dissolution wherever it is forgotten that Holy Scripture is a valid, normative and authoritative testimony to the revelation, that is, wherever the Church ceases to hold fast to the Bible and imagines it can know and acknowledge the revelation of God without reference to the Bible.

What is the true Church? The true Church is the multitude of those who are called, called out, called together and called up by the revelation of God in Jesus Christ, as the Word of God to which the Bible testifies.

'Called': they are therefore men and women who understand the call of God in His revelation so that it becomes part of their lives, so that what they have heard concerns them as intimately as their own bodies.

'Called out': that is, separated from the mass of the still vaster number of human beings in general; set in a special place; set on a special path; qualified in a way that others are not, so that in the midst of the whole human race they form a group apart.

'Called together': they are called with one another and to one another. They are called by the revelation of God to faith and obedience and thereby called *together*, made into brothers and sisters, set in a fellowship of hearing and receiving, in the special community of those who are called by the revelation of God.

And, lastly, 'called up': for those who are called, called out, called together, are given a special duty to perform, a task which they have to undertake together. Their being called apart is not an end in itself. Its purpose is that they shall be given a share in a Word and a task, called into a single ministry.

The true Church is the assembly of those who are called in these ways. To be means here being *in actu*, in life. The Church is a living Church or it is no Church at all. And a member of the Church is a living member. It follows that wherever and however we have to do with any body that calls itself a Church —whether it is an established Church, a free Church, a Lutheran or a Reformed Church—we have cause to ask: is it really a Church? It is quite possible for a 'church' to be called a church and to look like a church and yet not be a church at all. No form of Church can escape this crucial question. The true Church does not exist where people are called, but called by something other than the Word of God to which the Bible testifies. The true Church does not exist where the actual life of its members is not in accordance with this call.

The Church is constantly faced by the twofold question: Does this so-called Church really live by the revelation of God and by that alone? And does it really *live* by it? The Church lives in the world, in a neutral, indifferent or even hostile world. Nothing appertaining to the outward shape of the Church is without secular analogies and even secular relationships. The problems of the Church—whether understood or not—are open for all the world to see. The two questions: What does the Church live by? And does it really live by it? are not only familiar to the Church but very well known in the outside world too, among ordinary people, in the papers and wherever secular man lives and moves and has his being. Secular man is quite familiar with the question whether the Church is not fundamentally unnecessary. What is the point of the Church? Is not everything else more urgent and more necessary than the Church? And the other question is equally familiar: is not the Church unfitted for and hostile to life in the world? Is not the Church antiquated and out-of-date, is it not a terribly uncreative, unoriginal, terribly dull affair? And, furthermore, is not the Church in any case quite powerless? Such questions may arise because those who ask them do not know what they are talking about or are irritated by something they cannot understand. But such questions may also mean that the Church is being asked a question by the indifferent and the godless which really concerns it, though not in the way the questioner has in mind, but rather because of the hidden meaning in the question: Church, it asks, are you really *alive*? And do you really live by that whereby alone you can live? In any case, it would be better for the Church not to evade such questions but to take them desperately seriously. Even if the people who ask them are blind and deaf, the Church must face them with deep concern and not start talking plaintively about the 'godless world', but rather ask itself: Do we really live by that by which we *must* live and do we really *live* by it? Is it true? Is it true in every sense that we live by the revelation of God in Jesus Christ, or do we get no further than our creeds and constitutions? Do we really practise our faith?

The Church ought to profit from the questions of the 'wicked worldlings' by making them its own questions. Its whole existence is based on revelation. But as far as the eye can see it is also a human reality like any other natural or historical phenomenon of human life. Since the men and woman in the Church are also human beings, life in the Church is bound to be only too human, and it is inevitable that the question about the possibility of revelation in the Church will not only be put, but put in this form. It is of vital importance to the Church that the question of apostasy, great or small, dangerous or less dangerous, and of the renewal that apostasy necessitates, should be faced. The Church which does not ask itself whether it is not threatened by apostasy, and therefore in need of renewal, should beware lest it become a sleeping and a sick Church, even sick unto death. But where the Church understands the question it will listen with constant attention to the warnings which come to it, explicitly, or possibly only indirectly through a great silence. It may be that the Lord has bidden those outside the Church to say something important to the Church. The Church therefore has every reason not to ignore the questions and warnings of the outside world. Whatever befalls the Church from outside, it should take as a stimulus to renew itself from its own foundations. The Church must enter into the questions and movements of the age, but in order, by so doing, to understand anew and to understand better what the true Church is. Any Church that is too tired to do that, or that simply wants to jog along in the old, or even the new, ruts, is a sleeping Church. Any Church that tries to escape the reformation (not the sixteenth century Reformation, but the one that is again and again the vital need of the day) is a sick Church, sick unto death.

This is the vital and critical question, which, when rightly understood, can only serve the Church. By harassing the Church, from without or within, its function is to prove to the Church that it cannot live without the revelation of God in Jesus Christ. If the Church could do that it would have the 'peace' for which it so often yearns. Goethe says somewhat maliciously that the history of the Church is 'a hotch-potch of error and violence'. That is a fact. And one cannot even open Heussi's handbook without being forced to agree with Goethe. But he did not concentrate the whole of the Church's history in that remark. It is just as true that the whole history of the Church is an un-broken chain of unbroken replies to, and reactions against, this 'hotch-potch of error and violence'. In an astonishing way there are always forces at work to counteract the error and violence. Such forces may be of a polemical or irenical nature. Let me illustrate this with a few examples.

It is true that the Church is often helpless in the midst of human society, but it is just as true that faith enters the lists again and again with its *Credo unam sanctam ecclesiam*, and that its profession has historical power and strength. It is true that the Church degenerates into faithless impotence again and again, but it is just as true that again and again it is revived by the unpretentious, death-and-life-giving profession: *Credo in Spiritum sanctum*! Defiant and humbling faith in the Holy Spirit has never confronted the Church in vain. It is true that again and again we have seen the emergence of a way of life in the Church which can only be called a way of godlessness. But it is just as true that we have seen this godless piety confronted by a profession of faith in Jesus Christ as the living Son of God which was stronger than all godlessness. It is true that the Church often turns its back on the troubles and sorrows of the age in which it lives, but it is also true that again and again it has heard and responded

to the voice that says: 'Inasmuch as ye have done it unto one
of the least of these my brethren, ye have done it unto me!'—
a word that has often called the Church down from its imaginary
heights into the depths of human need. It is true that often enough
the Church has become secularised, that is, only too similar to
the surrounding world, that it has adapted itself to the culture
and science of its time. But it is also true that the cry, 'Here
have we no continuing city, but we seek one to come', has set
itself against all the secularising influences which play upon the
Church. It is true, again, that the Church has often shut itself
off from the world in an exclusive preoccupation with its own
dogmas and worship. But it is also true that a voice has resounded
from the gospel: 'Everything is yours but ye are Christ's.' And
wherever this voice was heard, for a while the ghostlike unreality
of the Church was destroyed. It is true that there has always
been, and still is, a politicised Church. But it is also true that
again and again the Church has been reminded that 'My Kingdom is not of this world!' And if the politicised Church has
often been confronted by the danger of a non-political Christianity which evaded its share of the burden of political responsibility, yet again and again the words of Rom. 13 have been
rediscovered and, above all, the words of Christ Himself: 'All
power is given unto me in heaven and in earth!'

For many people, particularly outsiders, the Church means
clericalism, the rule of parsons and their friends, who seem to
think they are talking down to the world from heaven itself.
But where that kind of clericalism springs up, the cry of the
freedom of the Christian man resounds and the fellowship of
free Christian men enters the lists against all clericalism and
papalism, with the reminder that 'One is your Master; and all
ye are brethren'. There is a prophetic word in the Christian
fellowship which has authority and demands obedience even in
the free Church.

Furthermore, the Church can become spiritless. The salt can
lose its savour. There is a great deal of insipidity in the Church.
But there is a cure for that too. The New Testament contains
the Corpus Paulinum, and the exegesis of the Pauline writings
has always opposed the effort of deep thought to the shallow-
ness and cheapness of conventional Christianity. As long as such

exegesis is pursued an over-insipid Christianity will not fail to be confronted by a number of conundrums! And if Christianity has sometimes been threatened by an excess of scholarship and degenerated into the heights or depths of gnosticism, sooner or later a Saint Francis has appeared on the scene to summon the Church to the simplicity that befits the Christian. It may even be called a sign of a really mature and deeply considered theology that it ends by returning to the great simplicities of the faith.

The Church can also become lazy. Theologians, parsons, parishes can all become lazy and neglect the tasks that are waiting to be done. The Bible says we are created for good works. And it is fortunate that alongside Paul we have a James to call us quite simply to work. On the other hand, however, the Church can become too busy and degenerate into a round of ceaseless activity, like a great factory, with its parsonages like antheaps! When it reaches that state it is time for it to hear the words from the First Epistle of Peter: 'Be sober, and hope to the end for the grace that is to be brought to you'—words which will somehow make themselves heard and spread their peace.

Finally, the Church can be paralysed by a too literal and too legalistic interpretation of its faith or by too much externalism. Where that is the case, it is opposed by the faith that 'God is Spirit and they that worship him must worship him in spirit and in truth!' On the other hand, it can also happen that the very substance of the Church may be dissolved into a society where there is no longer any trace of Christ and the revelation of God. Then law and order will be recreated in the Church by the word that God is not the author of confusion but of peace.

With these few examples we have touched on the aspect of church history which Goethe may have overlooked. In his age and country opposition to the degeneration of the Church—of whatever kind—was heard again and again. Excesses were not allowed to spread and destroy the Church. The Church preserved a certain, though at times almost invisible, continuity. And in the process of grappling with such dangers and degenerations new, positive and significant modes of church life became possible and real. It is true that heresies have a positive significance to the extent that they call the Church to bring to light again neglected elements of the truth. But why is that? Why does the history of the Church offer this spectacle of danger and degeneration on the one hand and life-giving resistance on the other? Evidently because what we have come to know as revelation in the Christian sense is an active power. In the midst of all the other powers the revelation of God is *the* power which again and again calls man back to the unity which prevents individual elements gaining the upper hand and bringing about ultimate dissension and disintegration. It is this power of the revelation of God which appears again and again, of which the *Heidelberg Catechism* declares that it 'protects and preserves us from all enemies'. God's revelation is on the battlefield of human life, correcting and suggesting, soothing and disturbing, restraining and promoting. The Church lives by this power. And in spite of all that can be held against it, the history of the Church has been, until the present day, a witness to the reality of what we have described as the Christian meaning of revelation.

Three conclusions follow:

1. The Church need not be afraid of critical questions, even when the question which disturbs its whole existence comes not from within itself but from without, perhaps as a result of certain developments in science, economics or politics, and even when the question is suggested by heresies within its own bosom. It has no need to be afraid if it is attacked. Persecution of any kind is certainly no cause for fear, and the more violent the persecution, the less reason there is for fear. Attack and persecution mean that the Church is thrown back on its own foundations, that it is forced to begin again from its own beginnings. And that is no loss and no impairment but pure gain.

2. The Church must not try to protect itself from critical questionings. It must not try to make itself immune or get itself into some position beyond the range of awkward questions. It must not attempt to tie itself down to one definite system for all time, even though the system in question may have stood the test of an age of struggle and suffering. That might mean that the Church was trying to entrench itself against the instructions of its Lord and surrendering its very self in an effort to safeguard itself. And an all-embracing system intended to provide against all eventualities might be the most dangerous of all forms of 'protection'. The Roman Catholic Church owes a

great deal to what has been called its *complexio oppositorum*. Many Protestants find there is something fascinating about the Catholic system of thought and life. But we should be clear that this all-embracing, all-intercepting system means that the living spirit may be obstructed in its course. It is of course just as true that the same danger exists, even more acutely, in a Church where indifference is the rule and every possibility open. This is the special danger of the Anglican system. All-embracing systems can mean that the Church may be sealed off from the exposure to danger which it needs as its daily bread. A Church which is not afraid of its Lord will certainly not attempt to safeguard itself in either of these all-embracing ways.

3. The Church must not spare itself the ordeal of facing critical questions again and again. It must not wait for the initiative to come from outside. When things are going well in the Church, it is always astir. It does not leave it to providence to see that everything comes right. That would be tantamount to surrendering to the world and heresy, and running blindly into the arms of one exotic 'revelation' after the other. The Church is never simply *ecclesia reformata* but *semper reformanda*!

This *reformatio continua* does not imply that the Church must always be 'progressive'. On the contrary, the Church must not allow itself to be swept away by the movements of the age; it must remain loyal to its own sources, but not allow itself to be paralysed by them. It may well be that in certain situations the Church must remain stationary or even go back a few steps. There is no inevitable law of development. The important thing is that the Church shall remain a true Church. This applies above all to exegesis, the central department of theology. It is right that the Bible should be read anew again and again. The Bible demands to be read again and again with new eyes. The same is true of systematic theology and dogmatics, preaching and the language of preaching—woe betide the Church if the language of preaching becomes rigid!—and it is true of every single Christian and every single theologian. Do not become enslaved to men! This applies to the discoveries of others as well as one's own. To become a 'frozen' Christian is to quench the spirit. The best remedy against that is to be diligent. The same applies to the organisation of public worship, the so-called liturgy. There

is a habit of speaking of classical ages of the liturgy, and why
not? But in this field to stand still or return to earlier forms which
can only be revived artificially today, is dangerous. Liturgical
'arts and crafts' are a risky business. Where prayer and man's
intimate life with God are concerned, we cannot rest content
with venerable forms. Here, if anywhere, we must sing a new
song to the Lord. And the same is equally true of the Church's
constitutions and creeds and dogmas.

Readiness to learn from the Early Fathers must not lead to
a rigid orthodoxy. We are not called to be orthodox but living
evangelical Christians, attentive to the confession of the Fathers,
but not merely repeating or reciting it. The relationship of the
Churches among themselves and of the Church to the State or
to particular ideologies will never be definitive. The *ecclesia
semper reformanda* should be constantly 'en route' with its own
questions, asking what the Holy Spirit and the Word of God
require of us today, ready to revise its whole fund of knowledge
and experience. It is founded on and preserved by the Word
of God alone, and therefore it must be unconditionally faithful
to this foundation in order to be free and flexible.

These are the three demands which must be fulfilled by a
living Church, that is, a Church moved by the Word of
God.

Of such a Church it may be said that it is the fellowship of
those who are called apart by the Word of God. To the extent
that the Church in this sense is a living Church, it can be said of
it that it is the dwelling place of God's honour. One cannot
esteem the living Church too highly. It is the place where the
Lord speaks, where the revelation of God is testified to the world,
though it must be remembered that the Church stands under,
not beside Holy Scripture. It can never boast of the directness
with which Holy Scripture testifies to the revelation of God. It
stands under the Bible, obedient to it as the source and the norm
which it cannot forgo. A vigilant Church will always be searching the Scriptures very concretely. It is there that the Spirit
reigns, not in some free choice or other. The Spirit exists in the
letters and words of Holy Scripture, and from these letters and
words it bloweth where it listeth. Bearing in mind all the time
that the Church is subordinate to Holy Scripture, it may be said

of the Church that it is the witness of revelation because Holy Scripture must also be heard in the preaching of the Church.

8

Let us end by considering the question of 'Revelation and Man'. It is man to whom the revelation is revealed. It is a light or a sound or a word to be received by his eyes, his ears or his heart. It is man who is affirmed and made new by the revelation of God; it is man whom the revelation unites with his fellow-men. And it is man who is confronted, in this revelation of God, by an authority that is absolutely above him, in his past, present and future. God is man's Creator and Redeemer: God wants to sanctify man. God is the God of man. For man's benefit the Son of God became man in Jesus Christ, and died and rose again. And the Word that was Jesus Christ Himself is addressed to man. Our last question is this: what is the significance for man of this event which we have described as revelation in the Christian understanding of the term? The question is not whether and to what extent man knows about God's revelation, whether he has heard about it and can speak about it, whether man acknowledges the fact of revelation and accepts it, whether he makes it his own and becomes one of its witnesses—though all these are certainly important questions. We are not going to enter into the whole series of historical and psychological problems and possibilities that they raise at the moment, however. The first thing to see is that the fact of revelation has an objective significance for man which persists whatever man's attitude to it may be, which exists long before he has accepted or rejected it, long before he was in the world, indeed, before man existed at all. We have to do with a decision which is independent of all subjective attitudes towards it. We do not pass judgment on the revelation: it passes judgment on us. Revelation as understood by Christians is an objective judgment on every human being, since it is a reality at the centre of humanity and human life—it is man's limitation and his destiny.

1. Revelation in this sense is the limitation of man. I said at the beginning that revelation means the unveiling of something veiled. The covering which revelation removes is the delusion, man's great self-deception that he, man, is the one and only

being, the real being. Whether man is taken as meaning the individual who fulfils his lower or higher instincts, or a collective, a class or some form or other of human society, or man the living creature in his relation to the cosmos, is unimportant. The crucial thing is man's assumption that he is the sole purpose of the universe, the delusion that he is the lord of all things. Objectively, revelation in the Christian sense is the destruction, the abolition of this delusion. Man's arrogant assumption that he is the sole master of the universe is brought low by the Christian revelation. Revelation in the Christian sense puts an obstacle across the path of all -isms, whether it be the -ism of materialism, or monism, or militarism or Communism. It puts paid to all -isms, it makes them null and void. And man who lives by such -isms and regards himself in their light as the lord of all things, is brought low by Christian revelation, whether he knows it or not. One might also say that fundamentally he is set free by this revelation. After all, he is not really the lord of all things, and therefore not the lord of himself—nor, however, the prisoner of himself. There is no necessity which forces man to posit his own absoluteness. He need have no fear of the demons with which he darkens and complicates his own life and that of his fellow-men. This whole world which man constructs for himself, is judged by the revelation of God, put in the shade by it, fundamentally and finally. Man is also limited in a relative sense by the failures and disappointments of his life, by the fact that he must one day die, and also by the great catastrophes which befall the human race from time to time. The strange thing is, however, that in the long run all these limitations fail to make an impression on man. He raises his head again and again as if nothing had happened. But this revelation of God is the fundamental and the final limitation of man, for here he is no longer confronted by a relative quantity—he can even interpret his own death as relative!—but by an authority which is absolutely superior to man himself and his whole world, his microcosm and his macrocosm. It is no longer a question of one opinion against another; this is an ultimate encounter: here man is brought to a stop by a fact. This revelation is no inimical force, no denial or condemnation of man, however, but an affirmation of man, addressed to man. It is not a revelation by which man is consigned to an uncertain darkness, or which confronts him with a puzzle which he could really solve on his own. He who meets man in this revelation is God the Creator, who by His action in Jesus Christ has set man up again, who takes care of man and against whom man has no cause whatever to rebel like a little urchin—Promethean rebellions are a fundamentally hopeless undertaking anyway! In this revelation man really comes to the frontier beyond which he cannot pass, beyond which he has no chance of continuing on the path of delusion and self-deception. God who exists for man and loves man confronts him here as a sovereign Lord. Man is shown that he is the creature for whose life God has undertaken to provide, and whose life he has undertaken to forgive and to determine. The limit which man encounters here is not a negative, but a positive and therefore a strong and an absolute limit.

2. This revelation of God is also man's destiny. If man's self-deception is the covering which revelation removes, what it reveals underneath the covering is the destiny which results from man's limitation. *The Destiny of Man* is the title of a famous book by Fichte. We can learn from this book what happens when a thinker attempts to consider the destiny of man regardless of the limitation which God imposes on him. According to this book man is really God, and his destiny is to exist in solitary divinity. One might set against this anthropology another, that of Martin Heidegger, according to which man exists in solitary nothingness, the prey of anxiety and at the mercy of fear. In both cases we have an interpretation of man which ignores his limitations. The revelation of God in Jesus Christ, however, is the objective irruption of the simple truth: Thou man, every man, all men have their beginning and end in God. Since He has acted in Jesus Christ, He has acted for man, and now man may really live. God has testified to Himself before man in Holy Scripture and the preaching of the Church. It is man's honour and privilege to accept this testimony. In its strength he can stand erect in his own age. The destiny of man is to be allowed by God to be free, to believe, to love and to hope. That is what the revelation of God has to tell man about himself, about his past, present and future. The revelation of God means that man is destined for faith, for freedom and therefore

for God. The freedom of God is to become free for God. All other freedoms are captivity in comparison with that fundamental freedom. Man is not compelled to know God, but he is allowed to know God, to trust Him and obey Him. His life can only receive its true goal, its fullness and its support from this fact that he is allowed to know, to trust and obey God. And furthermore, man is allowed to confess God and live a life in which his small existence becomes important and significant for God Himself. As a confessor man participates in the cause of God. Revelation in the Christian sense is the permission to share in the cause of God.

On the basis of the revelation man is also destined for love. Love too is a freedom, freedom for our fellow-men, for the other man. We do not have this freedom by nature. If there is a wall between God and man, there is an even greater wall between man and man. Loving one another means that this wall falls down, that we see the other as our fellow-man. For God's revelation tells us that we are allowed to be with our fellow-man. Why? Because he is in the same situation as we are. He is related to me because God's revelation takes place for him too; whether he knows it or not, it is addressed to both of us. When one knows that, one's fellow-man immediately becomes more interesting. And then everything that may still be hidden in the concept of love becomes self-evident. Because I like being with my fellow-man I can help him a little and allow him to help me. Not because I believe in his goodness and excellence or in mine, but because of our common situation before God. I have to see in my fellow-man the touchstone and at the same time the guarantor of my faith.

My fellow-man is a living witness that God lives. And if I should forget that God lives, he is there to remind me. That is the source of the joy man has in his fellow-man. And to have joy in another is love. It is not a compulsion but a freedom which, from this point of view, is self-evident.

3. Hope too is a freedom, man's freedom in time, the freedom of man who is to today and may be gone tomorrow. Hope is the freedom for man's future. Man can face the future patiently, he can hold out, he can live one day at a time again and again when he has hope. Death will wear a different aspect. Man will

see death as the sign of man's limitation, but he will go to meet it with courage and confidence. Not indifferently and apathetically, not because he has had enough of life, but because he knows that the God who has saved him is waiting for him there. And whoever lives in this hope in the great issues of life, will not be without hope in life's smaller anxieties. With this hope man will not despise the smallest opportunities; he will not be dejected. It is God's revelation that allows us not to be dejected by life's failures and limitations.

Great stress must be laid on this concept of freedom. We are living today in an age of much constraint and compulsion and fear and we have every reason to hearken to the words: 'If the Son shall make you free, ye shall be free indeed.' But let us be clear that this freedom really is something man cannot get for himself and does not possess in himself. Faith, love and hope, the great destiny of man in the light of God's revelation, are not factors of human existence which man can do what he likes with. No mere ideology can understand and grasp them. That we are able to believe, to love and above all to hope, is a fact beyond the sight of ordinary human nature. It is not an innate human faculty at all. To be able to believe, to love and to hope is man's destiny as seen in the light of God's revelation. In Christ it is true and valid for every human being. Through the grace of God it becomes a reality; through the grace of God man is allowed to believe, to love and to hope. Such is the freedom of man's destiny.

Because the freedom we are concerned with here is not a natural freedom but the freedom which is given to us, it is a fact that neither faith, nor love, nor hope can be called in question by any other authority. If a man's faith can be shaken by some mere ideology or other, one can safely say that what he had was no faith at all. For real faith stands as firmly as the revelation of God itself, and is absolutely certain of its cause. And so it is with love and hope as well.

This freedom of which we have spoken is the freedom, be it noted, beside which man has no other. If he does not take hold of this freedom he is not free at all. God's freedom is not an offer which we are left free to accept or reject. We are not free, and shall never become free unless our destiny is fulfilled by

God. 'If the Son of man shall make you free, ye shall be free indeed.' Beside that freedom all other 'freedoms' will always signify fear and captivity and demonism. Therefore the permission which God's revelation grants us to be free is also in the fullest sense a duty to be free. To be or not to be, that is the question.

We are only on the brink of the problem here. If we were to go any further we should have to speak of the event in which man's limitation and man's destiny is not only objectively valid but fulfilled in the life of faith and love and hope. New truths would open up before us: we should have to speak of the Holy Spirit and the Christian fellowship and Christian preaching, of Baptism and Holy Communion, of man's rebirth and confession, and of his prayer and the commandments which God has given him. We should have to enter the field of theology, for here we have been moving merely on its brink. But even in theology it is also true that the event can only be talked about. The event as such is inexpressible and can only happen.

We must not regret having to close at this point. Let me remind you of a story in the Old Testament. The Lord called Samuel: 'Samuel, Samuel', and Eli told him that if he heard the call again he was to answer: 'Speak, Lord, for Thy servant heareth.'

IX

POVERTY

An essay on 'Poverty' which
was printed in the Swiss paper
Atlantis, Zurich, December 1949.

POVERTY

THE word poverty is usually thought of in its sociological sense. It describes the state of a man who for one reason or another is lacking in, or is even entirely without, the material necessities of life; who, therefore, having to rely on the assistance —voluntary or other—of his fellows, has to do without a great many things. He may even have to go without those things most essential to him, which would be available had he adequate means. There are, however, also much to the fore in this world, still other instances of destitution and privation. Even a rich man can be poor in health. He can suffer from intellectual poverty, in contrast with which a poor man in the financial sense of the word may be rich. With all his wealth he may suffer from spiritual poverty and from poverty in his relations with those around him, whereas in comparison a financially poor man may be a veritable Croesus.

I have been asked, not for my own opinions, but for the Christian views on this subject. Therefore I open my Bible and immediately light on the calm and almost disconcerting assertion that poverty, taken in the sociological sense—usual in this world—exists in this life of ours, has always existed and will always exist. Although the Bible is certainly not lacking in pictures of material wealth, those who possess and enjoy such wealth can be seen at a glance to be really very 'poor people'. Throughout the Bible, however, the fact that there are both rich men and poor, in either sense of the word, appears to be a kind of divine ordering of events, which ordinance must serve as a basis for all further thought—just as in this world we have to accept the facts of illness, war and other such human deeds of violence, without question and without concerning ourselves with ideas of an essentially 'better future'. Let us not rejoice or be angry too soon! Without that starting-point in mind, however, we can comprehend nothing.

All the more striking is the fact which dominates the picture,

namely, the unmistakable and definite sympathy towards
poverty seen in the Old and New Testaments, also the sympathy with those who, according to that divine ordinance, in
this life are poor in one way or another, but above all in the
material sphere. If in accordance with God's will there are also
rich people, if, especially in the Old Testament, He includes
among His blessings the gift of riches to one man, He in no wise
takes up a neutral position between the poor man and the rich
man. The rich may take care of their own future, He is on the
side of the poor.

First, there is no place in the Bible where the rights of the
rich are proclaimed, where God appears as the Lord and Saviour
of the rich and of their wealth, where the poor are exhorted to
preserve the wealth of the rich and remain poor themselves
merely for the sake of the rich. There are, however, many places
in the Bible where the rights of the poor are proclaimed, where
God declares Himself to be the upholder and avenger of these
rights, where the rich are commanded not to forget the rights
of the poor, not to alter or ignore them just when they feel
inclined to do so, but rather to be rich only for the sake of the
poor and for their benefit. We cannot but recognise the high
principles and radical spirit of the Bible on both these questions.

Secondly, there is no place in the Bible where anything in the
nature of praise is accorded to riches, where the rich are upheld
and exalted. There are, however, many places where the poor
are extolled as blessed, where they are called the chosen of God,
where the words 'the poor' are synonymous with 'the righteous'.
The gospel was proclaimed to the poor, while on the contrary
the rich are often shown in suspiciously close proximity to the
mighty evildoers, whose pride goes before a fall. Because of their
wealth they at least run a great risk.

Just because they are rich men, they will in no wise enter into
the Kingdom of Heaven (as hardly as a camel can go through
the eye of a needle, as we know), but to this end they must
themselves sell all and become poor. In this respect the distinction
made in the Bible is as sharp as a knife: the blessings of wealth
cannot claim to be on an equal footing with the blessings of
poverty.

Thus the Bible is on the side of the poor, the impecunious

and the destitute. He whom the Bible calls God is on the side of the poor. Therefore the Christian attitude to poverty can consist only of a corresponding allegiance. This allegiance is, however, only the reflection, the likeness, the testimony of a much more comprehensive distinction. If one should wish to withdraw from that allegiance, then one cannot comprehend, nor be in sympathy with, that all-embracing distinction to which it testifies. By 'poverty' we—and the Bible too in these connexions, which have already been mentioned—mean financial, or some such form of poverty as is found in this world. Why then does poverty stand thus illumined, and wealth lie in the shadows? It is possible to give two answers to this question:

First, because poverty as seen from the background of human existence, that is, from the point of view of the coming Kingdom of God, and of the future life, is not a natural condition of life in this world, but is part of the evil which dominates that life. It is perhaps the most striking result of human sin. God's ordinance, whereby the rich and the poor live together side by side, is only temporary. His coming Kingdom will put an end to poverty.

Why, then, should this end not be proclaimed here and now, since the Word of God has already been heard? Why should God not here and now reveal Himself to and dwell with those who suffer from this evil which has been ordained to disappear? Why should He not comfort and encourage the poor, simply because they are poor in this world, with the realisation that their rights are the very mirror of His eternal justice? And why should He not give the rich of this world to understand anything other than that the rights of the poor—those who in this life are lacking in wealth and all things necessary—must be sacred to them for the sake of His righteous judgment and of the approaching release from poverty?

The other side of the question is this: that here and now not wealth but poverty is the mark of our present life and of the future Kingdom promised to both rich and poor. For this Kingdom is not still in the future, but has come already. Christ was born: the Son of God, eternally rich, Himself the source of fullness of life for everyone. But the Kingdom is come in poverty because it is now become a reality to us men, who—rich or poor—are all greatly poverty-stricken in comparison with the abundant riches of the Kingdom. Christ was born in poverty in the stable at Bethlehem, and He died in extreme poverty, nailed naked to the Cross. He is, then, the companion, not of the rich men of this world, but of the poor of this world. For that reason He called the poor blessed, and not the rich. For that reason He is here and now always to be found in the company of the hungry, the homeless, the naked, the sick, the prisoners. For that reason those who are rich must cleave to them, if they would be close to Him. Therefore, in order that they themselves may be blessed, the rich must become poor, or at least in all earnest be ashamed of their wealth; if they have to part with that wealth, whether gradually or all of a sudden, they must not show surprise, nor horror, nor yet try to ward off poverty. Not wealth but poverty is the mark of Heaven, the mirror of eternal salvation.

For Christ, in whom eternal salvation has come to those who in this world are rich or poor, is the Christ of poverty for all who are poor, all who are truly destitute and suffer any privation: such a one is the conqueror, who makes all poor men rich, and only such a one! In great humility did the most High God become the Lord of mankind. Man will have to follow the example of this humility, will have to confess his poverty, in order to grow rich in Him.

One of St. Paul's sayings sums all this up: 'Ye know the grace of our Lord Jesus Christ, that, although He was rich, yet for your sakes He became poor, that ye through His poverty might be rich.' That is, briefly, the Christian attitude to poverty.

BIBLIOGRAPHY OF KARL BARTH'S WRITINGS IN ENGLISH

Christian Life (S.C.M. Press, 1930)

The Epistle to the Romans (O.U.P., 1933)

The Resurrection of the Dead (Hodder & Stoughton, 1933)

Theological Existence Today (Hodder & Stoughton, 1933)

*Come, Holy Spirit (T. & T. Clark, 1934)

*God's Search for Man (T. & T. Clark, 1935)

The Word of God and the Word of Man (Hodder & Stoughton, 1935)

God in Action (T. & T. Clark, 1936)

Credo (Hodder & Stoughton, 1936)

The Doctrine of the Word of God (T. & T. Clark, 1936)

The Church and the Churches (J. Clarke, 1937)

The Holy Ghost and the Christian Life (Muller, 1938)

The Knowledge of God and the Service of God (Hodder & Stoughton, 1938)

Trouble and Promise in the Struggle of the Church in Germany (O.U.P., 1938)

Church and State (S.C.M. Press, 1939)

The Church and the Political Problem of Our Day (Hodder & Stoughton, 1939)

* In collaboration with E. Thurneysen.

A Letter to Great Britain from Switzerland (S.P.C.K., 1941)

The Germans and Ourselves (Nisbet, 1945)

The Teaching of the Church Regarding Baptism (S.C.M. Press, 1948)

Dogmatics in Outline (S.C.M. Press, 1949)

Prayer (Westminster Press, U.S.A., 1952)

GENERAL INDEX

ADENAUER, 155
Amsterdam, First Assembly of the
World Council of Churches
(1948), 76, 135
Anglican Church, 233
Anti-semitism, 115, 140, 168, 196ff.
Arabs, 197
Augustine, 15

BAPTISM, 74, 240
Barbey, Lt-Col., 115
Barmen Declaration (1934), 17, 21,
22, 26, 50, 117f., 142, 149, 156
Barth, Karl, reply to Emil Brunner,
113ff
Beethoven, 169
Bereczky, Pastor, 123
Berlin,
Soviet zone of, 150
West, 150
Bible, The, 89, 90, 153, 160, 174, 177,
196, 217, 218, 219, 220, 221, 222,
224, 225, 226, 231, 233, 243, 244,
245
Protestant theology and, 217
Roman Catholic theology and, 217
Bismarck, 40, 49, 128
Bonhoeffer, Dietrich, 151
'British Empire', 128
Brunner, Emil, 125
Open letter from, 106ff.

CALVIN, 94, 216, 219
Calvinism, 102, 173
Canterbury, Dean of, 104
Capitalism, 109
Catechism, 89, 153
China, 128
Christian 'parties', 44ff., 99f.

Church, the
and Bible, 220f., 234f.
and Communism, 106, 111, 113ff.,
142ff.
and defence of the Sabbath, 47
and democracy, 44
and dictatorship, 37
and education, 30
and freedom, 37f., 75, 87ff., 119,
145
and gambling, 47
and Kingdom of God, 31ff.
and peace, 41
and politics, 26, 29, 31, 34, 35f.,
39, 41, 42, 45, 47, 77ff., 80ff.,
90ff., 143, 149ff., 232
and Revelation, 225f.
and social justice, 36, 153
and State, 15, 17ff., 94ff., 143, 149,
159, 234
and use of alcohol, 47
as Christian community, 15ff., 127
as congregation of Christ, 66f.
as fellowship of the Holy Spirit,
37f., 71ff., 75ff., 157, 163, 229
as true human solidarity, 69f.
as Visible, 63f.
between East and West, 127ff.
Christian political parties and, 44ff.
in Germany, 48f., 62, 150ff.
in Hungary, 53ff.
'neutrality' in, 143, 155, 157, 158
nourished by the Word of God,
39f., 85ff., 87ff., 227, 234
One, Holy, universal, apostolic,
76f.
persecution of, 232
real, 62ff.
under the order and government of
its Lord, 74ff.

Churchill, Sir Winston, 114
Citizens, Christians as, 82, 99
Collectivism, 188
Communism, 104, 106, 107, 108, 109,
    110, 111, 112, 113, 115, 116, 117,
    138ff., 153, 170f., 184, 236
Community
    Christian, 15ff., 53ff., 77ff., 200
    Civil, 16ff.
    Concept of, 15, 84, 95
Confession, a new, 142f.
Co-operativism, 36
Cullmann, O., 20
Czechs, 104

DEATH, 238f.
Decline of the West, The 171
Democracy, 44, 133, 170
Destiny of Man, The, 237
Dibelius, Bishop Otto, 62
Diem, Hermann, 106
'Disillusionment', Christian, 131f.

EASTERN EUROPE, 102, 106, 108
Eckhart, 169
Ecumenical movement, 63
England, 171
Enlightenment, 60
Europe today, Christian message in,
    167ff.
Evangelism, Christian, 172
Existentialism, 187, 226

FAITH, 178, 239
Fichte, 237
France, 168
Franco, 138
Free trade, 36
Freedom, 37ff., 58, 59, 61, 82, 84, 95,
    96, 129, 134, 135, 139, 140, 144,
    161f., 188, 215, 238, 239, 240
French Revolution, 139

GERHARDT, PAUL, 131
'German Christians', 156
German Communists, 145

Germany, 103, 114, 115, 116, 149,
    150, 168, 169, 175, 176
    the Church in, 48f.
    Confessional Church in, 50
    Eastern, 153
    Evangelical Church in, 118, 121,
        150, 151f., 155, 153
    Protestant Church in, 62
    remilitarisation of, 151, 152, 153,
        155
    West, 153
Gladstone, 128
Gnosticism, 231
Goebbels, 139
Goethe, 60, 169, 214, 219, 223, 229,
    231
Good Friday, message of, 53ff.
Göring, 139
Grace, 189
Grob, Rudolf, 114
'Guilt problem', 103

HEIDEGGER, 189, 211, 226, 237
Heidelberg Catechism, 76f., 232
Heinemann, 151
Hess, 139
Himmler, 139
Hitler, 40, 108, 109, 111, 113, 114,
    118, 139, 151
History, God and, 154
Holland, 168
    Protestant Church in, 62
Holy Communion, 74, 108, 122, 240
Holy Scripture, canon of, 220
Hope, 179, 238, 239
Hromadka, Josef, 107, 111, 112
Humanism, 183ff.
    of God, 185, 186
Hungary, 53ff.
    Reformed Church in, 101ff.
    religious revival in, 105
    Roman Catholic Church in, 103,
        120, 121

'IDEOLOGIES', 132, 139, 239
Individualism, 188

Indonesia, 138
'Iron Curtain', 101ff., 117, 129, 150

JAPAN, 128
Jerusalem, 198
  Fall of (A.D. 70), 196
Jews, the, 195ff.
  Christian attitude to, 200f.
Journalism, Christian, 48

KANT, IMMANUEL, 60, 104, 153, 169,
  223
Kierkegaard, 226
Kingdom of God, 20, 25, 26, 31, 32,
  33, 42, 71, 81, 160, 176, 177, 178,
  180, 245
Kirschbaum, Charlotte von, 101
Kutter, Hermann, 62

LABOUR PARTY, BRITISH, 140
Law, 35f., 82, 84
  equality before the, 36
League of Nations, 143
Liturgy, 233f.
Love, Christian, 70, 71, 179, 238, 239
Loyalty, 179
Luther, 149, 169, 173, 219

MARX, 188
Marxism, 36, 139
Maydieu, P., 183
Metternich, 128
Mochalski, 151
Moses, 222
Mozart, 60
Munich Crisis (1938), 169

NATIONAL SOCIALISM, 107, 108, 114,
  115, 118, 136, 137, 138, 139, 140,
  149
Nationalisation, 109
Natural law, 27ff., 31, 43
Nero, 81, 96
New Testament, 94, 99, 161, 162, 200,
  216, 217, 218, 219, 220, 221, 222,
  241

Niebuhr, Reinhold, 106
Niemoeller, 151, 155
Nietzsche, 188
Nihilism, intellectual, 59, 115, 168,
  215
Norway, 168
  Protestant Church in, 62
Noth, Martin, 221
Nuremberg Trials, 12

OBEDIENCE, 178, 187, 215, 238
Old Testament, 83, 161, 162, 200, 210,
  216, 217, 218, 219, 220, 221, 244

PAUL, 81, 82, 222, 231
Peace, 144
Peter, Pastor Janos, 119, 124
Philosophy, history of, 210f.
Plato, 219, 220, 223
Political change, 77ff.
Political decisions, 149ff.
Political parties, 99f.
  the Christian and, 99ff.
Political systems, 80f., 82, 92
Poverty, 243ff.
Power, 40, 82, 84, 95
Preaching, 74
Progress, 35
Protestant Church, the, 62f., 91f.

RAVASZ, DR., 119, 122
Revelation, 205ff.
  as the Word of God, 215f.
Ribbentrop, 139
Richelieu, 128
Roman Catholic Church, the, 58f.,
  62, 91f., 103, 112, 156, 173, 232f.
  and Communism, 112
Roman Catholics and Protestants in
  Christian parties, 44, 46
  in struggle against Hitler régime,
  112
Roman Empire, 167, 211
Rosenberg, 139
Rothe, 22
Rousseau, 43

Russia, Russians, 102, 106, 117, 128ff., 153, 170f.
  Communism in, 138ff., 170f.

SARTRE, JEAN-PAUL, 59, 189
Scandinavian countries, 171
Scepticism, 59
Schweitzer, Wolfgang, 163, 164
Sincerity, 178
Social-liberalism, 36
Socialism, 109, 110, 132, 133, 171
Society, a stateless, 95
Socrates, 219
Spain
  Protestants in, 138
Stalin, Josef, 139
State, the, 94ff.
  and Christian 'parties,' 44ff.
  and freedom, 37, 119
  and the Kingdom of God, 31, 33, 81
  as 'civil community', 16
  as Visible, 63
  Christian doctrine of the just, 25
  Church and, 15, 17ff., 143
  Communist, 110f.
  constitutional, 95f.
  democratic, 44
  divine ordinance of the, 21ff., 43, 81
  'natural law' and the, 28
  Nazi, 110, 111
  power in the, 40
  Russian, 110

State, the totalitarian, 37, 107, 108, 109, 110, 111, 149
Streicher, 139
Stuttgart *Kirchentag*, 164
Swiss Confederation, 60
Swiss neutrality, 105, 131, 137, 143
Swiss Zofinger Society, 114
Switzerland, 111, 114, 115, 116, 119, 169, 171
Syndicalism, 36

TECHNICS, 56, 58
Ten Commandments, 59
Thales, 211
Third Reich, 139
Tildy, President, 102, 113
Totalitarianism, 107, 109, 110, 115, 117, 138
Trianon, Treaty of, 103

UNDERSTANDING, 177f.
United Nations Organisation, 143
United States of America, 128ff., 170

WEBER, KARL, 115
Weimar Republic, 150
Writing, Writers, Christian, 48

YOUTH, MODERN, 56ff.
  freedom of, 61

ZWINGLI, 15

INDEX OF BIBLICAL
REFERENCES

Deut.
30.19...154, 164

I Sam.
3.9...240

Eccles.
7.16...145

Isa.
19.24, 25...146

Dan....130

Matt.
5.5...53
11.28...198
22.21...25
23.8...230
25.31f....19
25.40...230
28.18...21

Mark
1.15...191

Luke
10.36f....34
18.8...66

John
1.1f....213

1.3...215
1.5...212
1.18...213
4.24...231
8.12...212
15.5...213
15.16...213
18.36...29, 230
19.11...22

Acts...218
2.9...225
17.30ff....212

Rom.
3.23f....212
8.37f....21
12...75
12.2...157
12.6...154
13...27, 96ff., 230
13.1...24
13.1b...21
13.2...22
13.3...20
13.4, 6...22
13.5...24
13.6f....24

I Cor.
3.21...230
12...75
15.58...124

II Cor.
8.9...246

Eph.
2.10...213

Phil.
3.20...19
4.5...71

Col.
1.16f....21

I Tim.
2.1–7...19

Heb.
1.3...215
1.13...26
11.10...26
13.8...213

Jas....89, 220

I Pet....231
2.14...20

I John
2.1ff....212

Rev....173
13...27, 96ff.
21.2, 24...19